Failures of Feeling

Failures of Feeling

Insensibility and the Novel

Wendy Anne Lee

Stanford University Press
Stanford, California

STANFORD UNIVERSITY PRESS
Stanford, California

Printed in the United States of America

ISBN 9781503615014

First paperback printing, 2020

The Library of Congress has cataloged the hardcover edition as follows:

Names: Lee, Wendy Anne, [date]– author.

Title: Failures of feeling : insensibility and the novel / Wendy Anne Lee.

Description: Stanford, California : Stanford University Press, 2019. | Includes bibliographical references and index.

Identifiers: LCCN 2018009022 | ISBN 9781503606807 (cloth) | ISBN 9781503607477 (epub)

Subjects: LCSH: English fiction—History and criticism. | Emotions in literature. | Fiction—Psychological aspects.

Classification: LCC PR830.E46 L44 2018 | DDC 823.009/353—DC23

LC record available at https://lccn.loc.gov/2018009022

Typeset by Kevin Barrett Kane in 11/14 Adobe Garamond

*For Jong Sook Noh, Colin Christopher Bridge,
and Delia Noh Bridge*

The uneasiness of being contemned depends on sympathy.

DAVID HUME, *A Treatise of Human Nature*

Contents

Failures of Feeling

INTRODUCTION

The Bartleby Problem

AN IRRESISTIBLE BUT UNSEDUCIBLE young woman who would rather die than marry. A burnt-out altruist who must stop his ears to the inflicting cries of others. A would-be sovereign whose license to rule is predicated on her capacity for indifference. A pale and emaciated scrivener who would prefer not to. Unfeeling, it turns out, takes many shapes in fiction's history, but the perverse logic of insensibility remains the same: nothing incites the passions like dispassion. *Failures of Feeling* traces this axiom of emotion through a literary account of what some have called "The Bartleby Problem," that is, the encounter with a human subject who lacks volition or desire, who is neither moved nor moves.[1] I argue that what philosophers and critics alike have grappled with as the limit-case of character is not the advent but the culmination of a dilemma in fiction. Not only does Herman Melville's listless scrivener have a history, but his antecedents mark a consistent vexation for philosophy and narrative. Indeed, insensibility seems to express the philosophical problem *of* narrative.

We might begin by defining *insensibility* as unfeeling combined with inaction—in other words, not moving on the inside or on the outside. In

Melville's text we meet someone who does not move and so, presumably, has no volition. But, because he *will* not move, he seems also to possess a cache of thoughts and feelings. Insensibility names this unnerving oscillation between impassivity (no feeling) and contempt (bad feeling) that inheres in the Bartleby problem. This "flickering" between apathy and hostility aggravates fiction's otherwise capacious program for emotional life.[2] An ontological and ethical impasse that compels narrative's drives and compensations, insensibility upsets the novel's promise to deliver the goods of human interiority at the same time that it foments that very mission. *Failures of Feeling* thus elaborates how the phenomenon that would appear to halt feeling, relation, and narrative, in effect, incites them. Just as insensibility comes to provoke others' sensibilities, it is the impassive, nonresponsive, inscrutable subject of fiction who generates narratives of penetrating interiority and hauntingly intense relation. As the uncle of the "hard-hearted" Clarissa Harlowe puts it in Samuel Richardson's prime demonstration of the doomed logic of unfeeling in the history of the European novel: "How can you be so unmoved yourself, yet be so able to move everybody else?"[3] This signature accusation, like a dye shot through the colorless waters of unfeeling, is the trace of the insensible.

To study insensibility's changing figurations is to follow a telling obsession of what we now call the psychological novel, whose uneven, hybrid, gendered, and unfinished history is attended to here.[4] In offering this slanted, skeletal, and multigenre genealogy of fiction, I am persuaded by Nicholas Paige's claim that "the novel" was never "born" and so never "rises." In his "morphological history of the novel," Paige insists that fictional texts cannot be treated as participating in a coherent or collective practice to achieve certain protocols of belief. Individual novels "are not feeling their way through the pseudofactual night toward the bright light of the fictional day. Nor have they intuited some truth about literature."[5] Insofar as my own study charts a course for what I call Richardsonian fiction, I do so without making any progressive claims about the nature of that project. More often than not, I convey the "stuckness" of fiction—a narrative attachment that, as my conclusion argues, George Eliot tried (without success) to amputate from the genre.

The "father of the psychological novel," Richardson distilled the raison d'être of the form into the tapping of the innermost recesses of the heart—the unbidden, involuntary "throbs," "glows," and "shudders" that attest to one body's susceptibility to another. Why, then, the persistence—even within *Clarissa*—of a subject who shuts down that process, who both goads and exhausts the novel's mandate to feel? The insensible, I argue, lays bare the dominant conception of emotion *as* responsiveness, as a story of how a moved body moves. Seen through the double lens of Enlightenment philosophy and literature, the insensible emerges as a charged figure whose very impassivity is a source of impossible power and intolerable resistance. "We cannot enter into his indifference and insensibility," complains Adam Smith of the "mean-spirited" impervious man (*TMS* 1.2.3.3: 42). Insensibility, as I shortly explain, spoils the entire mechanism of sympathy—without which there is neither moral sentiment nor moral society. Suddenly, the Keatsian "feel of not to feel it" assumes a criminal neutrality—contempt. A favorite emotion in both literary studies and philosophy,[6] contempt describes a peculiarly noxious movement between hatred and dispassion. This affectless affect, as I will discuss, reaches back to its complex and shifting articulation as an "exemption from the calamities of others" by Thomas Hobbes, first affect theorist of a competitive market society,[7] defining architect of the sovereign, and dark conscience of Enlightenment thought.[8]

Insensibility's conflation of inaction and unfeeling reaches back to that nonnarrative linchpin of any narrative sequence of events: Aristotle's unmoved mover, the first cause of the universe that makes all motion possible by not being subject to motion itself. If divinity is, in fact, the archetypal insensible (as Agamben suggests in his reading of Bartleby as a subject of divine "decreation" and "pure, absolute potentiality"), it also drives a host of other potent figurations: the outcast, the villain, the sovereign, and, of course, the dead.[9] Part human and part inhuman, the insensible traffics in what Descartes describes as "nothingness or non-being" (*du néant ou du non-être*), thus claiming an exemption from the play of will and desire that is animated by mortal life.[10] Such an implausible figure evacuates the conception of emotions as motives, disrupting the principle of causation that underwrites both our theory of mind and our theory of the novel.

Failures of Feeling revives an abundant Enlightenment discourse of the passions, beginning with Hobbes's definition of emotion as the invisible beginning of action. Committed to such primary explication, my study reopens the *question* of emotions in a long trajectory of fiction, from Madame de Lafayette's breathtaking and dolorous depiction of arrested desire in *La Princesse de Clèves* (1678) to *Daniel Deronda* (1876), Eliot's overtly sinister riff on Richardsonian form.[11] In tracking the always alarming appearance of the insensible from the seventeenth-century stock figure of the prude to the sentimental novel's traumatized man-of-feeling to the stone-cold heart of Jane Austen herself, my method is not to analyze character but to present feelings themselves as narrative phenomena—as situations that unfold over time through an intersubjective matrix of thoughts and actions, benefits and injuries, pleasures and pains—in other words, not strictly as backformations of psychic life. I rely here on the view that every philosopher of the Enlightenment was also a theorist of affect, laying the groundwork not only for psychoanalysis but also for much of the current framing of emotions as encounters or responses.[12] Thus, Michael Frazer pairs a "rationalist Enlightenment" with a "sentimentalist" one, "an age not of reason alone, but also of reflectively refined feelings shared among individuals."[13] For the novelists treated here, not only were such models of the passions at play in their work, but the dominance of a framework that posits all emotions as rooted in unconscious desires has rendered those conceptions inaccessible or uninviting to many contemporary readers. To ask the question of emotion is thus to unknow (to repurpose a Raymond Carver title) what we talk about when we talk about love, hope, envy, rage, dejection, fear, kindness, courage, and every other configuration of feeling. *Failures of Feeling* thus addresses the "presentist" tilt of affect theory, which has tended to simplify or overlook Enlightenment writers even as it relies, sometimes explicitly, on their treatments of emotions as relations of force.[14] Additionally, where eighteenth-century studies has attended meticulously to cultural discourses of sentiment and sympathy, my study turns to more philosophically rooted questions about what emotions are.[15]

The lineup of insensibles offered in this book reorients the conventional codependency between interiority and the novel, if not upending that relation then at least questioning its innocence. If, as Lauren Berlant writes, "desire is memorable only when it reaches toward something to which it can attach itself" (20), then why would it attach to the blank, nonstick surface of the insensible? Put differently, how does the insensible come to incite narratives of longing, sadness, and desire, as if only a figure of immobility could prompt an investigation of inner life? Catherine Gallagher—extending the insights of *Nobody's Story*, which argues that narratives about "conjectural, suppositional identities *belonging* to no one . . . could be entered, occupied, identified with by anybody"[16]—theorizes how readers cathect onto subjects who float free from historical reference. The epistemologically available figures of fiction, who "carry little extratextual baggage," can hop on and off flights of readerly imagination, enabling play in the "language game" of belief in which "flexible mental states [became] the sine qua non of modern subjectivity."[17] To Gallagher's crystalizing claim that "readers attach themselves to characters because of, not despite, their fictionality" (*Nobody's Story*, 351), I observe a countergravitation toward a seeming afictionality—characters with indeterminate antecedents who are somehow nonappropriable. In other words, if the nimble "nobodies" of the novel travel light, without any carry-on luggage, then insensibles are like fiction's dead weight: taped-up, hardshell suitcases marked "HEAVY." Their "givenness" (353) as characters cannot exactly be located in fictionality because their opaque self-determination keeps flagging the problem of their origins.

We might say that while theories of fictionality address how relations with characters are like or not like ontologically real human relations, a theory-of-emotions approach still wonders what an ontologically real relation is.[18] Gallagher ends her essay with a similar turn, as it shifts to a fluid meditation on the fictionality of "any representation of consciousness" (quoting Ann Banfield) and, thus, the fictionality of intimacy itself (359, 357). Gallagher here formulates the necessary "incompleteness and disjunctions" of character as "inviting gaps for the reader to slip through" or "subjective blanks to be overcome by her own idealized ego" (360). In my variation those blanks and gaps feel more like black holes, enabling less pleasurable ego consolidation than existential free fall following rabid pursuit. Without quite repudiating the terms of "familiarity, immediacy, and intimacy" of fiction's covenant (360), the literature of insensibility is a reminder of the work required by its inimitable pact, of the mess its participants keep having to make.

"Emotions work like stories do," writes Rae Greiner, engaging Martha Nussbaum's claim that the cognitive structure of emotions partly takes narrative form. "Embedded in 'narrative history,' [emotions] make sense in relation to what might happen and to what came before."[19] For Enlightenment writers the story of what happens now and what happened before was a story of passion and action, how moved bodies move other bodies. To understand those dynamics required a theory of mental causation, yet any account of why someone did what she did (or what she might still do) was fundamentally compromised by the fact that sensory experience only happens, as Smith writes, to "our own person" (*TMS* 1.1.1.2: 11). My senses are not triggered when you touch a scalding kettle. I do not feel the heat that you feel. Yet when I see you stretch your hand toward the piping-hot object, I wince in anticipation of the pain, and when the kettle burns you, I seem to feel it, too. I may shout, but it will be too late to prevent you from making contact—speech being slower than sight. Furthermore, when I later tell the story of your injury, I will be sure to include details like the fire-truck redness of the kettle, the unsuspecting look on your face as you reached for the nearby plate of brownies, and its grimacing horror when you hit scorching enamel instead. My goal is for others to experience the sensation, even if to a much lesser degree than you or even I did. Smith writes, "As we have no immediate experience of what other men feel, we can form no idea of the manner in which they are affected, but by conceiving what we ourselves should feel in the like situation" (*TMS* 1.1.1.2: 11).

Sympathy is the cognitive effort to reconstruct "like situation[s]." Sensations are fleeting, singular, and proprietary—I have almost no access to them, even sometimes to my own. Narrative helps me. By reconstructing "every little circumstance . . . with all its minutest incidents," my imagination reproduces the conditions that gave rise to your response, that is to say, your emotion (*TMS* 1.1.4.6: 26). Ideally, I would imagine not just the scene itself but a whole history of scenes—*your* whole history: how you burned your other hand last week on a blue kettle or how, as a baby, you fell into a hot tub and still have a phobia of boiling water. Conditions will explain causation. If I can answer "as perfect as possible" the question, "What has befallen you?" I will be able to perceive your feelings, almost as you perceived them yourself (*TMS* 1.1.4.6: 26; 1.1.1.9: 14).

A century before Smith's theory, Spinoza's detailed narrative breakdown of affects (not just sadness and joy but timidity, ambition, gratitude, devotion, dread, disdain, and weariness) upheld a situational model of emotions. Longing, for example, is a "sadness, insofar as it concerns the absence of what we love," but this sadness triggers another pathway, a desire to return to the scene of love, when and where the object was present: "He who recollects a thing by which he was once pleased desires to possess it in the same circumstances as when he was first pleased by it" (*E* P36: 89). Spinoza's observation does not just associate place with feeling but makes the more extreme claim that circumstances make the passion—that, as in Smith's account, if you could just reproduce the circumstances, you could engender the feelings they once produced. The inability to do so, to recover the situation of love, is equivalent to the loss of love itself, leaving us with only our longing as a record of its absence. This book concerns the essential absence of any emotion, as well as the narrative tenacity with which we try to reconstruct it.

I begin with a reading of Melville's "Bartleby" through the lens of Hobbesian contempt in order to establish a conceptual touchstone for understanding insensibility. This introduction appends the chronological trajectory of literature that begins in Chapter 1. In reframing the Bartleby problem from a picture of capitalist abjection to a philosophical riddle about narrative, I advance the book's overarching theory of insensibility: what it is, how it works, and what it has to do with fiction. The opening chapter then moves back in time to an unlikely precursor to Bartleby, the stock figure of the prude, whose ubiquity in early print culture attests to a primary connection in the history of the novel between insensibility and gender. Linchpin to an elaborate, seventeenth-century taxonomy of female subjects who come to populate English literature, the prude bears the brunt of dualism, embodying and (in her punishing transformations) repairing a misalignment between inside and outside, motive and action, feeling and speech. Returning us to the feminocentric scene of the *précieuses*, prude fictions, I argue, conjure the dream of female sovereignty and its unbearable, heretical, and anticonjugal aspirations.

Such concerns link these early, rangy protofictions to Richardson's *Clarissa* (1748), the marble-hearted subject of the second chapter and *echt* prude narrative of Western literature. Newly framed, Clarissa Harlowe's tragic case of unfeeling can be understood through a doomed metaphysics of emotion, explored here mainly through Lockean "indifferency." This chapter also explains my understanding of a Richardsonian project as synonymous with psychological fiction in what I discuss as Frances Ferguson's crucial theorization of the novel as a self-cancelling form, whose double purpose is both to construct and to eradicate the inner life. To this end I argue that Clarissa's life as a transparent, urban rape survivor installs a trenchant self-critique and sweeping countermodel within a Richardsonian tradition.

My third chapter turns to the sentimental novel's man of feeling, radically reinterpreting his fine-tuned capacities for public sympathy through the insensible who loomed largest over the eighteenth century, Charles I. Alternately public enemy and slaughtered sovereign, Charles inspired narratives of enigmatic unfeeling, which could be read as either regal tranquility or landmark contempt. This chapter examines, in particular, the insensibility of laughter, what Hobbes controversially defined as a triumphant glorying in the infirmities of others and Bergson a "momentary anesthesia of the heart."[20] My analysis features two works by Oliver Goldsmith: his sentimental but unfunny *The Vicar of Wakefield* (1766) and his "unfeeling" but very funny *She Stoops to Conquer* (1773). Unable to resolve the mutual exclusions between emotion and laughter in his only novel, Goldsmith realized that the problem was the genre itself, whose characteristic humorlessness, he complained, had already infected the theater. His solution was to reappropriate Puck, comedy's ready-made insensible, as the delightfully "unfeeling monster" Tony Lumpkin, a character who revives sovereign exceptionality as "Humour, my dear: nothing but humour."[21]

From Goldsmith's hero of comic misrule we turn to that figure of godlike dispassion who presides at the apex of the novel form. Endlessly diagnosed with world-class heartlessness, Jane Austen, like Clarissa Harlowe and the prudes before her, stands accused of heresy and abuse, of spoiling the plot for herself and for others. In this chapter we see how the reception of Austen's fiction—a history crucial to the reputation of the genre at large—exemplifies the ways in which failures of feeling are entwined with narrative failure. Once again, the charge of insensibility marks a disruption to protocols of fictionality, here the plaiting of narrative with conjugal felicity.[22] My analysis moves to the curdled plot of *Sense and Sensibility*, whose stalwart heroine, Elinor Dashwood, has been so closely identified with Austen herself. In my reading of Elinor I intervene against a nearly unavoidable assumption about her psychic repression by engaging an alternative framework of emotions in Hume's *Treatise of Human Nature* (1738), a text considered the philosophical companion to Austen's oeuvre. *Sense and Sensibility*, I argue, extends and revises the *Treatise*'s influential account of sympathetic relations, distressingly completing Hume's picture of intimacy. My interpretation features Hume's tangled lines of resemblance, contiguity, and causation—what, in Austen's novel, makes emotion a contagion, or one sister's pain feel like the other's.

Failures of Feeling concludes by turning to the afterlife of insensibility in a late nineteenth-century novel that flags its own Richardsonian descent. *Daniel Deronda* makes an ideal bookend for this study. It not only features a heroine who declares at the outset, "I can't love people. I hate them" (after strangling her sister's canary), but, more profoundly, offers an anguished meditation on the legacy of the insensible to the project of fiction. For Eliot, this subject—now brought to the breaking point of mental and narrative health—cannot be extricated from the "history of a young lady" begun by

Clarissa and put to rest, Eliot hopes, in her "history of a young lady hitherto well provided for" (253). *Deronda* offers multiple takes on novelistic unfeeling, most memorably in the figure of the Alcharisi, a brilliant conflation of Diderot's paradoxically dispassionate actor and Defoe's flagrantly unmaternal mother. All told, Eliot's late work draws together the different strands of the Bartleby problem explored by this book: the ridiculed dream of female sovereignty in prude fictions, the anxious and sadistic logic of the Richardsonian plot, the inevitable burnout of the man of feeling, and the compromising ethics of intimacy in Jane Austen. Eliot, I argue, brings these elements to bear in order to euthanize a genre that relies on the now thoroughly pathologized principle by which insensibility inflames the passions. Insofar as Eliot sketches alternative pathways for the English novel, then, they would appear to involve leaving behind both England and the novel, two forms whose very nonrehabilitation only testifies to their dogged endurance.

THE SCANDAL OF IMMOBILITY

In the first part of *Leviathan*, "Of Man," before Hobbes defines a commonwealth and prophesies the philosophical "Kingdome of Darknesse" into which it can descend (4.44: 956), he proclaims that "to have no Desire, is to be Dead" (1.8: 110). As a motto for the passions, the phrase resonates as a defense of desire, a call to understand strong feelings as on the side of life. To have no desire is to be dead or as good as dead. Of course, in Hobbes's philosophy, it means to be clinically dead, since life is defined as a state of motion, and desires (into which all passions can be distilled) are "the Interiour Beginnings of Voluntary Motions," the very first stirrings of action that move us either toward objects that are good for us or away from objects that are bad (1.5: 78). In opposition to a scholastic view of sense perceptions as taking place within the immaterial soul, Hobbes redefined all interior responses (thoughts *and* feelings) as physical movements.[23] Put simply, emotions are motions. As Thomas Spragens writes, "Not only are the passions motions, in Hobbes's view, but cognition also can be conceived as a form of motion. That is, the intellectual faculties as well as the emotional strivings of living creatures are, at bottom, nothing but motion."[24] In this ontology of life, cognition, emotion, and action are continuous and inseparable phenomena.[25] Thus, insensibility as an absence of interior motion that arrests the possibility of action, would appear impossible to conceive except as death. "For there is no such thing as perpetuall Tranquility of mind," writes Hobbes, "because Life it selfe is but Motion, and can never be without Desire, nor without Feare, no more than without Sense" (*L* 1.6: 96). Susan James observes that for Hobbes "we can never be without a susceptibility to passion," and "when the internal motions that are our appetites and aversions cease, we die, and become corpses rather than human beings."[26] James makes apparent the tautological thrust of Hobbes's saying that "to have no Desire, is to be Dead." To cease feeling desire (including its negative form, aversion) is to cease feeling anything at all, to stop distinguishing what will help you from what will hurt you and thus to become not only a physical corpse but—in a Hobbesian world where one must always be on the move—a social casualty as well.

But if feeling is moving, and moving is living, how can we account for those who do not move and who are thus, according to a Hobbesian physics, not themselves moved? If an unmoving body is by definition a dead one, then what do we do in the face of an immobile subject, who should not be alive to begin with and should certainly not be alive for long? And if those who do not act do not feel, then why does insensibility—as the conflation of inaction and unfeeling—seem like an all-out form of hostility, both an action and emotion expressing the deepest contempt? The insensible cannot be verified as existing and, even worse, cannot confirm the existence of others. "The human mind," Spinoza writes, "does not perceive any external body as actually existing except through the ideas of the affections of its own body" (*E* 2.P26). Unaffected, insensibles negate the actuality of bodies; they do not, cannot, perceive others as existing. The insensible thus pulls the plug from any Enlightenment system of ethics. Without perception routed through the interior ("the ideas of the affections of its own body"), the subject is both an emotional and social cipher. For Hume, such blankness claims immunity from not only personal passion but also public evaluation. It is by people's "intention [that] we judge of [their] actions, and according as that is good or bad, they become causes of love or hatred" (*T* 2.2.3: 226).[27] Insensibility disables judgment, aborting the processes of standardizing response or establishing benchmarks for praise or blame.[28]

Yet insensibility involves another negation that, if puzzling to philosophy, becomes tinder for the novel. The problem is not just that the insensible cannot acknowledge the existence of others but that it cannot acknowledge the existence of itself. In an earlier postulate Spinoza states, "The human mind does not know the human body itself, nor does it know that it exists, except through ideas of affections by which the body is affected" (*E* 2.P19). To put the two claims together, I can only perceive that objects exist by way of their impact on me; I can only perceive that I exist by my responsiveness to other objects. If, then, my body is unmoved, my mind cannot confirm either that I or others exist. Hume pointedly equates such insensibility with annihilation, or what it would mean to be "a perfect non-entity." The fuller passage, which precedes his theory of personal identity, is a remarkable advance from Descartes's dream:[29]

> When I enter most intimately into what I call myself, I always stumble on some particular perception or other, of heat or cold, light or shade, love or hatred, pain or pleasure. I never can catch myself at any time without a perception, and never can observe any thing but the perception. When my perceptions are remov'd for any time, as by sound sleep; so long am I insensible of myself, and may truly be said not to exist. And were all my perceptions remov'd by death, and cou'd I neither think, nor feel, nor see, nor love, nor hate after the dissolution of my body, I shou'd be entirely annihilated, nor do I conceive what is farther requisite to make me a perfect non-entity. If any one upon serious and unprejudic'd reflexion, thinks he has a different notion of himself, I must confess I can reason no longer with him. (*T* 2.4.6.3–4: 165)

Like Hobbes, Hume posits that to be without affect is to be without life—except that the impossibility of sensing oneself apart from one's perceptions, or "catch[ing] myself at any time" without affects, suggests a primary insensibility. In other words, if human beings "are nothing but a bundle or collection of different perceptions," then there is no *there* there.[30] Insensibility thus flags the great "fiction" of the self: "Ourself, independent of the perception of every other object, is in reality nothing. For which reason we must turn our view to external objects" (*T* 2.2.2.17: 221). It should not surprise us, then, that the object we turn to with the greatest need is itself insensible.

INERTIA AND THE FORCE OF RESISTANCE

Recent debates in affect studies about whether emotions are intentional or nonintentional states return us to Enlightenment philosophies of the passions, beginning with Hobbes, who conceived of emotion as extensive of intention as well as subject to unpredictable relations of force.[31] Here I am engaging a fraught distinction between narrative and nonnarrative phenomena that emerges in the debate sparked by Ruth Leys's trenchant critique of affect theory.[32] In one exchange a central division between cognitive and noncognitive experience maps onto a more subtle difference between what Charles Altieri describes as action-oriented "emotions" and perception-oriented "feelings." Emotions, he writes in response to Leys, "lead agents to shape experience in terms of plots with points of incitement leading to projected action." By contrast, feelings or affects apply principally to the realm of "aesthetic" experience, as "states of sensation that involve the imagination but that do not enter into the structure of cause and consequence because the state of attention becomes an end in itself."[33]

The difference Altieri sketches between action and perception, or emotion and feeling, relies on an implicit binary between narrative and aesthetic experience, or emplotment and nonemplotment ("end in itself").[34] Miranda Burgess recasts Altieri's distinction as one between subjective and nonsubjective states: "Emotions are subjective to the precise extent that they take teleological form; affects, in contrast, are non-subjective but personal, orienting individuals toward objects without causing the individuals so oriented either to analyze their own responsiveness or to act on it."[35] Burgess's compelling account of transsubjective and nonfigural migrations of affect begins with Hume. In starting with Hobbes I am constructing a terrain in which underlying distinctions between narrative and nonnarrative phenomena (emotions and affects, acts and feelings) fail to register because sense and imagination are already theorized as causes.[36] For those still working through Aristotle's ideas about the motivational qualities of reason and desire, mental states "that involve the imagination but that," as Altieri posits, "do not enter into the structure of cause and consequence" (880) would be hard to conceive since feelings *are* accounts of causes and consequences, agents and patients. Descartes writes that "whatever takes place or occurs is generally called by philosophers a 'passion' with regard to the subject to which it happens and an 'action' with regard to that which makes it happen" (*PS* 218). Likewise, Hobbes comprehends "this progress of causation that is of action and passion" (*EP* 124).

Hobbes redefined suffering as material impingement, part of a cosmological order in which an "agent" is a body "said to work upon or *act*, that is to say, *do* something to another body" and a "patient" is a body "said to suffer, that is, to have something done to it by another body" (*EP* 120). The passion of suffering thus illustrates more the unfolding of a structural relation than a dolorous predicament of pain.[37] As Daniel Gross observes, "Hobbes treats the soul by way of an interpretive political science where passions are a function of power."[38] Moreover, this schema, in which one man's passion is another man's action, opens several narrative pathways: not only insofar as there are always two sides / two stories to every emotion but also in the fracturing *within* each subject, especially for Descartes (voluntary or involuntary, body or soul, cause or effect). A dual or split model of emotion further entails an abiding commitment to figure, even if that figure—as in the case of the insensible—upholds the circular logic of allegory. "What is distinctive about personification," Jonathan Lamb cannily observes, "is its coalition of causes and effects in the one phenomenon, such as Death that appears as its own victim."[39] A figure of insupportable self-determination (cause *and* effect), the insensible is a glitch, in other words, a malfunction or corruption endemic to the system in which it appears.[40]

Relatedly, Hobbes interpreted liberty not as the reaching of a specific goal but, instead, as the experience of unimpeded motion, a condition foreclosed by the fact of endless and inherent resistance against the motion of others. His theory of inertia, a "sweeping transformation" in the historical conception of movement, reframed the meaning of immobility through a narrative about force (Spragens, *The Politics of Motion*, 57). Inertia, formulated by Galileo as the tendency of any body to resist change to its course and velocity, describes the property whereby either an unmoving object remains still or a moving object continues its course until it meets with an interference. Rest is thus not the telos or fulfillment of motion; instead, both motion and rest are changes of state caused by the exertion of other bodies. As Spragens writes of Hobbes's theory, "'Rest' was purely a relative situation, and it came about in a moving body only through the imposition of an external force" (176–77). States of motion therefore describe how one body begets the motion or change in motion of another body. Even if a body is at rest, one should understand that it came to rest by the force of something else. As Spinoza restated: "A body which moves or is at rest must be determined to motion or rest by another body, which has also been determined to motion or rest by another, and that again by another, so on, to infinity" (*E* 2.L3).

Two dynamics are at work in Hobbes's physics: a movement inward and a movement against. When in Hobbes's scheme a subject senses an object, the motion of that object radiates from the outside to the inside of the sentient body: "For when the uttermost part of the organ is pressed, it no sooner yields, but the part next within it is pressed also; and, in this manner, the pressure or motion is propagated through all the parts of the organ to the innermost" (*EP* 390). Moving begins by being moved, touching by being touched. Feeling in this account would appear equivalent to yielding, to a state of being "pressed" one layer at a time until the motion of the object reaches one's "innermost" part. Yet Hobbes clearly regards feeling as the meeting of force with force—in other words, as an active state of resistance. Thus, the experience of the motion of other bodies is always an experience of "contrary" motion. As James, quoting *The Elements of Philosophy*, writes, "A human body does not passively receive the motions caused in it by external objects; it also resists or reacts 'by reason of its own internal natural motion'" (*Passion and Action*, 128; *EP* 391). Here human bodies do not vibrate sympathetically with the motions of foreign bodies. Unlike the transfer of or identification with others' emotions described in later accounts of sympathy, Hobbesian sensibility involves an essential barrier to and negotiation of others' powers to move us. Hobbes thereby loops feeling to unfeeling, or motion to immobility, somehow equating the action of self-preservation with the traction of resistance. As one historian records, Hobbes advanced the claim that "like any other physical action, resistance is also motion"[41] Even if Hobbes's principle of resistance seems more remote to us than the rhetoric of fellow feeling that emerged in reaction to his ideas, we are hardly far from his views of the senses.[42] A psychological understanding of emotions retains the basic assumptions that actions originate from deep inside us, that these inner states are responses to social and material situations, and that such responses can register conflict, if not violation, of personhood.

Dualism, in its bifurcation of the human subject, gives shape and urgency to a belief in undivision—in Spinoza's emphatic response to Descartes, for example, that "the Mind and the Body, are one and the same Individual, which is conceived now under the attribute of Thought, now under the attribute of Extension" (*E* 2.P21S: 467). Spinoza's monism consisted not in reattaching mind to body, as in some reparative gesture of suturing, but rather in positioning them on parallel tracks of human apprehension, as distinct modes of grasping a unified being or "substance" ("the thinking substance and the extended substance are one and the same substance" [*E* 2.P7S: 451]). As Catherine Malabou writes of Spinoza, bodily "affects do not belong to the human mind as such but appear as *natural ontological phenomena*, the causes of which have to be rigorously determined."[43] Spinoza's and Hobbes's insistence on the ontological status of the passions makes plain the newly troubling premise at stake in the relation between body and mind: the interpretation of human behavior as part of the physical world and the contested belief that actions can be traced back to and explained by their invisible "Interiour Beginnings."

THE CONTEMPTUOUS INSENSIBLE

The story of insensibility expresses how the problem of interiority is a problem about other people's interiority. Because one cannot guess what insensibles feel, there is no way of knowing what they will do. The reverse is also true: because insensibles do not move, there is no way of knowing what or, more important, whether they feel. Insensibility would thus appear immune to narration (no effect and therefore no cause), yet the passionate scene of its occurrence reveals the surprising impact of an unmoving body. In the philosophy of emotions the scene of insensibility is played out in the story of contempt, which appears throughout *Leviathan*. Hobbes, in an early chapter delineating the variety of emotions that stem from the primary states of appetites and aversions, acknowledges a condition explicitly void of the passions, a living immobility in which one exerts neither force nor counterforce: "those things which we neither Desire, nor Hate, we are said to *Contemn*: contempt being nothing else but an immobility, or contumacy of the Heart, in resisting the action of certain things" (*L* 1.6: 80). A state in which we do not experience desire or hate, in which we perceive but do not move toward or away from an object, would seem to defy a Hobbesian physics, in which bodies are constantly reacting to the motion of other bodies for the sake of keeping themselves intact. For a moment in Hobbes's philosophy, "perpetual tranquility of mind" seems possible, an instance of dispassion, inaction—but only for a moment. Hobbes immediately construes such "immobility" as resistance, a "contumacy of the heart" that reacts to "something" by willfully stopping its own motion.

Yet, unlike Hobbes's theory of inertia, in which a body comes to rest by the force of another body, the subject of contempt is responsible for his or her own immobility. If an object fails to move someone, it is the fault of the unmoved someone. To be unaffected by an object turns out to be against it, to be full of hard feelings and not just empty of all feelings. Hobbes's *Elements of Law*, for example, posits the "contrary of pity" not as its absence but as a "hardness of heart, proceeding either from slowness of imagination, or from extreme great opinion of [one's] own exemption of the like calamity, or from hatred of all, or most men" (*EL* 40). An ostensibly neutral state of pitiless indifference, in which someone does not move you, becomes an active state of hostility, in which you are a combination of dullness, delusion, self-regard, and hate. (Other synonyms for *contempt* are *contumely* and *impudence* [234, 90].) Hobbes's description turns immobility—the state of having no voluntary, interior motions—into passion. Such a ready conversion of impassivity into hatred anticipates similar gestures in the history of affect—a hermeneutic impulse to make literal sense of insensibility. After defining contempt as immobility toward an object, Hobbes immediately hedges that such a state may reflect a "heart [that] is already moved otherwise, by other more potent objects; or from want of experience of them" (80). Thus, instead of dwelling on the enigma of what it would mean not to feel, Hobbes shifts the emphasis to a state of preference or ignorance, to feeling nothing toward *this* object.

I am not claiming that insensibility is a single, coherently understood state that poses problems for the ontology of emotions as the interior origins of human agency. Rather, I am arguing that the event of nonresponsiveness exhausts this model, eliciting the illogical charge of an absence of motion that exerts force, an immobility that also applies what Hobbes calls "counter-pressure" (*L* 1.1: 22). Hobbes thus reconceptualized stillness as a result of force and imagined such response as taking the singular form of resistance. Under this rubric the immobile body must be understood as having moved before and as movable still—a quality that distinguishes it from insensibility and simultaneously voids the very concept. To be clear: inaction is not controversial. The scandal arises when stillness does not result from external force, as if the living subject had *never* moved. Such a situation refuses to corroborate not only a theory of passion as motion but also the definition of life itself, illustrated, for example, by Descartes's claim that the "difference between the body of a living man and that of a dead man" is purely motion (*PS* 219).

Importantly, the nonnarrative phenomenon of immobility, in which there appears to be no motivation, action, or interaction, becomes a story through the charge of insensibility. The construction of a culpably resistant subject turns the philosophical problem of stillness into overt narrative conflict, replacing an ontological question about what feeling is with a character-based inquiry about who it is, along with the ethical quandary of what to do with him or her. The insensible as that which has never moved initiates a desperate search for signs of interior motion and a clashing dynamics of persuasion, coercion, seduction, and persecution—all bound, of course, to fail. The insensible does not, will not, and never did move—an intolerable situation, as made clear by Adam Smith, who takes up Hobbes's touchstone of contempt.

Whereas for Hobbes the insensible is understood as having contempt *for* others, Smith relates how the insensible draws the contempt *of* others—not the objects of contempt but the third parties to the scene of emotions who feature so prominently in *The Theory of Moral Sentiments*. Smith's chapter "Of the Unsocial Passions" begins with a fight. One man has provoked another into hating him, and Smith describes how we come not just to sympathize with but, indeed, to "applaud" and "delight" in the man's animosity (*TMS* 1.2.3.2–3: 42). Initially, he explains, our sympathy is divided between the hater and the hated since "our fear for what the one may suffer, damps our resentment for what the other has suffered" (*TMS* 1.2.3.1: 42). To tip the balance of our fellow feeling, the injured party must render his hostility "graceful and agreeable," demonstrating "his patience, his mildness, his humanity" in the face of harm (*TMS* 1.2.3.1–2: 42). Forbearance yields sympathy, as gentleness puts such an agreeable face on bad feelings that resentment "may be admitted to be even generous and noble" (*TMS* 1.2.3.8: 47). The more likable the victim, the more keenly we feel for his injury. So when the victim's forbearance finally breaks, we are licensed to "rejoice to see him attack in his turn," to soak in the fullest pleasures of punishment, "as if the injury had been done to [our]selves" (*TMS* 1.2.3.3: 43). That said, his forbearance must break.

Smith clarifies: "A person becomes contemptible who tamely sits still and submits to insults, without attempting either to repel or to revenge them. We cannot enter into his indifference and insensibility: we call his behaviour mean-spiritedness, and are as really provoked by it as by the insolence of his adversary" (*TMS* 1.2.3.3: 42). Submission is not, in fact, an acceptable response to harm; the insulted party must react. Insensibility—as indifference denoted by inaction—alienates a willingly, indeed eagerly, sympathetic public and denies it the pleasures of emotional experience, whether sadness in distress or glee in vengeance. As Smith observes, "It is always disagreeable to feel that we cannot sympathize" (*TMS* 1.1.2.6: 19). By contrast, the unsocial passions of hatred and resentment may appear difficult to share, but, if "brought down" to an agreeable pitch, they become perfectly sympathetic. For Smith the difference between bad feeling and unfeeling centers in this: negative emotions may challenge sympathy, but insensibility obstructs it. Where, for example, raw hatred can be tempered into honorable indignation, thus paving the way for shared hostility, nothing can be done with unfeeling ("we cannot enter into" it). And for Smith's impartial spectator, who exists precisely to be moved out of his impartiality, to be left feeling nothing is inconceivably worse than being permitted to feel (deliciously) bad.

In the arena of emotions, Smith suggests, insensibility spoils play for all, which is why it amounts to a public offense instead of just a personal insult. Insensibility is intransitive: it denies the existence of objects and negates any relational space to "enter into." Disabling the circuitry of subject, object, and observer, unfeeling would appear to staunch all feeling. It is its provocation ("we call his behaviour mean-spiritedness, and are as really provoked by it as by the insolence of his adversary") that proves to be so emotional. We remember that for Smith, sentiments derive more from external than from internal pressures: "We should resent more from a sense of the propriety of resentment, from a sense that mankind expect and require it of us, than because we feel [it] in ourselves" (*TMS* 1.2.3.8: 46). Insensibility counts less as a failure to preserve oneself, as in Hobbes's view, than as a dismissal of the proprieties of feeling, of what "mankind expect and require" of its own species. Consequently, far from cauterizing sympathy, unfeeling comes to unite others in their resentment, even and perhaps especially in those who have no apparent stake in the conflict.

In spotlighting contempt, critics have picked up on the dysphoric turn that unfeeling can take. William Ian Miller in *The Anatomy of Disgust*, for example, associates the "intensely political" structure of Hobbesian contempt with a cluster of negative emotions like "loathing, horror, disgust, hatred, cruelty" (207, 215)—affects that appear to draw on the alternate definition posed by Hobbes of contempt as possessing "little sense of the calamity of others, [or] that which men call Cruelty" (*L* 1.6: 90).[44] Sianne Ngai, engaging Miller's reading, emphasizes the essential condition of indifference expressed by Hobbesian contempt, enlisting it as an "ugly feeling," more like "contemptuous tolerance" than disgust (*Ugly Feelings*, 336). Like Smith's, these accounts work by implicitly constructing a figure, someone who does not care and whose carelessness hurts others. Narrativizing insensibility thus renders senselessness a form of cruelty—no longer not feeling but not feeling *enough* for "the calamity of others." As Ngai observes, the subject of Hobbesian contempt, he who dismisses others as "too weak or insignificant to pose any sort of danger" (336), comes himself to pose danger, to threaten the peace of others with his indifference. We see how the insensible delivers a reprise of Hobbes's questions, backed by a fresh set of concerns: Is inaction a kind of action? Does immobility express resistance? Can bad feeling take the form of unfeeling? Thus, even as the problem of insensibility migrates to a tale of provocation, it always returns to the mystery of emotion itself, to the chicken-and-egg of outside-inside, or the unfathomable beginnings of voluntary motion.

LIVING WITHOUT DINING

The insensible perhaps most familiar to literary critics is a law clerk on Wall Street who stands behind a screen and prefers not to. Melville's "Bartleby, the Scrivener: A Story of Wall-Street" (1853) features a "motionless young man" whose impassivity sends the narrator, the lawyer who employs him, into a tailspin that ends in uncanny communion with his copyist's dead hand.[45] As in Hobbes's account, Melville's story defines emotion as physical motion, equating motionlessness with emotionlessness. Bartleby is "singularly sedate"; he "moved not a limb" and "refuses to budge" (19, 31, 38). Can he not or *will* he not move? The inscrutability of the scrivener's mind is premised on the immobility of his body. If he does not move—"*he was always there*," "he never went any where"—then what does he feel in "those dead-wall reveries of his" (26, 28, 29)? Melville's fiction elaborates the predicament of insensibility gleaned by Hobbes, the puzzle of unmotivated action, or what happens when life proceeds without interior motion. Like Hobbesian contempt, the scrivener's impassivity would appear to reflect his inexperience of either aversion or desire. But impartiality can denote force—an act of defiance or protest more disruptive than anger—but against whom or what? And how could Bartleby make such a demonstration if what is at issue is his very lack of motivation (to do anything)? Bartleby's "great stillness" somehow comes across as "point-blank" refusal, an internal resistance literalized when the lawyer tries to open the door but finds the keyhole "resisted by something inserted from the inside" (26, 25).

The problem with Bartleby is not simply that he shows no feelings but that he fails to recognize the encounter that should produce them—the demands, in other words, that the motions of one body make on another. While the lawyer construes his clerk's sudden policy of inaction as proceeding from some inscrutable directive from within, it is hard to say what interiority would even mean if it no longer referred to a space of responsiveness where one negotiates, resists, or otherwise processes external objects.[46] The clerk's defining impassivity involves neither an advance toward a beneficial object nor a retreat from a harmful one. As Bartleby tells the lawyer, "I like to be stationary" (41). But without evidence of either desire or aversion, no interior motion can be said to take place, and life cannot be said to exist. The anorexia that presumably kills him (he refuses to take dinner from the "grub-man" Mr. Cutlets [43]) reinforces a fundamental absence of desire (*an-*, "without," and *orexis*, "appetite"). To stop eating ("I prefer not to dine to-day," he specifies [44]) is to halt ingestion, the taking in of substance that is the most basic, fetal gesture of responsiveness. The lawyer's obsession with Bartleby's diet (there is evidence of cheese and cake, but no one sees him *eating*) captures how answering the question of what or whether Bartleby eats will attest to his sensibility or susceptibility to other bodies. Meditating on his staple of ginger nuts, the lawyer fantasizes a "hot and spicy" Bartleby—an active organism made of wildly motile parts (23).[47] But without proof of his actual digestive practices (of catching him in the act of internal motion), the scrivener's capacity for action remains unconfirmed. Thus, Bartleby cannot be "made to move" since there would be nothing *to* move, no matter the location of his body (behind a screen, in a yard, or being carted down Wall Street "in his pale unmoving way" [42]). The evacuation of volition implied by Bartleby's motionlessness collapses the distinction between voluntary and involuntary motion (what Hobbes calls "vitall" motions, or biological functions that take place without our awareness such as breathing, the circulation of blood, and digestion [*L* 1.6: 78]).[48]

The lawyer's pointless check for Bartleby's vital signs conveys a disrupted relation between surface and depth, an aberration evident in the open-eyed cadaver the clerk leaves behind. On the soft grass of the prison yard, "wasted" with "knees drawn up," lies the body of the scrivener, but it bears no mark of injury or trauma (44). There is no bruising to attest to the circulation of blood, only the slow violence of emaciation—a starkness of form that had long characterized his "cadaverous" appearance and manners (27, 30, 35). Although interpretations of Melville's text often focus on the significance of Bartleby's demise, the more salient question is not whether he dies at the end of the story but why he was thought to be living in the first place. In other words, if the body of Bartleby is now pronounced dead, then what did it mean for it to be alive? "Won't he dine to-day, either? Or does he live without dining?" Mr. Cutlets asks of the corpse. "Lives without dining," pronounces the lawyer, who closes its eyes. Is it the deceased or living incarnation of Bartleby who lives without dining, moves without being moved? Even though the scrivener's early days at the office evinced a certain hyperactivity (a flurry of copying in which "he seemed to gorge himself on my documents"), the lawyer's detail that "there was no pause for digestion" indicates the same absence of interior motion—eating without digesting (19).

Bartleby's cessation of action (retirement from copying means he no longer moves even his hands) raises the question of what *made* him stop moving. As the theory of inertia makes clear, bodies do not come to rest by themselves; rest is the result of having been stayed by the force of another body ("nothing," writes Hobbes, "can change it selfe" [*L*, I.2: 26). Where agents are bodies that "do something to another body," and patients are those that "have something done to it by another body" (*EP* 120), action and passion describe two experiences of the same event. Thus, the threat contained in the lawyer's warning to Bartleby that "either you must do something, or something must be done to you" reflects the sheer fact that to do something is *always* to have something done to you (41). But what was done to Bartleby? Who or what changed him from productive scrivener to stationary object? Did he, in fact, ever really change? The rumor passed on by the lawyer that Bartleby had formerly worked in "the Dead Letter Office at Washington" attempts to fill in a backstory of progressive alienation, but its details ("from which he had been suddenly removed by a change in the administration" [45]) only reinforce his passivity. Thus, the lawyer's theory of how "continually handling these dead letters" exacerbated the abjection of one already "by nature and misfortune prone to a pallid hopelessness" does not begin to explain the phenomenon of causeless immobility, a "long-continued motionlessness" that seems always to have been the case (45).

The Bartleby problem (comically previewed by Nippers' furniture-shaking "as if the table were a perverse voluntary agent" [18]) confuses basic distinctions between living and nonliving beings. Daniel Heller-Roazen, writing about the hierarchical differences among objects, animals, and human beings posited in Augustine's *De libero arbitrio*, recounts the three definitive states of being as existence (*esse*), life (*vivere*), and understanding (*intelligere*): "First on the ladder of creation is the state of things like the stone and the corpse, which exist but neither live nor understand. Then there is the condition of the animal (*pecus*), which lives and so also exists, even if it cannot be said to understand. And, at the highest level of creation, there are those like Augustine and Evodius, who understand and, by necessity, therefore also exist and live at once."[49]

The scrivener, whom the lawyer calls "a millstone to me" and whose body is contiguous with the "cold stones" on which his head lies (32, 44), would appear to occupy the lowest rung of beings: "the stone and the corpse" without sense or intelligence.[50] But Bartleby, a living being who appears merely to exist, also lays strange claim to understanding. Moreover, as corroborated by countless philosophical treatments of the story, he demonstrates an intelligence that eludes and surpasses the understanding of mortals. The lawyer describes Bartleby's knowingness this way: "It seemed to me that while I had been addressing him, he carefully revolved every statement that I made; fully comprehended the meaning; could not gainsay the irresistible conclusions; but, at the same time, some paramount consideration prevailed with him to reply as he did" (5). Instead of conveying madness or stupidity, the insensible gives the impression that it is others who are in the dark, that even after the lawyer closes Bartleby's dead eyes, the scrivener still sees something that we do not.[51]

The extensive theoretical attention Melville's story has received from continental philosophers (including Giorgio Agamben, Maurice Blanchot, Gilles Deleuze, Jacques Derrida, and Jacques Rancière) has focused on this state of supremacy as potentiality. In "Bartleby, or On Contingency" Agamben, who enlists Bartleby as a "new creature" in the history of philosophy, describes him as "the extreme figure of the Nothing from which all creation derives; and at the same time, he constitutes the most implacable vindication of this Nothing as pure, absolute potentiality" (271, 253–54). Agamben imagines Bartleby as an impossible "third term" between action and inaction, a state of "suspension" that describes foremost the potential *not* to be, the "potential not to (do or think something)" (250), the divine practice of "decreation" (253), as if the nothing from which God created the earth could have remained nothing. Nancy Ruttenburg, in a persuasive attempt to reconcile readings of Melville's text by continental philosophers and American literary critics,[52] responds to what she sees as a lapse in Agamben's reading by emphasizing how "the philosophically significant figure of Bartleby makes its appearance in a narrative, the story of an encounter" (143). Ruttenburg reads Bartleby as "the limit case of all character," as one who "interferes with" bildung (147). Echoing Deleuze's pronouncement that he performs a "radical, a kind of limit function" (Deleuze 68), Ruttenburg reminds us that the philosophical abstraction of Bartleby must be understood within the context of Melville's narrative. In my argument the philosophical abstraction of the insensible concerns the origins of narrative itself.[53]

UNMOVED MOVER

Smith's account of the insult of unfeeling demonstrates the unsettling effects of obstructed sympathy in an economy of moral sentiments. Sympathy relies on circulation. Likewise, in Melville's story the provocations of the other clerks serve the sentimental appetites of narrative. As the lawyer acknowledges, "Nippers, like his compatriot Turkey, was a very useful man to me" (17). Whereas the semi-useless Turkey still makes an "appeal to my fellow-feeling [that] was hardly to be resisted," Bartleby, as we know, makes no such appeal, authorizes no formula (emotional or narrative) based on overcoming resistance (16). The scrivener, as Branka Arsić writes, "is interested in neither self-recognition nor in seduction. . . . [He is] a body dedicated to a complete cleansing of the traces of otherness, a body that cleanses itself of life."[54] So it is Bartleby's refusal to play that rouses the lawyer's "unheard-of perplexity" and "distress of mind" (35, 25), followed by a cavalcade of fiercer, then softer, then fiercer feelings ("spasmodic passions," "overpowering stinging melancholy," "sincerest pity," "fear," "repulsion," and "nervous resentment" [35, 25, 26, 28, 29, 36]). The lawyer issues this understatement: "I trembled to think that my contact with the scrivener had already and seriously affected me in a mental way" (31). To elaborate Smith's claim: so disagreeable is it to feel that we cannot sympathize, that we simply override the nonsympathetic object, turning its nonengagement into the ultimate trigger. In this way stillness comes to generate action: here, an alternating compulsion to move as far away from or as close as possible to the insensible. After failing to move his employee (even into his own home), the lawyer announces, "Since he will not quit me, I must quit him" (39). And, as if relocating a legal practice were not sufficient measure to move away from a "stationary" "fixture," the narrator takes "flight" to the suburbs by car (41, 32, 42). Once Bartleby is dead, the lawyer heads in the other direction. He recounts of the now affirmatively unmoving body, "something prompted me to touch him. I felt his hand, when a tingling shiver ran up my arm and down my spine to my feet" (45). Death renders Bartleby touchable at last, but, in fact, the same demonstration is made as when he was alive: immobility inspires motion. Whether living or dead, Bartleby's hand does not move, and it is this very stillness that sends shivers down one's back.[55]

This final scene evokes the Aristotelian concept of the unmoved or prime mover—that is to say, the first cause of the universe that makes all motion possible by not being subject to motion itself. Such an entity introduces divine potentiality as the ultimate instance of immobility: "if there is something which is capable of moving things or acting on them, but is not actually doing so, there will not be movement; for that which has a capacity need not exercise it."[56] Aristotle's "something" is an object of *stored*, not missing, energy, a feature evoked in Agamben's reading of Bartleby's "pure, absolute potentiality" or state of "suspension." Like any object of "capacity," a first mover possesses force by virtue of its *position*. In a reformulation of Derrida's reading of Aristotle, Sean Gaston calls such an entity "*the untouchable that touches everything*."[57] Gaston writes, "We can never stop confessing the desire or temptation or even the hoped-for redemption of touching the untouchable" even as that desire produces a "discourse of impossibility and confession" (132). The lawyer's desire to touch his lifeless clerk expresses less a desire to move Bartleby at last (to prove finally his capacity to be moved) than an acknowledgment of the powers of the unmoved mover, the archetypal insensible. If motion is a chain reaction ("Something prompted me to touch him"), then something must start the chain, and that something must not itself be moving. In fiction the corollary to this figure is Melville's "Original."

"Original" appears at the end of chapter 43 of *The Confidence-Man: His Masquerade* (1857),[58] after the novel's silver-tongued "man charmer" swindles a barber out of the price of his shave through his signature confabulation about philanthropy and trust. The barber, left "in a maze, staring after" his "queer customer," later relates the story to friends, who pronounce the swindler "quite an Original" (237). Melville devotes the next and penultimate chapter to an elaboration of that phrase and, in particular, to an inquiry about "original characters in fiction"—a rare species not to be confused with merely "odd characters," who are "novel, or singular, or striking" (238). The essential difference rests not in some identifiable quality immanent to originals but in the nature of the response evoked by such figures—in their beholders' sudden concern with causation or, in other words, a pressing need to know the origins of the original. Whereas an odd character provokes a response along the lines of, "I have never seen anyone like you before!" an original always elicits the question, "*Where* did you come from?" (or, as the lawyer puts it, what are its "original sources"? ["Bartleby," 13]). "Wonder," as Sarah Tindal Kareem writes, "encompasses both stupefaction—'Ah!'—and recognition—'Aha!'—thereby pulling in two different directions simultaneously."[59] For Spinoza, wonder precludes recognition, refuses an "Aha!" The wonderful object is so singular that encountering it stops one's normal processes of mental association. It has no likeness and, therefore, calls nothing else to mind. "Wonder is an imagination of a thing in which the Mind remains fixed because this singular imagination has no connection with the others" (*E* 3.4: 352). To want to know where an unprecedented being comes from is to seek context, connection, as well as cause—whatever can unfix my attention, allow my mind to move on. Melville's original denies such resolution: it "cannot be born in the author's imagination" and is furthermore not even constructed but simply "pick[ed] up" somewhere "in town" with "much luck" (*Confidence-Man*, 238, 239).

Such glibness reinforces the status of originality as an effect rather than a quality. Whereas an odd character, in the following much-discussed passage, possesses "something personal—confined to itself," an original "is like a revolving Drummond light, raying away from itself all round it—everything is lit by it, everything starts up to it . . . so that, in certain minds, there follows upon the adequate conception of such a character, an effect, in its way akin to that which in Genesis attends upon the beginning of things" (239). As with the spirit of God that moves on the face of the waters before letting there be light, illumination is conceived as motion—here, as Melville scholars have discerned, as one of the limelights atop P. T. Barnum's American Museum whose searching incandescence had the effect of bringing a still city to life: "everything is lit by it, everything starts up to it." In the impresario's own words such devices, "in the darkest night, threw a flood of light up and down Broadway, from the Battery to Niblo's, that would enable one to read a newspaper in the street."[60] "The sense of originality" lies in those that are moved rather than in the mover (*Confidence-Man*, 238). The inert piece of quicklime that gets ignited by an oxyhydrogen flame (or the incandescence swiveled by a mechanical contraption or even the spirit of God in Genesis) has no meaning in itself. And like the novelist who only "picks up" characters in the "man-show" of the city, even Barnum, the driver of capitalist spectacle, cannot be said to originate his own limelight (238). The power of originality is not manifest in an agent but in the world of motions it makes possible. As Ruttenburg, engaging Arsić's study, observes, "the representative challenge inheres not in the Drummond light itself, but with those who live in and struggle to account for its peculiar illumination" ("Silhouette," 152). Like the newsprint suddenly set aglow by Barnum's device, that world is narrative itself.

Before propelling far backward to Bartleby's antecedents in this history of the novel, I want to conclude this introduction by suggesting that such high stakes for understanding the insensible call for a reconsideration of the relation of narrative and a particularly visible figure of unfeeling today, the autistic subject. Studies of fictionality, for example, have tended to premise the phenomenon of reading on emotional or psychological responsiveness, the very trait that goes missing in the insensible. Lisa Zunshine articulates this claim most clearly in positing the task or essence of fiction as "mind-reading," or as engaging "our ability to explain people's behavior in terms of their thoughts, feelings, beliefs, and desires."[61] A theory that equates reading fiction with inferring mental states, Zunshine writes, explains why autistic persons display "a lack of interest in fiction and storytelling" since they are challenged precisely in the activity of intuiting others' feelings and desires (8). But what if, as this book suggests, narrative relies on "autistic personhood" or "lifeworlds,"[62] on a vision of affective nonresponsiveness and illegibility in the form of a recalcitrant subject who defies fundamental concepts of agency, interiority, and ontology? Amit Pinchevski, in an important study demonstrating the embeddedness of Melville's fictional character to early clinical theories of autism, has described how "incommunicability breeds communication."[63] Relating the solipsistic, nonsignifying, and gendered "figures of Bartleby, the Muselmann, and the autistic," Pinchevski argues, "it is their failure to speak that summons the production of speech by others who set out to tackle that failure. It is their incommunicativeness that obliges others to speak for them, on their behalf, or in their stead" (38). As the lawyer declares from the start, "I was not insensible." Such claims suggest the stakes for a theory of the insensible (Pinchevski's incommunicable, Melville's original) as the unmoving center or "millstone" in a field of causes and effects, agents and patients. The dependence of narrative on such a figure makes certain elements surprisingly immanent to storytelling: a resistance to depth, the primacy of nonrecognition, and an absence of desire.[64]

We come back to the scrivener's undeniable and unaccountable claim to intimacy: "I know you," he tells the lawyer in their final living encounter, "without looking round" from his spot on the grass. As Bartleby and his precursors make disturbingly clear: the insensible is *not* antisocial. Melville's lawyer recounts, " 'Will you, or will you not, quit me?' I now demanded in a sudden passion, advancing close to him. 'I prefer *not* to quit you,' he replied, gently emphasizing the *not*" (32). To hear the insensible's call for relation without contact, for living in sheer proximity—the wish to remain "a fixture in my chamber," behind a "high green folding screen," out of sight but within earshot—is to apprehend the thoroughly disruptive possibility of sociality without sympathy and without, in particular, a sentimental program based on overcoming resistance (19).

Bartlebyan intimacy sketches the inverse of Anne-Lise François's important account of "recessive action" or "uncounted experience" in literature.[65] In her breathtaking reading of Lafayette's *La Princesse de Clèves*, a text taken up in the following chapter, François discerns a mode of "leaving open without actualizing," "disclaiming without foreclosing," and "acting out of unmet potential" (70, 67). Desire here is expressed and preserved through its nonrealization. "The fantasies by which [the lovers] possess each other in mind effectively bar them from ever sharing the same physical space; the characters themselves provide the safest barrier, keeping each other intact and separate, even as their unspoken mental life makes redundant any physical action between them" (68). The lovers and Lafayette's narrative itself, François writes, "walk away" from the scene of desire, making "a report on another's inner life we are invited to take note of and leave without follow-up" (69). The Bartleby problem describes no such narrative grace or light report of interiority. Instead of soft-spoken avowals and "weightless" actions that result in the most attenuated leave-taking, insensibility makes the reverse demand to share space without the possibility of mental possession, to induce and then withstand the self-exposing rage of the other, a relentless shouting in the ear:

> "Bartleby!" No answer.
> "Bartleby," in a louder tone.
> No answer.
> "Bartleby," I roared.

This picture of relation revisits an earlier and equally distressing portrait of unfeeling, Rousseau's insensate man-child, born fully formed and, therefore, without the capacity for growth (neither inward in depth nor outward in extension). This "perfect imbecile" makes the writer's emphatic point in the first book of *Émile* that education begins as infantile, even gestational, development. The subject who does not grow is someone lacking sense, touch, instinct: "He would see nothing, hear nothing, know no one, would not be able to turn his eyes toward what he needed to see." Without touch, Rousseau's insensible exists without relation, even to himself: "the bodies he touched would not be on his body; he would not even know that he had one."[66] Compare Rousseau's out-of-touch *homme-enfant* to the supreme understanding of Bartleby: his grasp, for instance, of language ("fully comprehended the meaning"), place ("I know where I am"), and minds ("I know you"). Only God, as Hobbes writes of the difference between observable crimes and unobservable sins, "seeth the thoughts of man" (*L* 2.27: 452). As Derrida riddles, *il touche ce qu'il ne touche pas* (*Le toucher*,82). In Hobbesian contempt's exemption from calamity and in Bartleby's "strange peculiarities, privileges, and unheard of exemptions," we discern the vantage of the sovereign (26). In *Romantic Intimacy* Nancy Yousef describes how eighteenth-century discourses of sympathy rely on an improbable confidence in knowing the thoughts and feelings of others. The radical epistemological doubts of Enlightenment skepticism are conspicuously nowhere to be found in the "genial emotional certainties of sentimentalism."[67] Insensibility makes short work of skepticism and emotional certainty and emotion. Ontological beliefs, the attribution of mental states, and conceptions of fellow feeling no longer avail. The principle of causation—its movements from inside to outside and outside to inside—seizes up. The insensible does not, as the lawyer fantasizes, mark the spot where "privacy and society were conjoined" but keeps working the pressure point of their codependency, a leaden finger on a panic button, continuously setting off the epistemic violence of the novel's mandate to behold interior motion, to make it show, speak.

CHAPTER 1

A Brief History of the Prude

A LONG POEM PUBLISHED ANONYMOUSLY in 1740, the same year as Richardson's *Pamela*, bears a title that sounds curious now but would have been commonplace then: "The Triumph of Beauty: or, The Prude Metamorphos'd."[1] In 233 sprightly heroic couplets, we hear how "the hateful Prude" Corinna, hell-bent on obstructing heterosexual happiness, disrupts the amours of her young friend. With Iago-like scheming

> . . . to fill the Virgin's Heart with Fears;
> With jealous Pangs her easy Mind infest,
> Destroy her Schemes of Bliss, and break her Rest,

Corinna poisons the matchless beauty against her suitor, but the power of love—literalized here by Venus riding shotgun in an ivory carriage—defeats the Prude's designs. "One soft Glance" at the beloved is all it takes to restore faith between "the Hero and the Fair." The goddess pronounces,

> For there are Wretches, who untouch'd with Grace,
> Unbless'd with Form, or past the Prime of Face,

Strive all they may to thwart the Lover's Joy,
Profane my Rites, and hop'd for Bliss destroy;
Of these *Corinna*, one (whose fruitful Brain
Could unattack'd, such deep-laid Mischief feign)
Shall stand a Warning to succeeding Times,
That Justice will at last o'ertake their Crimes. (423–30)

What kind of justice is meted out to perpetrators of causeless aggression—malicious revelers who (in Hume's definition of malice) experience "joy in the sufferings and miseries of others, without any offence or injury on their part"? (*T* 2.2.8.1: 240). "Untouch'd with Grace" and "Unbless'd with Form," Corinna is rendered a piece of early Georgian furniture:

Four Legs of curious Work her Form uphold,
Plumes grace the Top, the Sides are lac'd with Gold;
Her swelling Hoop the Surface smooth o'erspread,
And all the Woman is become a *Bed*. (453–56)

Justice takes the form of metamorphosis, the prude's aggressively material transformation into an "Inanimated being" that befits her inhuman stance against beauty and conjugality. All the woman becomes a bed—specifically, a marriage bed. As in the tradition of *contrapasso*, or "suffering the opposite," where Dante's sinners are punished by eternally acting out their crimes *or the reverse* of their crimes, Venus sentences "the wicked Prude" to feel again and again the literal force of heterosexual desire, physically to support the coupling she tried to block. Yet even as a four-poster canopy, the prude will hover over this scene of congress, her "Profane . . . Brain" still at work. As Lynn Festa writes in her revisionary account of anthropomorphic objects, "the wanton projection of self onto thing ricochets back onto the human."[2] Like Milton's Satan circling through chaos, the prude is restless, burdened, undeterred in her revolt against the ruling structures of happiness, peace, and freedom. Judgmental, hysterical, suicidal; killjoy, heretic, vulture, the eighteenth-century prude aspires to nothing less than a new world order, in defiance (as the subject of *The Prude: A Novel* sneers) of all the "happy Mothers, and the no less happy Lovers" who enjoy the favors of the narratorial gods.[3] In search of her own dominion, the prude crashes the plot with her "Hell-contrived Design" and "devilish Contrivance" (*The Prude* 3.40), in protest against the commonwealth: "Now fell Corinna, born to mar our Ease / Our Quiet poison, or disturb our Peace."

Far from an oddity in the salvage bin of early print culture, the prude is ubiquitous in the literature of the period. Database searches reveal a steady preoccupation with her form, not to mention an entire subfield devoted to its metamorphosis. A sampling from across the century includes *The Ramble Between Belinda a Demy Prude, and Cloe a Court-Coquette* (1716); *The Prude: A Tale in Two Canto's* [sic] (1722); *An Epistle to the Most Learned Doctor W—d—d; From a Prude, That Was Unfortunately Metamorphos'd on Saturday, December 29, 1722* (1723); *The Ball: Stated in a Dialogue Betwixt a Prude and a Coquet, Last Masquerade Night, the 12th of May* (1724); "The Metamorphosis of a Prude: A Poem" (1756); *The Prude: A Comic Opera in 3 Acts* (1777); *The Prude; or, Win Her and Wear Her, a Comedy* (1791). These selections take the form of ballads, court poems, ramble fictions, philosophical dialogues, one-act plays, and other hybrid forms that populate the era during which fictions stabilized into "novels," or, in J. Paul Hunter's terms, "the various traditions of prose and poetry, some fictional, some not; some narrative, some not; some long and comprehensive, some not, that ultimately came to fruition in long prose fictional narratives that we have come to call novels."[4]

This study's genealogy of psychological fiction, apotheosized in *Clarissa*, opens in this generic turbidity. In beginning my archive with the unlikely stock figure of the prude, I offer an early and apparently unkillable iteration of the insensible. Part of a breathlessly mixed-media culture, these rangy narratives tell a particular story about the insensible's deep and deeply gendered relation to the novel.[5] Whereas my introduction located in Melville's Bartleby a theoretical touchstone for understanding insensibility, this chapter looks to the prude as a historical precedent. But, as in any ever-receding history of the novel, the prude herself returns us to an earlier scene of literary production: here, the seventeenth-century salon culture so intimately identified with the beginnings of the novel form, *les précieuses*.[6] Elizabeth Wahl has detailed how *précieuse* culture was transplanted to early modern England by Charles I's unpopular consort, Queen Henrietta Maria.[7] Along with its cultivation of high literature, *préciosité* imported principles and practices of Platonic love, exquisite femininity, and disciplined virtue, which aimed not only at a "feminocentric model of social relations" but also "a mythology of feminine rule."[8] The habitual pairing of *la précieuse* with *la prude* reveals a vituperative libertine discourse kindled by *préciosité* and its untenable dreams of sovereignty. Eugenia Zuroski Jenkins and Patrick Coleman write that in the rocky transition between an ancient discourse of medical humors and a modern "sense of humor," the "humorous bodies" of eighteenth-century French and English literature "formalize a pervasive sense of uneasiness, restlessness, or ambivalence in a culture not at all certain of how to represent authorized ways of being."[9] What kind of being, then, is the prude? Where did Her Wretchedness come from? What cultural past explains her specific menace, and what is she doing in that charged landscape of writing "before novels"?

Another prude poem of the same year, "Honorio to Corinna: *Upbraiding Her Falsehood*" reinforces the name associated with female heartlessness.[10] In a roll call of the prude's "Coldness and Indifference; Disesteem, Neglect, and Scorn," the speaker blasts his beloved's imperviousness to heterosexual demand. As a 1756 fable more tentatively asks, "Tell me, Corinna, if you can, / Why so averse, so coy to man?" The original Corinna seems to belong to Ovid's *Amores* as the object of the poet-speaker's intense and complex desire. She is named during a felicitous afternoon tussle in the bedroom, whose shuttered half-light gives cover to the modesty of shy girls: "that light is to be provided for bashful girls, where shy modesty might hope to have a place to hide."[11] Rebecca Armstrong glosses, "Corinna puts on a show of resistance, but it is just a show." Armstrong translates, "She fought as though she did not want to win, and was conquered without trouble by her self-betrayal."[12] Ovid thus launches a female subject defined by a rift between feeling and action (putting up a fight in order to lose it). Less at stake for Corinna than sexual surrender is "self-betrayal," a slip of feeling that would deflate her lover's fantasy of seduction and thus end her power to stage it.

By early modernity, Ovid's Corinna has dispersed into different points along a misogynistic spectrum. Pope's "Rape of the Lock" immortalizes the prude's position at its furthest end:

> The graver Prude sinks downward to a *Gnome*,
> In search of Mischief still on Earth to roam.
> The light Coquettes in *Sylphs* aloft repair,
> And sport and flutter in the Fields of Air. (1.63–66)

Split into prude and coquette,[13] the latter inherits Corinna's physical charms and exquisite surrender while the prude assumes her suspect modesty. In her wide-ranging study of antifeminist satires from the period, Felicity Nussbaum writes of "Rape of the Lock" and "Epistle to a Lady": "women divide themselves into prudes and coquettes; they are inconstant and changeable; they pursue pleasure and power; they worship themselves at the expense of others."[14] Over time, the particular misalignment between thoughts and deeds, form and content that accrues to the prude hardens into the charge of hypocrisy. Jenny Davidson, defining hypocrisy as the opacity permitted by eighteenth-century manners, explores its moral and political benefits, which, among other virtues, helped women to negotiate relations of stark inequality. "By the start of the nineteenth century, women were not merely allowed, but actively encouraged, to cultivate an unreadable quality in their relations with men and with society at large."[15] The problem with the prude is her failure at any such relation. Early prudes do not play games of politeness. Yet, as predators they are profoundly interactive. Madeleine de Scudéry, herself a targeted *précieuse*, offers this sketch of prudes in *Clélie* (1654–61): "These scrupulous women who would not want even to see love in paintings, rip up all women, easily condemn the actions of the most innocent, cannot suffer any pleasures they do not enjoy, do not spare even their dearest friends, find fault with all that they do not do, and malign all that happens outside of their presence and all that they have not heard of."[16] Prudes, Scudéry observes, are "strangely curious, wanting to know everything that happens in other circles," even if only to slander them.

By the age of manners, the prude's antisocial aggressions have been tamped down, only to reveal a chilling indifference. Pope includes the "prudent" Cloe among "the Characters of Women" in his "Epistle to a Lady":

"Yet Cloe sure was formed without a spot"—
Nature in her then erred not, but forgot.
"With every pleasing, every prudent part,
Say, what can Cloe want?"—She wants a heart. (157–60)

The eighteenth-century prude "speaks, behaves, and acts just as she ought," "never slander[ing]" a single friend or betraying her secrets, yet: "Would Cloe know if you're alive or dead?" (161, 175, 177). "So very reasonable, so unmov'd, / As never yet to love, or to be lov'd," the prude is no longer vicious but worthless: "Cloe is prudent—would you too be wise? / Then never break your heart when Cloe dies" (165–66, 179–80). By midcentury, Corinna's "show of resistance" takes another turn in the construction of Pamela Andrews's "irresistible resistance," which goads Shamelists' tireless send-up of female "vartue." Such fictions of modesty, Ruth Yeazell argues, reveal how a culture produces shame, what "aggressive energies and desires" are foreclosed by the figuration of female innocence.[17]

FIGURE 1. *Four Times of the Day: Morning*, engraved by William Hogarth (1738). Courtesy of the Harris Brisbane Dick Fund, Drawings and Prints Department, Metropolitan Museum of Art.

In the rollicking archive of prude fictions we see cultures grappling with those energies and ambitions, still scandalously visible. One response is to turn Ovid's *pudor* into *pudeur*, or a "shame of nakedness."[18] As one of Molière's *précieuses ridicules* explains, "I find marriage a completely shocking thing. How can one stand the thought of lying against a truly naked man?"[19] Prude fictions seize on this picture:

> The Sight of Breeches shook my very Frame,
> And sooner wou'd I starve, that Cod-fish name:
> E'en now my poor Heart pants—do what I can,
> Convulsions seize me at the Thoughts of Man.[20]

But as Jean Claude Bologne argues, *pudeur* is irreducible to sexual feeling—less descriptive of individual qualities like shyness or modesty and more a litmus test of acute social discomfort. He explains that *pudeur* is a moment of blurred self- and social consciousness: not the state of Adam's or Eve's nakedness but their realization that they appear naked before each other and before the world. Sexual discomfort is social shame: "a dynamic process that must be defined in phenomenological terms, emerging only at the moment one realizes that one is naked" (*Histoire de la pudeur*, 15).

Hogarth's "Morning" from his *Four Times of Day* series (1736) would shape the representation of the English prude (fig. 1). A well-dressed woman of a certain age, Morning makes her way to church, a sniveling boy trailing with her Bible. As dawn creeps into the London sky, her gaze lands on an illumined couple in a fondling embrace. Around the pair, residual signs of nocturnal life (more lovemaking, a coffeehouse brawl, pick-pocketing) merge with the business of the day (vendors setting up provisions, children crossing the square). In their midst Morning stands quite still. Even as the ribbons of her headdress flutter and cross in the breeze, she is fixated by the dalliance taking place not two feet from her skirts. On the ground a mendicant lifts her eyes and raises her hand to the lady of fine dress and, presumably, finer feeling. But Morning's "over-rigid Carriage" is unbendable; she is riveted by public sex, oblivious to the beggar's appeal ("Metamorphosis of a Prude," 4). Hogarth's allegory captures the prude's tipping point between shame and shamelessness, neither achieving sublimation nor gratifying desire.

Fielding's *Tom Jones* (1749) invents a prequel to Hogarth's painting (turned into a popular etching in 1738) with its pivotal but underworked character of Bridget Allworthy. Of the budding courtship between the spinsterly Miss

Bridget and lusty Captain Blifil, the narrator remarks that neither "was remarkable for Beauty." Of Miss Bridget, he continues, "I would attempt to draw her Picture; but that is done already by a more able Master, Mr. *Hogarth* himself, to whom she sat many Years ago, and hath been lately exhibited by that Gentleman in his Print of a Winter's Morning, of which she was no improper Emblem, and may be seen walking (for walk she doth in the Print) to *Covent-Garden* Church, with a starved Foot-boy behind carrying her Prayer-book."[21] Cleverly superseding Hogarth's figure, Fielding invents a real-life model, but both subjects derive from the prude of false virtue, who feigns shock but is captivated by vice. Textbook prude, Bridget Allworthy is unlovely, middle-aged, and contemptuous. She "very rightly conceived the charms of person in a woman to be no better than snares for herself, as well as for others; and yet so discreet was she in her conduct, that her prudence was as much on the guard, as if she had all the snares to apprehend which were ever laid for her whole sex" (32).

A figure of sexual rejection (no snares are laid for *her*) but also repudiated shame (she would never succumb to them anyway), Fielding's Hogarthian prude is resurrected in "Yon ancient prude" of William Cowper's "Truth" poems (1782). In a detailed reading of Hogarth's portrait—

> Her elbows pinion'd close upon her hips,
> Her head erect, her fan upon her lips,
> Her eyebrows arch'd, her eyes both gone astray
> To watch yon amorous couple in their play,
> With bony and unkerchief'd neck defies
> The rude inclemency of wintry skies

—the poem consolidates the prude's various features: her spiritual pretensions, malicious pride, and bitter tongue ("her every word a wasp"). Cowper's own waspishness hard at work, he catches the prude in a moment of reverie and showcases the embarrassing fantasies of an "Old Maid":

> Conscious of age, she recollects her youth,
> And tells, not always with an eye to truth,
> Who spann'd her waist, and who, where'er he came,
> Scrawl'd upon glass Miss Bridget's lovely name;
> Who stole her slipper, fill'd it with tokay,
> And drank the little bumper every day.

Cowper's Bridget concocts ridiculous fictions, but at least her stories are her own. By contrast, Fielding's Bridget hushes up her highly romantic but still authenticated love affair with the handsome, genteel, and sadly dead Mr. Summer. Indeed, without Bridget's shame there can be no orphaned Tom Jones, no tale of two sons, no *éclaircissement*. The novel only speaks where the prude falls silent, yet it is still her story that it will not tell. Too much the gentleman, Fielding refuses to probe female interiority. At the moment when Sophia Western learns that Tom loves her, the narrator openly declines to represent her feelings: "As to the present situation of her mind, I shall adhere to the rule of Horace, by not attempting to describe it. . . . Most of my readers will suggest it easily to themselves" (180).[22] Fielding (pre-*Amelia*) leaves the task of unearthing women's motives to Richardson.[23] Yet Richardson himself relied on an earlier tradition of laying bare the female soul—a textual history that consists of exilic women's voices and the painstaking rhetoric designed to sabotage them.

DUALISM AND PSYCHOLOGICAL NARRATIVE

Before Lacan there was La Bruyère pronouncing the split that constitutes sexual difference. In his monumental *Les caractères ou les mœurs de ce siècle* (1688), La Bruyère declared that the essence of *les femmes* is, simply, that they are liars.[24] Whether through costume or cosmetics, their *métier* is to falsify appearances, to practice *une espèce de menterie* (79). The calling card of a libertine taxonomy, the prude hails all of her sisters: *la coquette*, *la galante*, *la femme savante*, *la volupteuse*, and *la femme sage*. Such classifications address the basic unintelligibility of women; their honed capacity (a product of their essential inferiority) to deceive: "to wish to appear on the outside what goes against the truth" (*vouloir paroître selon l'extérieur contre la vérité*) (79). Bruyère observes that while a woman dissimulates through her toilette, her most baleful tactic is to "speak against thought" (*parler contre sa pensée*) (79). The prude thus excels in verbal manipulation.[25] More hideous than even a woman's pallid, crinkled, rotting surface can express, the female mind can never be fully realized. "Unbless'd with Form," her soul is so denatured that it must undergo radical reupholstery to assume viable shape: "all the Woman is become a *Bed*." (For a visual demonstration see Thomas Rowlandson's etching "Six Stages of Mending a Face.") Contrary to the notion that the prude is the formal nemesis of the libertine—the "equal and opposite" force of virtue exacted against vice[26]—the prude emerges as his double: a merciless and loveless destroyer of innocents, laying waste to conjugal norms.

In conveying a fundamental incommensurability between feeling and form, or a ludicrous mismatch between motive and appearance, the prude captures and exorcises the essence of womankind. She is ridiculous not simply because she looks nasty but because of the futility of her life's work to hide it. Endlessly exerting herself, the prude keeps trying to pass off vice as virtue, old age as youth, deformity as beauty: "Prudery constrains the mind but hides neither age nor ugliness." (*La pruderie contraint l'esprit, ne cache ni l'âge ni la laideur*) (Bruyère 96). The inaugural issue of Eliza Haywood's *Female Spectator* reports that "the greatest prude in the nation" was mistaken at a masquerade for a *fille de joye* but then properly exposed. Ridicule is the prude's "just punishment for her appearing in a place so little conformable to the austerity she professed in other things."[27] What must be punished, in other words, is her signature dissonance, a masking of beliefs that must be sinister indeed to necessitate such a cover.

Across genres, prude fictions showcase how femininity plays out the anxieties, fantasies, and impossibilities that attach to an ontology of inside and outside. Again and again, the prude is made to bear the brunt of dualism's impasses, to enact and expel its worst implications. Her frenetic oscillation between a raging interior ("such an Uproar in her Soul") and an empty one ("her Heart was vacant") brings the teetering logic of insensibility to its breaking point (*The Prude* 3.21, 3.4). In another riff on "A Prude unfortunately Metamorphos'd," one pent-up specimen is transformed into a hermaphrodite after her roiling intestines expel a penis: "Restless they roll and bounce . . . Till all at once they burst with dreadful Roar, / And force out something—I ne'er felt before" (*An Epistle to the most Learned Doctor W—d—d*, 5–6). A "doubtful Sex" or "Animal amphibious," the prude disrupts the ontological standards of gender as well as of emotion (ibid., 4).

As I discussed in my introduction, dualism inspires the fantasy that one day, one way, the corporeal will fall into line with the mental—the dream that *res extensa* and *res cogitans* will be reunited. Prude literature features a breaching from an outside to an inside in order to harmonize the two zones—not content and form but two aspects of a single nature (the libertine's monism). What is so noteworthy about the prude is how much she chafes against this template even as she animates it. The prude abdicates from a paradigm of emergence. She is so highly exteriorized that she can only be surface-read:

In Flounces see the hateful Prude array'd,
Abhorr'd and fear'd by ev'ry trembling Maid.
Right well the very Notions of your Dress,
The cruel Pleasure of your Life express.
For ev'ry Flounce, that on your Vest is born,
As many Reputations thou hast torn. ("Triumph of Beauty")

Prude literature charges the "Cartesian Women" of *préciosité* with denying their own embodiment by grotesque substitution.[28] Unhinged from nature, the prude is all made up: *une mauvaise imitation, une imitation de la sagesse, une continuelle affectation* (Bruyère 55, 78, 77). Her penchant for literature is of a piece with her pretense, a perversion in which words come to move her more than men do. As Molière's principal exclaims after the recital of a quatrain in his immensely popular *Les femmes savantes* (1672): "One feels these verses to the bottom of the soul, / Flowing—I don't know what it is that makes one swoon" (*On se sent à ces vers, jusques au fond de l'âme, / Couler je ne sais quoi qui fait que l'on se pâme*).[29] Still, what animates satire is not the poor taste of the prude but rather her unbearably straightforward desire to dictate truths, to be boss. Molière's finale clarifies the stakes of her surrender: "It is not for women to prescribe, and I am / for giving way to men in all things" (*Ce n'est point à la femme à prescrire, et je sommes / Pour céder le dessus en toute chose aux hommes.*) (5.3.1065).[30] By flipping her linguistic command into its corruption, Molière discharges the threat of female authorship, upending her claims. The *femme savante* is reduced to a case of phallic envy. The learned lady's fine compositions and philosophical maxims are revealed to be copies of a bad copy, the work of a male charlatan, whose ultimate disgrace chastens the *précieuse* into accepting her husband's rule and her daughter's marriage.

The elaborate rage and unease of prude discourse exceeds the crime of female deception. Prudery, it seems, is not exactly dissimulation—spinning inner dross as outer gold—but a barely, if at all, concealed will to power. Bombing (she's not fooling anyone) strangely does not deter her from putting on the same show over and over again, with even more energy, more conviction than the last time. In so flagrantly and repeatedly failing to stage her own virtue, the prude's performance gives off a whiff of contempt—a certain disinterest in the audience. The real scandal may not lie in her dissemblance but in her failure to try hard enough to dissemble—in other words, the bad fiction of her performance. The prude's lame attempts at plausibility ("she hides her weaknesses under a plausible exterior" [*elle cache des faibles sous de plausibles dehors*]) flounder.

And it's one thing if no one buys the story of *her* goodness, but it's another if her lousy act chips away at the story of goodness period or of gender period or of heteronormative power relations period. The prude traduces femininity by hewing too closely to its grain, staying so exactly within its lines that she lays bare its entire shape.[31] Queen of camp, she conveys what Sontag calls "a seriousness that fails."[32] Or, we could say that the prude's repeated misfires qualify as what Judith (now Jack) Halberstam calls "the queer art of failure," a political negativity that refuses legibility and acquiescence "to dominant logics of power and discipline" and, in particular, to "forms of subjectivity within patriarchy."[33] Where Halberstam casts the queer as a repulse to "Enlightenment philosophies of self and other" (14), these early prude fictions, I am claiming, show her immanence to such theorizations, high and low.

The prude betrays conventions of inside/outside, true/false so constitutive of Enlightenment subjectivity and its manifestation in the form of the novelized individual. Insofar as novelistic language aims for, in J. Hillis Miller's phrase, a "one-to-one correspondence to psychological or historical reality," it also reflects an ongoing debate about the value and possibility of achieving such correspondence.[34] Any quest to write away the differences between internal and external reality, to render a realm of thoughts and feelings as "true" as any physical object, had long been considered to be a political undertaking. In theorizing a new state, Enlightenment thinkers prioritized linguistic clarity, a razing of terminological mumbo jumbo to construct fixed relations between words and things. Locke, in his tweaking of Descartes's "clear and distinct" ideas as "determinate or determin'd" ideas, aspired to a linguistic transparency that would underwrite a "commonwealth of learning" (*EHU* "Epistle," 13). Hobbes, too, railed against scholastic incoherence in his efforts to imagine a state that could immunize itself from the dense misprisions of civil war. Victoria Kahn observes, "We can't help being struck by his preoccupation with language, metalanguage, and genre rather than mathematics or geometry. Hobbes explained the causes of the civil war in terms of linguistic abuse and dysfunction. In response, his method of political science was metalinguistic and literary through and through."[35] The Enlightenment mandate to restore referentiality to language shaped the ambitions of early fictions, those "True Histories" that pledged, as in Aphra Behn's *Oroonoko* (1688), to deliver the goods of reality "and to render it diverting, without the Addition of Invention."[36] The prude's aggressive affectations and imitations expressed bad faith in that project.

THE PRUDE AND THE PRÉCIEUSE

To retrace the origins of the prude and her historical and ideological significance to the English novel requires an examination of her antecedents in the *ancien régime* that bred both the novel and the *précieuse*. As Françoise Jaouën explains of the ridiculed coteries, notoriously fastidious in their literature as well as in their morals: "No text, no author of the period is a self-described *précieux*; they are described as such by their enemies."[37] A group identity constructed by its satirists even as they targeted real individuals, *les précieuses* remain inseparable from the misogynistic panic induced by women writers in the early republic of letters. "Preciosity is at once a phantom, a construct, a figure, and a historical phenomenon, but one that can be traced only from its critique," restates Jaouën (106). The prude emanates from this discourse, as we see in Charles de Saint-Evremond's "La Prude et la précieuse" (1656). In what we recognize from the Corinna poems as a "*nuit et jour*" problem, the pair expresses La Bruyère's split between public appearance and private practice: the upright matron and the *volupté domestique*, who regularly wears out her husband. What distinguishes *la précieuse* from *la prude* is simply the depth of her dissociation. Whereas the prude is at least her true (sybaritic) self at home ("conjugal appetites chafe at her, and her modesty suffers the robust caress of a naked man"),[38] the *précieuse* is not herself to herself. The result is a chiastic cancellation of feeling: *De jouïr sans amour, d'aimer sans jouïssance*.[39] In her affective and behavioral contortions, the *précieuse* hollows out her heart, splits sensation from emotion and achieves an insensibility to which the speaker strangely comes to aspire: "Would that I, too, were a sister *précieuse*." (*Je pourrois bien aussi d'une sœur précieuse*) (306). The antifeminist satirist, as Nussbaum writes, "is not always fully in control of his persona."[40]

Having spent a lifetime honing her skills of dissemblance, the prude perverts the primary virtue of the statesman, prudence. In Abbé Michel de Pure's early novel *La prétieuse ou le mystère des ruelles* (1656–58), "a prude is a middle-aged woman who has all the ardors of her first bloom but who, with time and good use of that time, has acquired the art of disguising them so well that they do not appear at all."[41] A travesty of experience, the prude migrates across time and cultures from allegory of deception to undeniable fart joke:

> Those airy Particules in *Hippo*' pent,
> Try'd ev'ry Hole, resolv'd to find a Vent;
> Their Exit I forbid;—a rumbling Sound

From Vapours thus confin'd began it's [*sic*] hollow Round,
In restless Torments I the Op'ra pass'd,
Dreading some frightful Squeak or horrid Blast.[42]

Turned into an old bag of pressurized innards, the prude now aims not for sovereign mastery of the passions (which would license her to govern others) but for gastric self-regulation. "Full of internal mischief," the prude feels "such an Uproar in her Soul" that she is overwhelmed by the need "to give [it] vent" (*The Prude* 3.21–22).

The history of the novel replays the libertine's trick (perfected in Molière) of debasing political desires into thwarted games of love, matchmaking, and social acceptance. Prude fictions make this narrative program jarringly explicit. The anonymous author of *The Prude* (known only as "MA. A."), for example, followed its success with another novel, *The Female Politician: Or the Statesman Unmask'd*, which elaborates the joke of a female statesman and features more faked "Insensibility to Mankind."[43] The précieuse/prude/coquette formation, Wahl reminds us, was a mid-seventeenth-century reaction against the increase of women's sexual autonomy. Libertine discourse was satirical blowback against alleged proposals, including birth control measures, that signaled a "rejection of heterosexual as well as maternal norms" and an attempt by women "to remove themselves from the sexual economy upon which [patriarchal] society was predicated" (*Invisible Relations*, 221). Earlier, Joan DeJean introduced the crucial claim that *précieuse* culture originated in the failures of state action. According to DeJean, the aristocratic women who led and were defeated in the midcentury civil skirmishes known as *la Fronde* retreated into the *ruelle*, that exilic space between the wall and the bed that was ground zero of the *précieuse* scene of writing.[44] In this literary backstory, revolutionary aspirations became sublimated into plots of *narrative* insurrection that flouted scripts of conjugality and maternity. As a result, DeJean writes, "in the final decades of the seventeenth century, a new female icon replaced the Amazon, an image still firmly in place well into the following century, woman as home-wrecker, once again as threat to State security, but this time in the State's very foundation, the family" (10). Insensibility, what once registered the female sovereign's necessary rejection of "the safe Harbour of Matrimony," a stance closely identified with Elizabeth I, returns as hauteur, meddling, and malice.[45]

Nonconjugal and thus noncirculating, the prude opts out of a vibrant economy of exchange and pleasure.[46] A century after Saint-Evremond, in yet another poem devoted to "the metamorphosis of a prude" (1756), the gods insist that the "Unmov'd" and "obdurate" Phyllis "yield to Love." A messenger is sent to charge the "Maid perverse" of hoarding her gifts instead of allowing them to be used, as they were intended, by others:

"For whom does thou adjust that auburn Hair?
To whom display each brilliant Beam and Grace,
And all the Wonders of thy Neck and Face?
Those Gifts the genial Pow'rs would ne'er afford,
For Self alone, or Miser-like to hoard;
Bestow'd in vain if ne'er to be employ'd,
They only are in social Bliss enjoy'd."

Miser and spoiler, the "Narcissus like" prude replies to the divine messenger:

"From me demand no Dues.
Those Pow'rs may seek them of their Subject Stews;
And quickly quit thy insolent Embrace,
Or tenfold Vengeance shall imprint thy Face."

To paraphrase her message: "Don't tell me what I owe to the gods. They can redeem their gifts at the whorehouse. And if you don't leave me alone, I will take it out on your face." At this, the messenger "drew back, and with Amazement view'd / Within so fair a Form a Mind so rude." The lovely, auburn-haired, rude prude shocks the gods, resulting in her transfiguration into not a bed but a cat: her "inward Savageness of Mind" captured this time by the "hairy Paws" and "crooked Claws" of a distempered tabby:

Now by her Tail is understood no less.
As erst, when courted by the am'rous Male,
With screaming Voice her Custom's still to rail,
To spit, and scratch, and shew her spiteful Spleen,
And all the Prude now in the Cat is seen.
("Metamorphosis of a Prude," 10–12)

This brings me to *The Prude: A Novel* (1724–26), a sprawling, three-part best seller that went through four editions in two years but whose nearly incoherent *entrelacement* would disqualify it today from any bookstore classification of "novel."[47] Prudes abound in this text, the most treacherous of which is a bloodless sister named Elislnda ("with a Complexion of the purest

White, without the least Tincture of Red" [1.14]). Handsome, clever, rich, and untouchable: her "eyes, moving with a heavy Deadness, are generally fix'd on the Ground, with so conscious a Shame, as if afraid to advance their Lids, as dreading to encounter Looks too amorous, and too warm for so cold Chastity and so strict a Virtue, as that which she possesses" (1.14). In public Elisinda wards off contact (apart from staring at the ground, she also prays and fasts). In private she seethes with elaborate schemes (to have her sister raped, procure an abortion, and finagle a threesome with her maid and footman). *The Prude* showcases its subject's defection from any narrative program, a residue of *précieuse* ambition to surpass conventions of intimacy, felicity, and property. (Of her sex life, the narrator reports, "It would be endless to relate all the Rencounters she and [her female companion] had" [1.29].) Importantly, this "female *Machiavellian*"—who likens herself to "the great Queen *Elizabeth*," who "*dy'd a spotless Virgin*"—inherits a "vast Fortune" from her grandmother, "and as soon as she became of Age, she had had her own Equipage and Servants, living by herself" (3.69, 1.19, 1.5).

Novel readers recognize the predicament of the would-be female sovereign in another fiction of female estate, Jane Austen's *Emma*, whose cavalier heroine famously expresses a commitment to nonconjugality: "I am not only, not going to be married, at present, but have very little intention of ever marrying at all."[48] A self-proclaimed insensible ("I never have been in love; it is not my way, or my nature"), Emma Woodhouse surrenders not because an "arrow" of love "dart[s] through her" but because of the threat to her social precedence, what makes her "always first and always right" in the Hartfield of her dominion (90, 444, 91). As Mr. Woodhouse—"no friend to matrimony" himself—informs her, "A bride, you know, my dear, is always the first in company, let the others be who they may"—an axiom on which his usually insouciant daughter dwells a "long, very long" time (302).

While it may seem jarring to read Austen's masterpiece as a prude fiction (another throwback appears in the form of Lady Russell in *Persuasion*),[49] we might discern a generic preoccupation with the impact of emotional abandonment and socioeconomic precariousness on female character. In *The Prude: A Novel*, the inset stories of Morenia, the "adulterous divorc'd Wife of the injured Count Vilayne," whose "Heart was vacant," and Emelia, of independent estate and "frozen Heart," are marked by episodes of destitution and homelessness (3.4, 2.65). With Elisinda the novel goes further—not only defamiliarizing a stock figure and denaturing its virtuous countermodel but also proposing a darkly Defovian figure of entrepreneurship. The prude's ironclad virtue is not simply a disguise for her passions ("how different were the real Sentiments of her Heart, being fill'd with Desires quite contrary to all this outward Piety" [1.15]) but, more crucially what allows her to refuse marriage and maintain her own estate. Her virtue is "proof against every Scandal" such that no one minds that "she chose to live by herself, to be under the less restraint, not omitting the setup of an Equipage, tho very unusual in a Lady so young" (1.17). Across its several plotlines, *The Prude*, like *Clarissa*, like *Emma*, connects the problem of female dispossession and its ensuing dream of sovereignty directly to the plot of compulsory marriage. The open derelictions of the prude set off a reaction formation in the shape of a "reveal" of her roiling insides—the making of a subject of sexual shame that eclipses the scandal of her political aspirations with the lesser one of illicit desires. But the cover-up never quite works with the prude. That she's always showing her cards or refusing to play requires the invention of even more prodigious splittings and transformations. Anthropologist Elizabeth Povinelli writes, "Love, as an intimate event, secures the self-evident good of social institutions, social distributions of life and death, and social responsibilities for these institutions and distributions. If you want to locate the hegemonic home of liberal logics and aspirations, look to love."[50] At stake in early prude fictions is only its wholesale repudiation.

In the final scene of *The Prude*, Elisinda's "long-worn Hypocrisies" have been exposed, and she appears before her sister and her sister's entourage (82). "All that could be said on her shameless Vices, her pretended Piety, and assuming Vertues, whilst her blacker Heart was practicing unheard of Crimes, was utter'd." When her do-gooding accusers "come to preach Repentance," she snarls at all "the happy Mothers" and "happy Lovers" who mar her vision. Glaring in turn at each "insipid Ideot," Elisinda falls silent and then pours herself a drink: "Elisinda, without speaking, cast on each a wild furious Look.—And indeed, her haughty soul being possess'd with Despair to find—to find herself disappointed in her Design: Unable to support it, she immediately . . . pour'd into a Glass a large Draught, which drinking down, she said to them with Fury, I am now past Insults; and then with a violence breaking from them, she went directly to her Chamber" (84).

When "the Company" intrudes on her private death scene (that cocktail was poison), Elisinda unleashes what the narrator can only describe as an avalanche of unprecedented obscenity ("many horrid Blasphemies . . . in the most abandon'd Language" [3.84–85]). Although the priest-like Olarius manages to administer some last rites by extracting "a sense of [her] Crimes," Elisinda remains a figure "past Insults," or immune from disgrace, not only minutes from suicide but also impossible to shame. Like the deposed sovereign featured in Chapter 3 herein, the insensible enters no plea, makes no concession, and refuses to acknowledge the authority of the court. With one request (that they leave her the hell alone), the prude declares simply, "I . . . shall disappoint you" (3.85). Far from frozen with self-consciousness, the prude is past the pale of social feeling. But the story of the insensible, as we know from Bartleby, is not about its "Deadness" but rather its oddly galvanizing effects. As Adam Smith explains, others compensate for insensibility, supplying what the subject either disregards or was born without: "We blush for the impudence and rudeness of another, though he himself appear to have no sense of the impropriety of his own behavior; because we cannot help feeling with what confusion we ourselves should be covered, had we behaved in so absurd a manner" (*TMS* 1.1.1.10: 15). To "have no sense" of what constitutes good or bad behavior (what will be well- or ill-received) signals a failure of imagination, the faculty that regulates ethical and economic life. Such failure triggers instinctive recoil, as well as involuntary substitution: "we cannot help feeling" the shamefulness of his behavior, to "blush" on his behalf. Elisinda's sister, the sympathetic and sympathizing Bellamira, "feels a greater Shame for her, than that Lady could be sensible of, for all her monstrous Crimes" (3.67).

The prude animates shame by owning none of her own. She refuses to be accommodated by narrative's social embrace, even as her secession initiates everyone else's group hug: "But whatever Confusion that Family might be in concerning *Elisinda*, yet the Respect all the neighboring Gentry had for *Emelia* and *Bellamira*, could not prevent their being visited and congratulated on their Delivery, and the other happy Events" (3.86). Deviant, villain, scapegoat, the prude unites the Company in virtuous felicity. Notwithstanding, it is "her black Story," including "the manner of her Death," that they must "[take] care, as much as possible to conceal . . . from the World." The prude, like Bridget Allworthy, is hushed up, the spoils of her fortune silently divided, her body "buried privately" (3.86). Her very accomplices are released in the spirit of clemency—sent off to fiction's witness protection program. As a shower of "happy Events" falls on the shallow grave of the prude, the targets of her negation (marriage, patrilineal inheritance, heterosexuality, class exclusions) are newly fortified.

Lee Edelman writes that the queer subject "comes to figure the bar to every realization of futurity, the resistance, internal to the social, to every social structure or form."[51] The prude, that "Third Sex" or "animal amphibious" of the English novel, wages a tooth-and-nail contest for sovereignty. She has another story to tell, but it would probably kill us to hear it. Fiction preempts that violence while keeping its potentiality usefully intact: the prude is laughed off the stage, turned into a cat, sent to her room to die. Outrageous, overblown, and offensive in every register, prude fictions are important because they tell the story, as Edelman writes, "of why storytelling fails, one that takes both the value and the burden of that failure upon itself" (7).

DEATH, INDIFFERENCE, DESIRE

If *écriture féminine* had an answer to the misogynistic depravity of prude fictions, it would be Madame de Lafayette's *La Princesse de Clèves* (1678), a text that redeems the split between feeling and action decried by La Bruyère as the cursed nature of *les femmes*. Where *la prude* disavows desire, *la princesse* makes an *aveu* cataclysmic to the history of the novel. Lafayette manages in this sublime fiction both to construct erotic feeling and to redeem insensibility as a philosophical good. The reading that follows will elaborate that narrative achievement in order to bridge the gap between early prude fictions and *Clarissa*, the subject of Chapter 2. I will also develop the novel's concerns with dualism, in conversation with Descartes's *Passions of the Soul* (1649).

For both Descartes and Lafayette, the difference between passion and action lies in the distinction between involuntary and voluntary motion. Desire, like illness, just happens to you; it throws your insides into commotion, twisting your pineal gland this way, then that. In this state of body and soul your options are (1) to go where it takes you, which is no real option for a married princess; (2) to resist its impulses (what Descartes conveys as the cauterization of passion through sheer willpower, or "the force with which the soul, by its volition to avoid this thing, pushes the gland in a contrary direction" [*PS* 236]); or (3) in Lafayette's "unprecedented" twist, to tell your husband about it so that you will not be tempted by the first option.[52] Far from the essence of deception, the princess's strenuous separation of passion from action, what Anne-Lise François calls her "antiacts,"[53] defines her extraordinary virtue ("so austere that it is almost without parallel"): "if I have feelings which are displeasing to you: at least I shall never displease you by my actions"; "none of my actions has revealed my feelings" (Lafayette, *Princesse de Clèves*, 95, 97, 150). Furthermore, where prude discourse aims to delegitimize its subject's language, Lafayette explores how writing—indeed bad writing—can be a site of intersubjective pleasure that is close to, better than, and still deliciously unequal to erotic intimacy.[54] Her text suggests that writing is not a relay between feeling and action but, like a prude, some third thing, which partakes of but also takes the pressure off the other phenomena. Finally, *La Princesse de Clèves* revives a conflict between narrative and philosophy, claiming insensibility as an escape hatch from the novel's pummeled terrain of love and war, in which unfeeling emerges as fiction's shimmering death-drive. While the princess is no clear-cut instance of Bartlebyan impassivity, her case engages the same framework of causation in which a body is moved from the outside to initiate a response on the inside. Lafayette's narrative examines the choke points in that process: where feelings might be staunched, redirected, or exorcised.

Desire records the singularity of encounter with a specific object, what for Descartes makes the pineal gland move in a certain pattern: a "particular movement which is ordained by nature to make the soul feel this passion" (*PS* 232). In his important qualification, motion can also be attributed to inorganic objects: "we do not doubt that there are inanimate bodies which can move in as many different ways as our bodies, if not more, and which have as much heat or more" (*PS* 219). Descartes here disaggregates motion from life. Contrary to Hobbes's materialist definition of emotions as "the Interiour Beginnings of Voluntary Motions," Descartes sketches mental life as largely made of involuntary, quasi-immaterial phenomena. Heat and motion "belong solely to the body," but thoughts (perceptions and volitions) fall under the more ambiguous precinct of the soul. Furthermore, the passions—a distinct but also hybrid strain of thinking—agitate the soul, marshaling a "close alliance between the soul and the body" that renders affective experience ("joy, anger and the like") "confused and obscure." Feelings thus seem to take effect "in the soul itself" even if they are largely perceptions of external objects or of one's own bodily states (227).

Murky and incorporeal, passions still conduce to action: "the principal effect of all the human passions is that they move and dispose the soul to want the things for which they prepare the body" (*PS* 233). The spacing introduced here between feeling and action—the soul's preparation, or priming, of the body to want what it does—allows Descartes to wedge in the heroics of the will, an experience of autonomy ("our ability to do or not to do a given thing") that not only feels completely free but is, in fact, divine in its unboundedness. Whereas the faculty of understanding is limited and error-prone, "it is only the will, or freedom of choice, that I experience in myself as so great that I can form the idea of none greater, so much so that it is chiefly on account of the will that I understand that I bear a certain image and likeness of God" (*M* 41). Only this godlike faculty to choose (so much stronger than our shaky sense of knowing anything) can intervene in the helter-skelter of the passions.

Descartes posits that the "one special reason why the soul cannot readily change or suspend its passions" is an unstoppable "disturbance" within the heart, blood, and animal spirits (those rarefied bodies of the blood that, like clouds of fairy dust, flit over and infiltrate this pore, then this fiber, then this nerve, essentially controlling the dilations of the human organism to sensations, thoughts, and feelings [*PS* 231]).[55] In the full-throttle grip of the object (conveyed by the passions as if the object were pressing on the soul itself), the will retains a power to resist: "The most the will can do while this disturbance is at its full strength is not to yield to its effects and to inhibit many of the movements to which it disposes the body." Resistance takes place not against the body of the object but *within* the soul, in "battle against itself" (237). Thus, insensibility, or the refusal to be moved, works against "the principal effect of all the human passions" to dispose the soul and prepare the body to do what it does. The will holds down the soul in a tug-of-war with its own propensities for action.

This devastating triumph of the will is the premise of *La Princesse de Clèves*. Lafayette's initial configuration is striking: take the two most exquisite people in the world, mix them together, and observe incomparable passion. The problem is not so much that the princess is married (her husband is easily dispatched) but that the same formula for producing love dooms it: So breathtaking is M. de Nemours that others must love him, too. Eventually, he will respond to another object, and this redirection will kill me. In her second notorious *aveu*, this time to Nemours himself, the princess explains, "I should no longer be able to make you happy; I should see you behaving towards another woman as you had behaved towards me. I should be mortally wounded" (149). As Spinoza writes, "sickness of the mind and misfortunes take their origin especially from too much Love toward a thing which is liable to many variations and which we can never fully possess" (*E* 5.A2.P20: 606).

Having already (albeit mistakenly) experienced this sickness, the princess believes it to be "the greatest of all evils"—the same, in fact, that destroyed her husband, who "was so desperately in love with her that he believed everyone else had the same feelings" (149, 96). Reflecting on her marriage, the princess lands on the logic of insensibility: "M. de Clèves was perhaps the only man in the world capable of remaining in love with the woman he had married. . . . Perhaps, too, his passion only endured because he found no answering passion in me" (148). Nonresponsiveness, Hobbes conjectured, proceeds from a heart that is either not moved at all *or* "already moved otherwise, by other more potent objects" (*EL* 80). As M. de Clèves complains, "I have never been able to inspire love in you," but "I consoled myself in some measure for not having moved you by the thought that you could never be moved; now another man succeeds where I have failed" (95–96).

Reflecting on her own jealousy, the princess wonders what the point of desire even is: "She felt that it was almost impossible for her to find happiness in his love. But even if I could, she said to herself, what can I want with it? Do I really want to tolerate it? respond to it?" (91). Desire splits the soul, makes one a stranger to oneself: "I am conquered and overcome by an inclination that carries me with it in spite of myself" (91). Later, the princess announces, "my passions may govern me, but they cannot blind me" (149); but, indeed, they do blind her, or at least they so command her vision that she can hardly perceive, much less understand, anything else: "She could not help being disturbed at the sight of him, and yet taking pleasure in seeing him; but when he was no longer before her eyes and she reflected that the enchantment she experienced when she saw him was the sign of a new-born passion, she came near to believing she hated him, so sharp was the pain this thought gave her" (39). The commotion brought on by desire—the agita produced by the perception of the object—is no different from the experience of pain. "Involuntary, passive, motiveless, and generally painful" is how Jonathan Lamb describes the faculty of second sight, in which "the immediacy of the image" makes an impression that is "sudden and total, immune to reflection, comparison, and conjecture." Of a piece with what Adam Smith calls the "tumult of imagination," Lamb argues that "the social form taken by this kind of experience is not authorized, reflective, narrative or historical: in short, it is not civil and it is not modern."[56] The object that elicits unbearable, uncontrollable feeling ("What can I want with it? Do I really want to tolerate it?") deranges joy with sadness, what Spinoza defines respectively as "that passion by which the Mind passes to a greater perfection" and "that passion by which it passes to a lesser perfection" or as what "increases or diminishes, aids or restrains, our Body's power of acting, increases or diminishes, aids or restrains, our Mind's power of thinking" (*E* 3.P11: 500–501). "Today all my feelings are wrong," says Sancerre, the subject of the novel's embedded fable of treacherous passion (49).

You do not choose your object; your object chooses you. As Sancerre says of the faithless Mme de Tournon: "her image" was "the most perfect thing that ever existed, and the most perfect for me in particular" (47). The involuntary nature of desire underscores the singularity of the object—only *it* can move the pineal gland just so, prompting that "particular movement which is ordained by nature to make the soul feel this passion." This pre-ordained quality should gratify the object: "you may at least enjoy the pleasure of having won the heart of a woman who would have loved no one if she had never seen you" (151). Love's fantasy, as it was in "Bartleby," is to awaken the insensible: "I confess that you have aroused in me feelings I knew nothing of, indeed scarcely knew existed, before I saw you" (146).

Again and again, including in elaborate scenes of ekphrasis,[57] Lafayette emphasizes the visual nature of desire, as if the pineal gland lay just behind the optic nerve. The physical presence and proximity of the object floods the soul: "there was nothing that would protect her now; she would only be safe if she went away" (65). The princess must remove Nemours from her field of vision: "I must tear myself away from M. de Nemours's presence" (92); "I intend to remove myself from your sight" (150). Even immured in a convent, "she did not expose herself to the danger of seeing him and destroying, by the effect of his presence, sentiments that she was obliged to preserve" (155). Beholding the object is an experience of ecstatic pleasure; the problems begin when it leaves the room: "As soon as she was no longer sustained by the joy of being with a person one loves, she awoke as from a dream. She contemplated with astonishment the immense difference. . . . She could scarcely recognize herself" (90–91). The object out of sight, other passions (embarrassment, guilt, remorse) creep in. Locke observes, "Because the abstinence from a present pleasure that offers itself is a pain, nay, oftentimes a very great one, the desire being inflamed by a near and tempting object, it is no wonder that that operates after the same manner pain does, and lessens in our thoughts what is future; and so forces us, as [if] it were [a] blindfold, into its embraces" (*EHU* 2.21.64: 276).

Lafayette offers one passage of benediction, when both lovers bask in each other's company.[58] It is a scene of writing. They are forging a love letter to help the princess's uncle out of a bind with the jealous queen:

> Finally, after a great deal of discussion, they decided to write out the letter from memory. They shut themselves away to work on it, giving orders to the servants at the door not to let anyone in, and dismissed all M. de Nemours's people. This atmosphere of mystery and secrecy had no small charm for Nemours and even for Mme de Clèves. The presence of her husband and the aim of protecting the Vidame's interests helped to silence her scruples. She felt only the pleasure of seeing M. de Nemours, a pure, unmixed delight that was new to her, and from this delight came a mood of gaiety and freedom which M. de Nemours had never seen in her and which increased his love many times over. (89)

Writing does not simply provide an alibi for love (to look at and sit beside the object), but the activities it entails (discussing, deciding, ordering, remembering, revising, remarking) make desire *work*. This is all Spinozan joy—increasing and aiding the body's power of acting and the mind's power of thinking. The bliss of their cocreation derives from their sense of freedom and not, unfortunately for the Vidame, from the quality of their prose. Their letter "was so ill done, and the writing in which they had it copied was so unlike the one they had intended to imitate, that the Queen would have had to be very careless in her inquiry in order to fail to discover the truth. And in fact she was not deceived" (90).

The lovers' delight generates an implausible fiction, and its failure as writing (down to its unconvincing orthography) has material repercussions, inducing hatred, persecution, and exile. As the novel's opening makes clear, the court's web of shifting and high-stakes alliances overlays the map of European powers: "There were countless interests at stake, countless different factions, and women played such a central part in them that love was always entangled with politics and politics with love. No one was tranquil or indifferent; all thoughts were on seeking advancement, gaining favour, helping, or harming" (14). Insofar as seventeenth- and early eighteenth-century fictions track the play of power and interest (passion and action) that inhere in erotic plots, they also record fluctuations of war and peace, in which the stakes of individual feeling are shown to be no less than the stability of Europe itself. Indifference in this sphere is not an option. Whereas in the dialogue mistakenly attributed to Lafayette, *Le triomphe de l'indifférence*, three young women choose "generous indifference" over marriage and other affective entanglements, in Lafayette's novel the "desire for tranquility of mind" cannot be realized—at least not in a minefield of countless interests, proliferating factions, passions without end (150).

Theorists have shown how Lafayette's narrative structure plays out the possibilities for liberation. In April Alliston's reading the glass house at Coulommiers, to which the princess retreats from court life, reproduces "the architecture of her own heart of glass," which, like the "open-ended narration of her own desire," can only be controlled in the privacy of her own estate (*Virtue's Faults*, 61–62). "The new 'state' established by the princess of Clèves is a feminine space of retirement in which women have the power to determine the meaning of their own plots within the terms of a private exchange of personal narratives that are recognizable as true because freely offered, not subject to a prior demand that would predetermine their meaning in patrilineal terms" (73). According to Alliston, the novel's distinctive mode of tergiversation, or "endless delay in response to the unanswerable demand for a return," establishes "a purely narrative relation, a relation that cannot appear, cannot be represented, legitimized, or reproduced through resemblance" (72, 75). In François's interpretation Lafayette's structure of the "open secret" upholds "a chaste and chastening mode of interaction: chaste in the double sense of bearing little or no material consequences and of belonging to those who engage in the least possible intercourse, chastening in the sense of limiting anyone's power to do more than leave and be left alone" (*Open Secrets*, 81). Both Alliston and François highlight the incandescent zones of constriction and privacy that radiate in Lafayette's text, giving rise to its glassy narration, untethered to demand, not accountable to power. What, then, do we make of its final statement on desire: not the purity of nonreciprocation or the sufficiency of self-terminating speech but a creeping retreat into the hermitage of a sick woman?

Descartes ends *The Passions of the Soul* with a meditation on "the case of language": "Words produce in the gland movements which are ordained by nature to represent to the soul only their sounds when they are spoken or the shape of their letters then they are written; but nevertheless, through the habit we have acquired of thinking of what they mean when we hear the sounds or see the letters, these movements usually make us conceive this meaning rather than the shape of the letters or the sound of the syllables" (238). The habits acquired through language (shape → sound → movement → meaning) testify to our capacity to rewire the brain's patterning of responses, that is, to alter our desires. Like a public service announcement, Descartes's conclusion reassures us that new habits of feeling "can be acquired by a single action and [do] not require long practice" (238). It takes just one event (one story) to reconfigure our passions: to sever the links between the perception of an object, the movement it creates, and the emotion that attaches to that movement. Finally, by reattaching the feeling to other, "very different" objects, we come to control our desires. Such cognitive therapy works even on animals, like the reverse-conditioning of hunting dogs who learn to stop at the sight of prey and to run toward the sound of gunfire. Descartes insists that "we are able, with a little effort, to change the movements of the brain" (238).[59]

After confessing her love to Nemours and then pledging never to act on it ("I wish you to know and that I find it sweet to tell you. . . . For my confession will have no consequences."), the princess assures him that "my feelings for you will exist eternally and unchangeably whatever I do" (146). But, in fact, doing nothing for so long extinguishes them and, eventually, Nemours's as well. The process is not as effortless as Descartes would have it, but it is initiated by two discrete events: the death of her husband and, later, her own grave illness. "This long, close look at death made Mme de Clèves see the things of this life differently. . . . Knowing she must soon die, she grew used to detaching herself from the world, and as her illness continued the habit became ingrained" (154). How does a practice of detachment reconfigure the passions? What severs the links of desire if no new object exists to bind it? By what principle, in other words, could unfeeling even work?

After she recovers from her near-fatal affliction, the princess finds "that M. de Nemours had not been erased from her heart." In reminding herself of her reasons not to marry or, as we know, even to see him, "a great combat took place within her. At last she overcame the remains of a passion already weakened by the sentiments her illness had inspired" (155). Sickness, like the will, disposes the mind and prepares the body to want what it wants. Pain's insistent reminder of the corporeality of being abrades joy, relation, volition, and, finally, narration—a monism that transcends the libertine's agenda. Illness, like desire, draws body and soul into "close alliance": one experiences the approach of death as immaterial ("in the soul itself") even as it exploits the weakest points of the body (*PS* 229). Without room for further suffering, the princess finds a trace of her old desire, but it is overcome by a broader wish to end sensibility. She conveys to Nemours that on finding her "peace of mind to be irreconcilable with her desire to belong to him, all other things of this world had appeared so indifferent that she had renounced them for ever: she thought of nothing now but the life hereafter" (155).

Locke describes how pain occludes the possibility of every other feeling: "we have so great an abhorrence of pain, that a little of it extinguishes all our pleasures." Pain focuses the mind on the single purpose to eliminate it, *now*: "our whole endeavours and thoughts are intent to get rid of the present evil, before all things, as the first necessary condition to our happiness; let what will follow" (*EHU* 2.21.64: 276). The body in pain is heedless of the future, careless of narrative, seeks only the remedy of unfeeling. Oliver Goldsmith's *The Vicar of Wakefield*, a text I take up in Chapter 3, describes how "the man of sorrows lays himself quietly down, he has no possessions to regret, and but few ties to stop his departure: he feels only nature's pang in the final separation, and this is no way greater than he has often fainted under before; for after a certain degree of pain, every new breach that death opens in the constitution, nature kindly covers with insensibility."[60] As either unconsciousness or death, insensibility is the body's felicitous capacity for stopping its own receptivity. As in Freud's account, where the death drive is the defining attribute of the organism, on par with the instinct to preserve itself, unfeeling is feeling's own fail-safe mechanism. (Incidentally, this explains why impeccable happiness can look "too much like joy, senseless joy!" or what blacks out all your faculties ["For a few minutes she saw nothing before her. It was all confusion. She was lost."] so that you are glad to be sitting down in a window seat at Mollands when the "overpowering, blinding, bewildering" sight of Captain Wentworth walking down the street suddenly overtakes you [*P* 182, 190–91].) Goldsmith's description, in which pain ends simply by turning off the lights of consciousness, upholds the integrity of the body: each new breach is connected to and shut down by the whole. We return to our touchstone definition of emotions as "the Interiour Beginnings of Voluntary Motions." What is volunteered, or willed, at the end of life is the end of that motion, an end to being moved and to moving, a gentle switching off of that faculty: nothing, no one to regret.

Goldsmith's passage revisits Johnson's *Rambler* 32 on the topic of suffering and "the armies of pain" that overwhelm the human subject—body and mind—over the course of its life.[61] For Johnson existence means being forced to bear every variety of calamity. To deny this necessity is to affect the "wild enthusiastick virtue" of the Stoics, who "pretended to an exemption from the sensibilities of unenlightened mortals" (174). Johnson states definitively that "the cure for the greatest part of human miseries is not radical, but palliative" (175). He endorses what we half-recognize as the Princess de Clèves's practice of detachment: avoiding expenditures of consciousness that offer little consolation, like "the fruitless anguish of impatience," while pursuing those that do, like "conversation or advice [by which] we might be amused or helped" (179, 177). And yet, as in cases of "diseases intensely painful," there are times when consciousness maxes out: one may "suffer such exacerbations as seem to strain the powers of life to the utmost stretch, and leave very little of the attention vacant" (178).

Acute pain unites body and soul in the totality of its depletion, exhausting the body's powers to respond while also leaving no room to philosophize, to practice that "art of bearing calamities" (174). This precipitous decline in both mental and bodily capacity completes a Spinozan picture of sadness, to which unfeeling then enters as a remedy. In life's final stage, Johnson proposes, "the vital frame is quickly broken, or the union between soul and body is for a time suspended by insensibility, and we soon cease to feel our maladies when they once become too violent to be borne" (178). Like an internal morphine drip, insensibility kicks in just when we need it, suspending the ties between body and soul that confuse and compound our suffering. But Johnson goes further, like Lafayette, honoring the division that has garnered so much vitriol and anxiety: "I think there is some reason for questioning whether the body and mind are not so proportioned, that the one can bear all that can be inflicted on the other, whether virtue cannot stand its ground as long as life, and whether a soul well principled will not be separated sooner than subdued" (178). It makes sense in Johnson's theory that the princess dies, not because her virtue is about to crack and, therefore, so too should her vital frame but because the soul bears only as much as the body can and vice versa. "Separated sooner than subdued," the one finds the level of the other, and when it cannot, its connection is either snapped or held in suspension. Virtue stands its ground in the soul, pushing back on the susceptible pineal gland, until the body hits its limit, lays itself down, and nestles into insensibility.

Where prude fictions acted out the anxieties of dualism, *La Princesse de Clèves* plays out its dream of mysterious integration. Susan James details the feedback loop of passions and volitions, sensations and perceptions, body and soul in Descartes:

> To claim that our passions are in the soul is not so much to point to a place where they are as to indicate the absence of a spatial component to this class of feelings. Where is this joy? Spatially, nowhere; it is in the soul. Yet, taken as a whole, the definition presents the passions as lying between two categories, sharing some of the features of each without answering completely to either. Once we take account of their phenomenological as well as causal character, the passions, like nomads, traverse the border between perceptions and volitions, between passions and actions of the soul, between states that are, and are not, directly dependent on the body. Disorderly yet fascinating, they turn up on both sides of the line. (*Passion and Action*, 96)

Writing, too, is nowhere in *La Princesse de Clèves*. It flits between conceptions of desire as material and immaterial, searing and joyful, present and absent. "Untouch'd with Grace, Unbless'd with Form," the eighteenth-century prude is an undoing of the strange grace of Lafayette's text—as if an angry Nemours, instead of extinguishing his own passions, retaliated in prose and verse. Richardson will stage just that retaliation but will also keep intact the elusive form of the insensible. In *Clarissa* the prude turns up again like a bad penny, still worrying the line between true and false, body and soul, language and *repos*.[62]

CHAPTER 2

Clarissa's Marble Heart

AFTER THE LONG-SUFFERING Clarissa Harlowe finally dies and her rapist, Robert Lovelace, appears to lose his mind, a fellow libertine reports in a letter that "he was actually setting out with a Surgeon of this place, to have the Lady opened and embalmed.—Rot me if it be not my full persuasion, that if he had, her heart would have been found to be either iron or marble."[1] Famously impervious, Samuel Richardson's iconic character has garnered accusations from fictional libertines, eighteenth-century readers, and present-day critics alike. Sarah Fielding, tracking readers' responses, corroborated that "her Heart was as impenetrable and unsusceptible of Affection, as the hardest Marble."[2] Hard-heartedness offends not because it reflects an inability to love but because it betrays an absolute unwillingness to do so. The hard-hearted person is not just unfeeling, affectless, and inhuman (to take a few of Merriam-Webster's synonyms for *stonyhearted*), but she refuses to feel, to express affect, to be human.

This chapter follows the path begun by the prude and the *précieuse* into the uncomfortable intimacies between insensibility, power, and narrative so influentially charted by *Clarissa*. It is no stretch to claim its heroine as a literary descendant of the *précieuse*. If Richardson's landmark novel stands as a record of false charges against its subject, then the specific accusations made against her (of unnatural femininity, exaggerated prudence, and intolerable pretense as a "high-souled and high-sensed girl") all tap into the flights of misogyny set in motion by *préciosité* (5:301 [889]).[3] Eighteenth-century British fiction, as we've seen, inherits from seventeenth-century France this cultural discourse as much as the literary form of the *roman* itself. The prior chapter tracked one vector of literary historians' claim that the legacies of *préciosité* and the novel are inseparable.[4] Revisited from the angle of prude fictions, Clarissa's notorious insensibility—her endlessly debated contempt and shamelessness—can be recognized as principal feature of the would-be female sovereign. Her upsetting nonrelationality ("there is no dealing with you"; "There was no talking to me"; "There is no holding her") reflects her putative governance—the flouting of patrilinearity, in the form of "my Estate, the envied Estate, which has been the original cause of all my misfortunes" and which launches the novel's protracted plot (2:186 [301], 2:214 [316], 2:228 [324], 5:51 [754]).

Richardson turns what Joan DeJean describes as the "literary estate" of the *précieuses* (their retreat into a republic of letters following political defeat) back into real estate, which consists of subjects, as well as property ("*My Poor*, as I have had the vanity to call a certain set of people" [5:51–52 (755)]). Once again civil war, in which Lovelace is the self-identified usurper ("as Cromwell said, if it must be my head, or the king's"), puts rulership at issue in the appearance of unfeeling.[5] (We will touch on headlessness at the end of this chapter.) Lovelace reminds himself to "remember her indifference, attended with all the appearance of contempt and hatred. View her, even *now*, wrapt up in reserve and mystery; meditating plots, as far as thou knowest, against the Sovereignty thou hast, by right of conquest, obtained over her" (4:223 [657]). Enmeshed in plots of revolution and counterrevolution, Richardson's plot spirals out the precept by which unfeeling drives the passions. Prude fictions express this logic in libertine terms: "It was impossible for him to hear so much talk of *Elisinda*'s cold Indifference, without being fired with a desire to try if she could prove a Rock against all his artful Batteries" (*The Prude* 1.20). But, of course, the prude is the artful one. As Uncle Harlowe angrily marvels, "How can you be so unmoved yourself, yet be so able to move everybody else?" *Clarissa*'s exposition of the violence and futility of this question turns the novel into what Frances Ferguson depicts as a self-cancelling form, whose double purpose is to construct as well as erase interior life.[6]

My reading of *Clarissa* begins by setting out the problem, within and without the text, of its subject's desires. I then look to an alternative model articulated by Anna Laetitia Barbauld, revived by contemporary theorists, and advanced by Richardson's own postrape incarnation of his character. Examining Clarissa's phase of "indifferency" before the rape and her life of transparency after it, I argue that this central insensible in literary history first consolidates and then jettisons novelistic thinking about interiority as it considers what it might mean to live on without one.

THE PROBLEM OF LOVE

Richardson's immense fiction opens with the correspondence between Clarissa and her best friend, Anna Howe, a demanding reader who wants all "the particulars" about what her friend says, does, and thinks amid the scandal that the rogue aristocrat Lovelace has brought upon the Harlowes (1:1 [39]). As the story escalates into an abduction and rape narrative—with Clarissa fleeing an arranged marriage to one man, the odious Roger Solmes, only to find herself forced into cohabitation with another—Anna's need to know intensifies. From the famous "throbs" and "glows" Anna imputes to her friend, to her sober recommendation that Clarissa marry her rapist, Anna investigates what she is already convinced of: "It is my humble opinion, I tell you frankly, that on enquiry it will come out to be LOVE" (1:62 [71]).

Like Anna Howe, Richardson's readers discredited Clarissa's account of her own feelings, convinced that she did love, or at least should have loved, her rapist. Richardson wrote to two young female fans, "Would you not wonder . . . that there are Numbers of your Sex, who pity the Lovelace you are affrighted at, and call Clarissa perverse, over-delicate, and Hard-hearted; and contend, that she ought to have married him?"[7] Challenged to make dying a more attractive option than coupling, Richardson found himself in the awkward position of a scold. In his correspondence with Dorothy Bradshaigh, who famously expressed her disinclination to finish a novel in which Clarissa dies rather than marries, Richardson acidly observed that Lovelace had clearly succeeded with some women. Reading to the last volume, he wrote Lady Bradshaigh, "will cure you for your Love for the Man—Perhaps however you would not wish to be cured."[8]

In the end Richardson denied readers the only outcome that could make good on the relentless brutality of his plot. In response they simply disbelieved or even overwrote *Clarissa*, determined to marry her off, whether by rehabilitating Lovelace or by undoing his rape.[9] Readers' debates about whether Clarissa was a sexual prude, narrative killjoy, or paragon of virtue created a confusion that Richardson loved to hate. According to Sarah Fielding, "the many contradictory Faults that [Clarissa] was at once accused of, is almost incredible."[10] The bottom line seemed to be: if Clarissa could just love Lovelace, readers might then love her. Their experience of the novel boiled down to the question, "Is she in love?"—with most answering that yes, as Jean Hagstrum writes, "Clarissa was indeed in love with the person of Lovelace and contemplated a deeply satisfying union of body and soul" with him.[11]

Yet *Clarissa* is a demonstration of the many ways there are to say no: "Let me then repeat, that I truly despise this man! . . . I love him not, therefore!"; "I cannot but hope that I never, never more shall see him in this world. . . . I cannot consent"; "I have taken [the resolution] never to marry *this*, and if not *this*, *any* man"; "I must tell you, Sir (it becomes my character to tell you) that, were I to live more years than perhaps I may weeks, and there were not another man in the world, I could not, I would not, be yours" (6:376 [1116], 6:423 [1191], 6:378 [1141], 7:98 [1117]). Repetitiousness undermines the force of her negation. Each utterance chips away at Clarissa's credibility—no match for the tide of her own feelings, which are already so apparent to everyone else. "I once indeed hoped . . . that I might have the happiness to reclaim him: I vainly believed, that he loved me" (6:376 [1116]).[12] Scholars have interpreted at length the novelist's baiting of his readers.[13] *Clarissa*, Tom Keymer argues, encourages within the reader "a heightened awareness not only of the dangers represented in Lovelace but also of his own susceptibility to them."[14] Accordingly, the reader's purported experience of loving and then unloving Lovelace after the rape coheres with Richardson's moral and didactic purpose. Yet it is readers' precise inability to stop loving Lovelace and their refusal to believe Clarissa or to forgive her for not doing the same that mark the novel's reception. Clarissa's imputed desire—the love Anna Howe discerns, which readers experience vicariously and everyone expects to see manifest at long, impossible last—generates the dissonance so closely associated with the text's history.[15] A major counterresponse is recorded in 1804.

Forty-three years after Richardson's death, a London printer purchased his letters "at a very liberal price" from the author's grandchildren and commissioned Anna Laetitia Barbauld to oversee their selected publication.[16] In her edition of his letters Barbauld privileged the achievement of *Clarissa* (a gesture repeated in Barbauld's influential, fifty-volume *British Novelists* anthology). What Barbauld so admired about Richardson's heroine was the same quality that his contemporaries had found so objectionable: her unrelenting heart. Barbauld points out that unlike Pamela Andrews, who maintains her chastity but then says yes to life with Mr. B., Clarissa loses her chastity but does not waver in her commitment to be alone: "In circumstances the most painful and degrading, in a prison, in a brothel, in grief, in distraction, in despair," Clarissa says no. Love is not realized with the speed of an arrow, and marriage does not erase a rape. "With Clarissa it begins,—with Clarissa it ends" (lxxxiii).[17]

If Richardson's famous attempt at "a new species of writing" in *Pamela* was to catch young minds "when Passions run high," then what was the demonstration in *Clarissa* when passions, if they ever existed to begin with, run bone dry?[18] Barbauld, like Richardson, took issue with readers who craved more romance from the plot. She records in her preface that "the generality of readers are perhaps inclined to wish, that Lovelace should give up his wicked intentions, reform, and make Clarissa happy in the marriage state. This was the conclusion which Lady Bradshaw so vehemently and passionately urged the author to adopt" (lxxxvii). The wish, Barbauld maintains, to extract a redemptive love story from a tale of such incredible "wickedness" defies delicacy and even rationality. Between Lovelace and Clarissa, "nothing takes place of that pleasure and endearment which might naturally be expected on the meeting of two lovers" (xcii). Clarissa, she argues, is simply hunted. Her achievement is to stay the course of nonconjugality, leaving the reader to appreciate "the greatness of mind with which she views and enjoys the approaches of death" (ciii). Searching Richardson's meaning ("That Clarissa is a highly moral work, has been always allowed; but what is the moral?"), Barbauld remained unfazed by the novelist's confusing and even punishing affective demands, convinced that Clarissa had done well to die (xcix). A minority voice, Barbauld asserted that Clarissa's firmness, her precise lack of any change of feeling, her unresponsiveness to others' desires are what win "our fondest affections" (cii).

Barbauld's account shifts the emphasis from a conflict between man and woman or body and spirit to a less legible kind of struggle. Clarissa's thorough refusal, the "greatness of mind" that orients her toward death and dying, not only confounds the marriage plot but also establishes the disconnect between agreeable scandal (she does love him) and estranging noncompliance (she would rather die). To Anna Howe's insistence that "a close examination of the true springs and grounds" of her feelings will reveal "LOVE," Clarissa responds: "Let me enter into the close examination of myself which my beloved friend advises. I did so, and cannot own any of the *glow*, any of the *throbs* you mention—*Upon my word*, I will repeat, I cannot" (1:63–64 [72]). In case her friend is not convinced, she spells it out once more: "This man is not the man. I have great objections to him. My heart *throbs* not after him; I *glow* not." But, as Richardson would soon learn, protesting at all was protesting too much. Howe lobs back, "It is no manner of argument that because you would not be in Love, you therefore are not" (1:66 [73]).

Confusingly, Richardson himself confessed to Aaron Hill: "I must still say, that I would not have Clarissa in Love, at setting out: And that I intended the Passion should be inspired and grow, unknown to herself, and be more obvious, for a good while, to every-body than to herself."[19] As Scott Paul Gordon writes, "The question of whether Clarissa *can* [quoting Mrs. Norton] 'know her own heart' is central to Richardson's project, which constructs a space that later readers have called 'unconscious.' "[20] This construction lends itself to reading Clarissa as a "hermeneutic casualty," to use Terry Castle's phrase, a subject of others' interpretations who can never signify her own pleasure or power—only her pain.[21] Not only eighteenth-century readers but also modern critics have blamed Clarissa for bungling her own story. Ian Watt's characterization of Clarissa as withholding sexual feeling posits a different subject from Castle's: one who experiences pleasure and power but perversely denies their existence. Watt complains, "Clarissa could perhaps have married Lovelace, very much on her own terms had she known her own feelings earlier, and not been at first so wholly unaware, and later so frightened, of her sexual component."[22] Richardson's suggestion that Clarissa's sexual component consists in aggressive social perception, or "every-body's" knowledge other than her own, reinforces the bind of reading her as either deprived or depriving others of love. Barbauld realized an alternative, opening up a countermodel that continues to resonate in what has amounted to a critique of psychological realism, a meditation specifically galvanized in 1987 by the appearance of Frances Ferguson's "Rape and the Rise of the Novel."

RAPE AND INSENSIBILITY

Ferguson's reading argues that "from the moment after the rape, when Clarissa begins dying and Lovelace begins longing for her consent, the novel is literally haunted by the specter of psychology, in which mental states do not so much appear as register the improbability of their appearing."[23] Engaging ancient Hebrew law alongside radical feminist accounts of rape, Ferguson formulated consent as a function of form. Defamiliarized, consent is no longer a representation of the contents of someone's mind but a back-projection of a relational structure like marriage or intercourse. Ferguson writes, "If rape parodies the formal features of happier sexual relations by disposing of the same body parts, Hebraic and Saxon law in their earlier phases were committed to the assumption that intention and consent were so far derivable from the forms of action that there essentially could not be a form that did not imply consent. . . . Consent, it was assumed, would always ultimately follow from the ongoing operation of the form" (92). Rape law, in Ferguson's complex argument, names those forms by constructing specific, statutory parameters (like age, capacity, and consciousness) that obviate the need to engage with actual mental states (93). "The law of rape continually draws and redraws its terms, as if to underscore the desire to identify the crime as a project of stipulating formal criteria ever more precisely, ever more thoroughly in an effort to minimize the problems that can arise in the effort to identify psychological states" (94). Thus, a discourse that exists to ascertain facts about mental life (did she want to or not?) works by constantly, obsessively negating their existence.

In likening "the intense formality" of rape law to Richardson's classic text, Ferguson articulated a new theory of the novel (95). Freshly understood as substituting instead of reflecting mental states, psychological fiction could be treated as a self-contradictory and even self-negating genre that seeks simultaneously to represent and abolish inner life. Thus the novel sets up a "reversibility" of terms (wherein "yes" means *no*, and "no" means *yes*) that gives rise to a singularly disorienting hermeneutics. Moreover, Ferguson argued, the truthfulness of rape narratives relies on desubjectification, in which the powerlessness of the victim licenses her credibility, such that "not counting makes her words count" (97). This logic (weak subject = true speech) is formalized, for example, by the statutory impossibility of minors to consent (they can only ever mean "no"). It is also formalized by Richardson's novel, in which "the importance of the notion of a mental state, the importance of the notion of subjectivity itself, may be guaranteed precisely by eradicating its relevance" (98). Ferguson showed how immanent to fiction's elaborate structures of interiority (like Clarissa's drug-induced unconsciousness during the rape) is the threat that they will be contradicted by actual feelings: "that one might never consent even if one wanted to consent, that the form might itself oppose the very mental state it was designed to represent" (100–101). Thus, in Ferguson's twist the premise of the Richardsonian novel is not to convey psychological complexity but to show how its very effect emerges from a gap between actual interior life and its textual counterpart: "the contradiction makes the difference between mental states and their formal stand-ins, stipulated states, visible" (107).

What is so arrestingly profound about *Clarissa* and its genealogy of fictions is thus a commitment to self-exposure. The psychological novel does not merely fail to match the mental with the formal, but it stages that incommensurability with Baroque gusto.[24] Ferguson succinctly observes that unlike "the *Bildungsroman*, with its project of maturation," the Richardsonian novel "can never get ahead" (107). Instead, it exists to "make apparent" its subjection to its own form in a world where "forms can never be outrun" (107, 109). The Richardsonian text incomparably binds affective failure to narrative failure. Like a trip wire constantly going off, its built-in spacing between story and emotion disables yet, I will argue, miraculously redeems it as an ethical project. The double purpose of psychological fiction doubles again such that it (1) posits interior states, (2) negates them with formal structures, (3) features the violence of that negation, and (4) attempts to do something else.

In the wake of "Rape and the Rise of the Novel," theorists of *Clarissa* have taken a compelling counterturn away from the investigation of interiority and toward a surface reading of intersubjective relations.[25] Examining the contemporaneous emergence of strict liability law, Sandra Macpherson reads the novel through the lens of felony murder and argues for "a formalist account of action indifferent to questions of motive and practices of interiority." In this view crime disrupts standards of intentionality and agency because it holds people accountable for acts that they did not directly do.[26] Similarly, Jonathan Kramnick shifts emphasis from the content or authenticity of emotions to, in his reading, broader assumptions about how actions and intentions work in the world. The achievement of *Clarissa*, writes Kramnick, is not "to establish an individual's psychology against its misperception by others, at least if we define psychology in terms of an interiority that surpasses what is available to the reader or, even, to the person herself."[27] Reviving the vexed topic of Clarissa's self-opacity, Peter DeGabriele redefines her insensibility not as unconsciousness but as "an absence of sense or feeling"—more "bodily descriptor" than (per Ferguson) an "account of a mental state."[28] In DeGabriele's intricate Derridean analysis, Clarissa's insensibility demonstrates the aporetic nature of touch itself, as that which testifies to the self's nonpresence to itself.[29] The persistence of Clarissa's body after the rape is further proof: "A surviving body survives precisely because there is more to it than its touchable and penetrable superficies, and yet that 'more,' that excess, is improper and inappropriable by the subject, and thus not a space of private interiority" (50).[30] What survives is less a remainder of the touchable or penetrable subject than, in my reading, its self-detonation or, in Barbauld's, its core. As rape survivor and public writer, Clarissa flips the "space of private interiority" into a zone of shocking transparency. She disables any incentives for psychological discovery: where nothing is hidden, there is no point—and no pleasure—in probing. Richardson's creation of this safe space within the interrogation room of the novel speaks to the genre's embedded self-critique, a turning of its back on its own theory of character—what historians of the novel have formulated as the implanting of a "bad subject," in Nancy Armstrong's phrase, or as the dialectic between "public subjection" and "private ethical subjectivity," in Michael McKeon's.[31] Narrative, in my account of *Clarissa*, somehow stumbles back into grace, in implausible but nonetheless merciful fashion.

CAN A PRUDE CONSENT?

In the last chapter I argued that the prude takes on the metaphysical fallout of dualism, first by embodying and then by refuting the mind-body split. The payoff of prude fictions to expose her insidious nature (she shows one thing but thinks and speaks another) reinstates a monistic order, wrenching thought back into line with action. To repurpose Ferguson's phrase, "forms can never be outrun." The rupture between inside and outside will not be repaired so much as proved never to have really existed. *Clarissa* showcases the primacy of this fantasy within the libertine's plot and within the domestic novel.[32] Like the organizing hatred of prude discourse, a distinctly Cartesian anxiety drives Clarissa's persecutors—the problem, as Lovelace puts it, that "the heart cannot be seen into but by its actions" (5:115 [789]). In wishing to see what "cannot be seen," the libertine seeks access to the other's visceral or unmediated experience of herself as a subject, her primary sensations of desire or aversion that get lost in the face-to-face of expression. What everyone wants to see, to know, is what Clarissa feels without knowing that she feels it—in other words, the raw cognitive material that will be served up by free indirect discourse.[33] In the social form of epistolarity, every emotion is compromised; there is no direct feed into the mind, the heart.

What does *not* count as raw feeling is intention. Insensibility, as theorized in my introductory reading of Bartleby, describes a paradoxical state of forceful inertia, neither aversion nor desire but resistance to any change of motion. Kramnick's reading of *Clarissa* asks precisely whether inaction counts as action, or, as he puts it, "Have I acted if I do not do anything at all?" (*Actions and Objects*, 194). The answer for Kramnick hinges on the disqualification of the category of intentions. Where Macpherson's reading of the novel through felony murder (instead of rape) replaces an agential framework of intention (or "logic of the subject") with a tragic model of causation, Kramnick understands the tragedy of the novel to be this very substitution, a new paradigm that leaves Clarissa behind (63). "Clarissa maintains that one ought to be held responsible for the actions one has intended; as a corollary, she also believes that one shouldn't be blamed for the ill fortunes that should befall" others, since "she has no intention to do anyone harm and thus has not acted" (195). In other words, if Clarissa did not mean to run away or have sex or cause harm or die, then, in her doomed view, she should not be blamed (205).

Toni Bowers's reading of the illogic of Clarissa's culpability reminds us of the novel's epistemological quicksand, in which "the myth of firm distinctions between rape, courtship, and seduction" (which had started to unravel in the first two volumes of *Pamela*) "is recognized as bankrupt from the very start."[34] Bowers describes Clarissa's defection this way: "Caught in a brutally dehumanizing world where dominance and subordination appear to be the only available positions, Clarissa does not choose to be courted rather than to be seduced or raped, as Pamela had. Instead, she refuses to choose at all among those false alternatives"—that is to say, refuses the "false choice" of "force or fraud," resistance or consent, which Bowers's comprehensive study treats as the situational bind of Augustan-period seduction fiction (266). Clarissa's singularly styled inaction, or "*refusal to act*," Bowers writes, clears "a space between action and passivity, a third way that partakes of the other two [elopement and abduction] but that cannot be reduced to either" (168, 267). Clarissa's immobility thus evokes the triangulation of body, soul, and writing explored in the last chapter's Cartesian reading of *La Princesse de Clèves* as a reclaiming of dualist anxiety. Descartes located the confusion of volitions and desires, actions and perceptions in the very phenomenon of the passions. Here, Bowers discerns a gap between action and inaction that inheres in the ambiguity over Clarissa's guilt or innocence. This muddle, Bowers suggests, leads to a wholesale rejection of the structure of desire—a structure, I argue in this book, that is premised on insensibility.

Intentions are the essence of prudence, the sovereign virtue of deliberation so unbecoming to the artless female and so travestied by the designing prude. When Lovelace extols Clarissa's "vigilant prudence" thus: "She has a world of knowledge; knowledge *speculative*, as I may say; but no *Experience*!" (5:115 [789]), he guts prudence of its meaning, replacing experience-based adaptability with innate inflexibility: "such an immoveable spirit!"; "a virtue so immovable" (2:195 [306], 6:103 [972]). If Clarissa is "the fair Inexorable," then it is her unbending inexorability, as we know, that makes her so fair (5:263 [868]). "My Charmer has no passions," her seducer laments, "that is to say, none of the passions that I want her to have" (5:316 [897]). Far more potent than a rake's insensibility is a Clarissa's.[35] His test to see "Whether her frost be frost indeed?" will prove whether or not it is *real*, that is to say, whether her inaction can be certified as unfeeling (5:283 [878]). Aunt Hervey, for one, accuses Clarissa's lassitude of being a put-on. She calls out her niece's *true* liveliness: "the moment you are down with your poultry, or advancing upon your garden-walk, and, as you imagine, out of every-body's sight, it is seen how nimbly you trip along; and what an alertness governs all your motions" (2:273 [347]). The more Clarissa is seen to move ("Limbs so supple; Will so stubborn!"), the more she is detected in prude-like deception (1:122 [103]). Mrs. Harlowe, decrying her daughter's curtseys as an "outward gesture of respect," speaks for all when she says, "The heart, Clary, is what I want" (1:121 [103]). It is the perceived disjunction between Clarissa's nimble parts and the inscrutable fixity of her will that makes her so dangerous. Impossible to read, the insensible is a pariah on the passions. "Oh thou ever-moving child of my heart!" exclaims her mother, who banishes said child from her sight.

Johnson's *Rambler* 97, a screed against "the gay coquet" who flutters her charms in public places, famously records the stretched logic that bars women from saying or even thinking yes: "That a young lady should be in love, and the love of the young gentleman undeclared, is an heterodoxy which prudence, and even policy, must not allow."[36] Richardson's novel similarly demonstrates that a subject who cannot accept will be hard-pressed to dissent. Insofar as a virtuous action must never be intended or premeditated, then consent—as the will to a specific action—cannot be owned.[37] Clarissa alights on this truth when she laments to her friend how taking precaution (stashing money and valuables) would only "amount to a demonstration of an intention which would have a guilty appearance to them" (2:153, [284]). In other words, any demonstration of intent would have a guilty appearance to it.[38] A vehicle for misprision, consent always undoes itself: "I must seem to compromise with my friends: But how *palliate*? how *seem* to compromise? You would not have me endeavour to make them believe, that I will consent to what I never intend to consent to! You would not have me try to gain time, with a view to *deceive*!" (2:252 [336]).[39] The incoherence of an "inten[t] to consent" and of "never intend[ing] to consent" flags its signature lag between thinking yes and saying yes. Clarissa characterizes this relay as a "time . . . to *deceive*," that is, the spacing between feeling and action that gives rise to the mind-body problem at issue in prude fictions. Clarissa signals the construct of consent only to bury it in impossibility: "I will consent to what I never intend to consent to!" Such grammatical chaos expresses consent's weird temporalities. When Clarissa negates all futures in the speech act *I never intend*, she smashes the clock of consent. Any relay between motive and action—the spacing that permits speculation, interpretation, error—is demolished: now is never, never now. A theory of mind premised on the time to deceive falls by the wayside. Uncle Harlowe complains, "You know *our* motives, and we guess at *yours*" (2:192 [305]). Clarissa quips, "God knows my heart, I do not!" (2:90 [252]).

CLARISSA'S INSIDES

The Bartlebyan subject moves neither on the inside nor on the outside, is both anorexic and paralyzed: "she cannot move hand or foot: For so much has grief stupefied her, that she is at present as destitute of will, as she always seemed to be of desire" (5:298 [887]). Clarissa cannot move, does not want to, and has never much wanted to before. Without aversion (protest, defiance, anger) or desire (throbs, glows), the insensible remains nonresponsive. Even in motion ("as much too lively, as before she was too stupid" [5:301 (888)]), she is unaffected by the impact of others. The script of rape, Lovelace assumes, should render its victim hyperconscious: "that it should so stupefy, as to make a person, at times, insensible to those imaginary wrongs, which would raise others *from* stupefaction, is very surprising!" (5:297 [887]). Stupid now himself, Lovelace ponders what to do with her. "What's the matter with me, I wonder! . . . But what shall I do with this admirable creature the while?—Hang me, if I know!" (5:298 [887]). Still as an experimental object, the creature is useful, cannot be given up.

Lovelace is fixated on the idea that Clarissa's virtue is innate, materially bound up with the seat of her soul: "her LOVE OF VIRTUE seems to be *Principle*, native *Principle*, or, if *not* native, so deeply rooted, that its fibres have struck into her heart, and, as she grew up, so blended and twisted themselves with the strings of life, that I doubt there is no separating of the one without cutting the others asunder" (4:224 [657]). The rhetorical operation to establish the innate quality of Clarissa's goodness requires Lovelace to physicalize an abstraction—to make the "love of virtue" into twisting, fibrous, organic matter, indistinguishable from her arteries. Lovelace's insistent materialism reappears in his infamous desire to embalm Clarissa's organs, to return her "bowels" to her friends and family, saving the best part for himself: "her *heart*, to which I have such unquestionable pretensions, in which once I had so large a share, and which I will prize above my own, I *will* have. I will keep it in spirits. It shall never be out of my sight" (8:44 [1384]). Self-appointed "chief mourner," Lovelace carries into perpetuity not merely his own passions but the seat of his beloved's, which will accompany him in a "golden" "receptacle" to the end of his days. Clarissa's pickled organs, her heart "blended and twisted" with her moral essence, will continue to furnish visual proof that body and soul are one, that interior is the same as exterior, that "a virtue so immovable" can be carted around "in spirits" encased in gold and glass (6:103 [972]).

Helen Deutsch, in her searching account of Samuel Johnson's body, coins the desire for "autoptic vision," in which we "are driven by a desire to see beneath the surface, a desire that demands that surface's violation."[40] Such a fantasy entails "an uncannily complex relation of the living to the dead . . . in which a desire to know the other . . . is supplanted by a desire to see oneself."[41] What is expressed by Lovelace's "crazed fantasy" for "Clarissa's bottled heart" is the wish not only for "an end to narrative" but also for its perpetual reenactment, "the libertine's longed-for self-reflection, his story's continuing end" (46, 48). Deutsch's haunting analysis spotlights the correlation at stake in insensibility between narrative/nonnarrative and living/dead, as well as the fundamentally queer nature of any project to confuse the two.[42] The endlessly moving target of Clarissa's trial does not, as we know, stop with the rape (when it should presumably "go no farther"). Lovelace instead wistfully revisits its design: "I had rather, me thinks, she should have retained all her active powers, tho' I had suffered by her nails and teeth, than that she should be sunk into such a state of absolute—insensibility (shall I call it?). . . . Have not I the worst of it; since her insensibility has made me but a thief to my own joys?" (5:297–99 [886–87]). Clarissa's numbness spoils the trial's purpose to prove either "active" desire or "frost indeed." Lovelace concedes the dishonor of having to rape: "Abhorred be *force*, be the *necessity* of force, if that can be avoided! There is no triumph in *force*—No conquest over the will—No prevailing, by gentle degrees, over the gentle passions!—*Force* is the devil!" (4:223 [657]). Yet, as he explains, Clarissa's insensibility simply called for insensibility: "I tried by Gentleness and Love to soften—What?—Marble. A heart incapable either of Love or Gentleness. . . . So my Scheme of the gentle kind was soon given over" (6:55 [945]). To force a body to move when it does not want to (to impose action from without) disrupts the emergence of mental states, or what makes for the slow joys of the libertine. To the Bartlebyan question of how an unmoved body moves, Lovelace would appear to answer, "Watch me make it move. However, making it move would also mean that it never moved for me, which was my wish all along. I wanted to see *interior* motion, but what I proved was dumb mechanics: push a drugged body and it will budge." Contrary, then, to Catherine Gallagher's insight that the "proprietary barrier of the other's body is what fiction freely dispenses with,"[43] the Richardsonian text showcases its mulish heft, a body that won't go.

It is important to see how Lovelace's scheme to sink his victim into "absolute" insensibility preserves the totality of the object. Blackout maintains the integrity of consciousness, keeps the deep fibers of Clarissa's virtue uncut. "And for what should her heart be broken? Her will is unviolated:—At *present*, however, her will is unviolated" (5:352 [916]). The pedophilic dream to possess without damaging, to violate without spoilage remains intact: "Is not this then the result of all, that Miss Clarissa Harlowe, if it be not her own fault, may be as virtuous *after* she has lost her honour, as it is called, as she was *before*?" (5:265 [869]). Of Clarissa's notion that she could only ever recover as much as "*one half* of her fame" by marrying him, Lovelace chimes, "And if she must live a life of such uneasiness and regret for *half*, may she not as well repine and mourn for the *whole*?" (5:264 [869]). As Deleuze writes, what drives the sadist is a fantasy of wholeness, the achievement of totalization, even at the subject's own expense.[44]

As my chapter on Austen will elaborate, totalization also characterizes the processes of sympathy, in which complete immersion is required to contemplate the circumstances of another. Clarissa anticipates Adam Smith's very language when she asks of Lovelace: "I appeal to your own heart, if it be possible for you to make my case your own for one moment" (4:220 [655]). In Clarissa's logic, if Lovelace could momentarily assume her position, he would, by definition, have sympathized with her. Yet Lovelace's cognitive reach is limited, extending only as far as a bemused observation of difference: "I must own, that there is something very singular in this Lady's case" (5:295 [885]). Thus, when Clarissa observes "too great a mismatch, as I may call it, in our minds, ever to make you wish to bring about a more intimate union of interests between yourself and CLARISSA HARLOWE," she calls out his mental deficiency. The inability to "make my case your own" forecloses any "intimate union of interests" since, presumably, you should recognize what my interests are before you come to share them. Lovelace may play at totalization, but he is stumped by immersion, reconstruction, fiction.

After his friends appear to renounce him, Lovelace engages in tactical self-recrimination: "I deserve it all: For have I not been as ready to give up myself, as others are to condemn me? What madness, what folly, this!—Who will take the part of a man that condemns himself?—Who *can*? He that pleads guilty to an indictment, leaves no room for aught but the sentence" (8:143 [1437]). Anna Howe, long noting his "specious confessions and self-accusations" earlier observes that Lovelace's "ingenuousness is the thing that staggers me: Yet is he cunning enough to know, that whoever accuses himself first, blunts the edge of an adversary's accusation" (3:126 [451]). Lovelace corroborates. He writes to Belford, "seest thou not, that the more I say against myself, the less room there is for thee to take me to task?" (4:225 [657]), and later, he announces his aim "to disarm thy malice by acknowledgement: Since no one shall say worse of me, than I will of myself" (a line, as we will see, repurposed by Clarissa) (6:103 [972]). The fullness of Lovelace's self-condemnation obviates further say. As he writes to Colonel Morden, "I own to you then . . . and I'll tell you further. . . . Nay, I will say *still* further. . . . And if you can say worse, speak it" (7:263 [1280]).

Anna Howe attributes Lovelace's campaign of self-abuse to an overall publicity war ("He owns therefore what it would be to no purpose to conceal. . . . 'Why, this madam, is no more than Mr Lovelace *himself* acknowledges' "), and she accuses him of being a "dissembler, odious as the sin of Hypocrisy" (3:125 [451]). Lovelace's repudiation of these charges ("*I don't take the care some do, to conceal my lapses*") does not, however, bolster his innocence but simply reinforces the totality of his cathexis (3:125 [451]).[45] Others are important only insofar as they supply an audience, a witness to the unalloyed nature of his attachment to one object: "I did bad by Clarissa. I did 100 percent bad by Clarissa. I did bad by 100 percent of Clarissa." The partitioning of spectators seals off the dyad of agent and patient, cocooning the couple in their own tragedy and no one else's. Lovelace refuses to share the blame, including with those "implacable relations" on whom he formerly relied as coconspirators (7:263 [1280]). He is answerable to his victim alone, having acted "unworthily by Miss Clarissa Harlowe . . . [of] baseness to her . . . culpable *as to her*" (7:263 [1280]). The only need Lovelace has of the social is punishment. "He that pleads guilty to an indictment, leaves no room for aught but the sentence" (8:143 [1437]).

Where Lovelace needs an audience for his sadistic melodrama, Clarissa constructs a readership for her novel.[46] This structure disrupts the libertine's dyadic fantasy, opening up the story's distribution of blame and destabilizing its field of knowledge. Suddenly everything, everyone is implicated in her downfall, and even nonsubjective forces (like patrilinearity, commerce, marriage, misogyny) can be seen to exceed and incorporate the "cold purity" of the libertine's demonstration (Deleuze, *Masochism*, 86). As Macpherson writes, once "it becomes clear that the crime for which [Lovelace] might be responsible is murder rather than rape, [the] acts of others bear a more proximate relation to Clarissa's death than any action of his own."[47] Authorship does not claim the kind of exclusivity that is sought by the sadist. Where the sadist must destroy "something outside itself again and again" to achieve his vision of total negation (Deleuze, *Masochism*, 126), the writer works independently, at a distance. Clarissa here resembles Freud's storyteller as one who applies "purely formal" "technique" to his dreams "so that they lose their essentially personal element."[48] More focused on research and composition than on direct sharing (or inflicting), Clarissa, too, "sits inside [her] mind, as it were, and looks at the other characters from outside." The sadist is stuck on himself, too invested in a personal project of complete negation. Lovelace loses when he himself becomes partialized—one piece of a textual puzzle that is open, fluid, and ambiguous—the farthest thing from a zero-sum game.

INDIFFERENCY, LIBERTY

If Lovelace engaged in aggressive self-stigmatization, Clarissa turns herself into Wretchedness, a similar procedure whereby "no one shall say worse of me than I will of myself" (7:263 [1280]). In a study of allegory in *The Pilgrim's Progress*, Cynthia Wall has challenged the reading of character "from the post-nineteenth century perspective of *expectations* of development—which presumes a different ontological worldview, a different, nonessentialist understanding of personal identity as something capable of change and, therefore, of characters able to be 'round.'" Characters of earlier fiction, Wall argues, "are rendered [with] minimalist indicative detail," drawing on allegorical and emblematic structures to create the psychological and emotional spaces in which they dwell.[49] To auto-allegorize, as Clarissa does, is a peculiar practice of enclosure, which renders the self at once saturated and blank, neither flat nor round. The picture of a mind neither full nor empty resonates in what Locke calls "indifferency."[50]

Indifferency appears in Locke's brief, posthumous treatise *Of the Conduct of the Understanding* (1706), the purpose of which is to address the "several Weaknesses and Defects in the Understanding, either from the natural Temper of the Mind; or ill Habits taken up, which hinder it in its progress to Knowledge."[51] As remedy for mental neglect and mismanagement, *indifferency* describes a mode of imperviousness necessary to evaluate truth claims.[52] Against, for example, Descartes's account of *l'indifférence* as error or Mary Astell's indictment of "indifferency" as misguided self-interest,[53] Locke maintained the connection between indifference and knowledge, asserting that "an equal indifferency for all truth" means "receiving it in the love of it as truth, but not loving it for any other reason before we know it to be true" (§12, at 44–45 [186]). For starters, remaining "indifferent to opinions" (of "Parents, Neighbors, Ministers") does not necessarily prevent one from adopting them in the end, but it does allow one to "enquir[e] directly into the Nature of the thing itself, without minding the Opinion of others, or troubling himself with their Questions or Disputes about it, but to see what he himself can, sincerely searching after Truth, find out" (§3, at 7 [169]; §34, at 105 [213]).[54] The search for truth is actively solitary work. To "receive and imbrace" evidence, one disregards—rather than, say, thoughtfully considers or takes into measured account—the views of others. The indifferent subject keeps herself open (the truth is out there) while also shutting herself down (just not in other people) (§34, at 101 [211]).

Yet the apparently antisocial operation of indifferency rests on the riddle of Assent, another topic in the *Conduct*. Just prior to the last two parts on indifferency, Locke observes that "in the whole Conduct of the Understanding, there is nothing of more moment than to know when and where, and how far to give Assent, and possibly there is nothing harder." We know that granting assent is hard because apparently so few people know how to do it: "some firmly imbrace Doctrines upon slight grounds, some upon no grounds, and some contrary to appearance" (§33, at 99 [210]). Descartes's Meditator had already endorsed suspending assent in his momentous call "to demolish everything completely and start again right from the foundations" (*M* 76). He further reflected, "There is not one of my former beliefs about which a doubt may not properly be raised; and this is not a flippant or ill-considered conclusion, but is based on powerful and well thought-out reasons. So in future I must withhold my assent from these former beliefs just as carefully as I would from obvious falsehoods, if I want to discover any certainty" (78–79). What Locke understood from Descartes was that a blanket withholding of assent is a cultivated, strenuous practice—one that most would rather forgo. As Locke writes, rarely do people "deal fairly with their own Minds, and make a right use of their Faculties in the pursuit of Truth" (§34, at 102 [212]). Adapting the path of the Meditator, Locke advises, "He that will know the Truth of things, must leave the common and beaten Track, which none but weak and servil Minds are satisfy'd to trudge along continually in" (§24, at 71 [198]).

Clarissa's mental landslide over the course of the novel resounds in the Meditator's opening story: "Some years ago I was struck by the large number of falsehoods that I had accepted as true in my childhood, and by the highly doubtful nature of the whole edifice that I had subsequently based them" (*M* 17). After her rape, Clarissa back-projects cracks in the edifice: "As to the *world*, and its *censures*, you know, my dear, that, however desirous I always was of a fair fame, yet I never thought it right to give more than a *second place* to the world's opinion" (6:419 [1139]). Now out of the running for fair fame, Clarissa demotes public consensus even further, from second place to last, as her own understanding takes urgent precedence: "what advantage would it be to me, were [my reputation] retrievable, and were I to live long, if I could not acquit myself to *myself*?" (6:419 [1139]). Indifferency is a position of irreverence ("Respect and Custom" count for nothing) but not hostility (§11, at 42 [185]). For Clarissa, as for Descartes and Locke, there is simply no social value to truth. Locke states, "common or uncommon are not the marks to distinguish Truth or Falshood, and therefore should not be any bias to us in our Enquiries" (§24, at 71 [198]). To detach oneself from the bind of "common or uncommon" is to defect, at least temporarily, from any claim to understanding: what one knows is nothing. Locke writes, "the surest and safest way is to have no Opinion at all," that is, to eliminate all ideas, all mental company—a risky proposition (§35, at 106 [213]). "The World is apt to cast great Blame on those who have an Indifferency for Opinions" (§12, at 45 [186]); "those that break from [them] are in danger of Heresy" (§34, at 103 [212]).[55]

If truth and freedom are the rewards of impartiality, then alienation and persecution are its costs.[56] "We are surprised at your indifference, *Miss* Harlowe," say Sally and Polly, two of Lovelace's female minions who visit her in prison (6:257 [1056]). After Clarissa's private investigation of Lovelace's "regular and preconcerted plan of villainy," she demonstrates the paradox of indifferency, shutting out other voices in an acceptance of hard facts, taking the lonely route back to social acceptance (6:132 [989]).[57] "Indifference" appears many times in Richardson's novel, mostly as a state of disaffection ("such indifference, such coldness") or apathy ("more miserable if she loved him, than if she could have been were she to be indifferent to him") (6:154 [1000], 7:42 [1161]). When Sally and Polly charge Clarissa with indifference, they remark on her focused disengagement: "Will you not write to any of your friends?" "No," she answers. Clarissa's worth will be restored but through the path of devaluation—she cannot count on others' opinions and has to stop caring about them. First subjected to and then actively sifting through layers of human corruption, she finally leaves off thinking about others. The seemingly narcissistic economy that takes over the text (the insular tracking of Clarissa's writing, belongings, and time) replaces the social practices entailed in epistolarity and exemplarity. She writes Anna Howe, "When Catastrophes are winding-up, what changes (changes that make one's heart shudder to think of) may *one* short month produce!" (6:382 [1119]). Postcatastrophe, Clarissa comes to understand the implausible story of her own disgrace, clearing the ground of psychological narrative, or what first makes a heart and then makes that same heart shudder.

Descartes describes indifference as "the lowest grade of freedom," the sign of absent understanding or insight. The Meditator reflects: "If I always saw clearly what was true and good, I should never have to deliberate about the right judgement or choice; in that case, although I should be wholly free, it would be impossible for me ever to be in a state of indifference" (*M* 102).

You do not choose the truth; you see it. To be free is to possess the clear-sightedness needed to grasp it. Indifference helps to achieve this clarity, but once you perceive what is "true and good," you are on its side. The liberty achieved by Clarissa in London attains this 20/20 vision by securing several underlying conditions: freedom from encroachment and harassment, physical mobility, the right to accept or refuse company, the ability to work and to write, and the choice to live or die. In this disarmingly exteriorized subject of Enlightenment, Richardson resets the terms for novelistic personhood, offering up a new version of the insensible.

IMPERSONALITY AND THE GIFTS OF WRETCHEDNESS

Of the phenomenon of impersonality, Sharon Cameron writes: "The person is a surface—nothing that *can* be penetrated, something that does not even register contact—is impervious as a stone would be. This hardness which comes about because there is no inside (nothing in which an inside might be situated) is a state without exception."[58] Where the indifferent subject refuses contact or penetration, the impersonal subject simply averts it. The person is "nothing that *can* be penetrated." An indifferent Clarissa initiates her own fact-finding mission, dismissing the concerns of others as she reconstructs the truth of what happened to her before embracing nonexistence. An impersonal Clarissa, untethered to the paradox of indifferency, is neither open nor closed, available nor unavailable: "the person is a surface . . . because there is no inside." This conception—unrecognizable in the violable young lady of virtue but also in the hard-hearted subject of indifferency—marks the most radical alternative to the staple of personhood perfected in *Pamela* and in the first half of *Clarissa*. If, I am saying, the meta-apparatus of the novel—its mandate to search for hidden feelings through the structure of subjectivity—was put on trial by indifferency's hard examination of the facts, then it is swept aside by the grander gestures of impersonality.[59]

Refusing assent is revolutionary, as made clear by Descartes and by Locke. In *Clarissa*'s history, that refusal has constituted a manifold heresy—against readers, against norms, against genre. After the rape, Clarissa repackages antisociality as a beatific preparation for death: "What then, my dear and only friend, can I wish for but death?" (6:377 [1117]). She observes at first how in not marrying Lovelace and in choosing "The Single-life" (the wish of every prude), she will appear to have placed herself in moral quarantine:

"must I not *now* sit brooding over my past afflictions, and mourning my faults till the hour of my release? And would not everyone be able to assign the reason, why Clarissa Harlowe chose solitude, and to sequester herself from the world?" (6:377 [1117]). A brief life oriented toward dying would solve the problem of how acceptably to live alone. Yet while Clarissa pushes us to interpret the rest of the novel through the lens of a death wish, resulting in a master narrative of Christian martyrdom,[60] such a reading may lead us to overlook the life she actually leads between her rape and her death.

In the final episodes of the novel, after Clarissa has escaped Lovelace a second time, she works away on her writing, in London, mostly alone. She wants to hear from the people in her past, but she does not want to see them. She asserts the metropolitan's privilege of being left alone. To Anna Howe's invitation to live near her (Clarissa's dream not long before), she respectfully declines, preferring now the consolations of urban anonymity to country life with friends. The freedom to refuse company may have started with Lovelace, but it widens to nearly everyone she knows. Her brief incarceration reveals the starkness of this need: "Cannot I be permitted to see whom I please; and to refuse admittance to those I like not?" (6:259 [1057]). Of her suitor-then-rapist-now-suitor-again, she declares "that I *can* and *will* forgive him, on this one easy condition, *That he will never molest me more*" (6:424 [1141]). To her old friend Judith Norton she appeals, "Say not then, that you think you ought to come up to me, *let it be taken as it will*:—For *my Sake*, let me repeat . . . you must *not* come" (6:130 [987]). She writes to Miss Howe, "Love me still, however. But let it be with a weaning Love. I am not what I was, when we were *inseparable* Lovers" (6:320 [1088]). As to what she is now, this "*Self*, this vile, this hated *Self*," she announces, "I will shake it off, if possible" (6:107 [974]). Clarissa puts the burden of selfhood onto her friend, calling Anna "my dearer Self," and adding, "for what is now my Self?" (6:196 [1022]). If Clarissa is not what she once was, is no longer even a Self, then what is she? Clarissa's "weaning" self-estrangement can certainly be read as "the consequences of rape upon the woman's sense of self," in which Richardson "figures the assault on her body as an equally brutal assault upon her identity."[61] But I am tempted by a more hopeful trade-off.

On her first evening of freedom she writes to Anna Howe: "Once more have I escaped—but, alas! I, my *best self*, have not escaped!"[62] Pseudonyms reinforce the change. Under the assumed Identities of "Mrs. Harriot Lucas" and then "Mrs. Rachel Clark, at Mr. Smith's, a Glove-shop, in King Street,

Covent-garden," she asks Miss Howe to send a line (5:53, 6:107 [756, 974]). Later, she assumes other covers: Mrs. Clark in Covent Garden, Mrs. Mary Atkins at the Belle Savage on Ludgate Hill, and Mrs. Dorothy Salcomb at the Four Swans Inn, Bishopsgate Street. Under these directions Clarissa dispatches a flurry of letters from London to reestablish contact with her friends and to fact-check the conspiracy against her. In an affectionate letter to Mrs. Norton ("Let me, however, hope, that you love me still"), she inquires after her family and confirms some details of Lovelace's plot (6:114 [978]). She then solicits information from Lovelace's aunt, Lady Betty Lawrance, "from your Ladyship's hand (by the next post, if convenient) in answer to the following questions" (6:120 [981]). To the Harlowes' servant Sarah Hodges, she writes under strict secrecy, seeking further authentication and signing only "Your friend" (6:124 [984]). To her former maid, Hannah Burton, Clarissa appeals for company: "Do you chuse to come and be with me? . . . I am a very unhappy creature, and, being among all strangers, should be glad to have *you* with me" (6:111 [977]).

But, as the circus of pseudonyms suggest, Clarissa is now a stranger herself, removed from those who know her and in the care of assorted cotenants (a poor widow, the owners of the glove shop downstairs). As the responses trickle in to her several inquiries, Clarissa learns to "expect everything bad" from friends and family (6:129 [987]). Her letter to Anna Howe is returned by an admonitory note from Mrs. Howe to stop writing her daughter, a turning point for Clarissa. "The Letter I received from your Mother," she later confides, "was a dreadful blow to me" (6:176 [1012]). The rheumatic Hannah Burton sends her sorrowful but inflexible regrets. The answers of Mrs. Norton, Lady Betty, and Mrs. Hodges all confirm Lovelace's "complicated wickedness" (6:129 [986]). Of her family's amenability to forgiveness, Mrs. Norton reports, "No evil can have happened to you, which they do not *expect* to hear of" (6:115 [979]). Even Miss Howe, when cleared by her mother to reply, betrays a cruel incomprehension: "What have you brought yourself to, Miss Clarissa Harlowe? . . . What an intoxicating thing is *this love*?" (6:141 [993]). It is not the rape but rather the responses to it (what G. Gabrielle Starr terms a "communicative nightmare") that bring Clarissa to the rock bottom of expectations, leading to an overhaul of one's "best self," of having been "a Clarissa."[63]

The philosophical practice of indifferency begins with the position of no longer knowing what is true and what (who) is false. Once Clarissa knows the worst, she can expect everything bad until, finally, she stops expecting anything at all. Replying to Mrs. Howe's reprimand, Clarissa repeats a particularly cruel phrase: "When distressed, the human mind is apt to turn itself to every one in whom it imagined or wished an interest, for pity and consolation.—Or, to express myself better and more concisely, in your own words, *Misfortune makes people plaintive*: And to whom, if not to a friend, can the afflicted complain?" (6:110 [976]). This question, it turns out, is not rhetorical. Within days Clarissa learns that for pity and consolation, you cannot turn to those in whom you "imagined or wished an interest." Neither her family (her father curses her, her siblings betray her, her mother will not look upon her) nor her household intimates (Mrs. Norton—"Surely you are my own Mother") are good for anything but communicating the most dispiriting information (6:127 [986]). Only her new, "honest and humane" neighbors alongside a trusty health-care team ("an excellent Physician, Dr. H., and as worthy an Apothecary, Mr. Goddard.—Their treatment of me, my dear, is perfectly *paternal*!") prove to be real caregivers (6:130 [987], 6:319 [1088]). Anonymity, the frightening condition of "being among absolute strangers," becomes a blessing for the rape survivor (6:113 [978]). Clarissa makes this clear enough in her directives to Mrs. Howe: "first,—that you will not let any of my relations know, that you have heard from me. The other,—that no living creature be apprised where I am to be heard of, or directed to. This is a point that concerns me, more than I can express.—In short, my preservation from further evils may depend upon it" (6:111 [976]). Clarissa, as Mrs. Clark in a glove shop or as Mrs. Salcomb at an inn or as nobody at all, inhabits the newly necessary, distinctly urban position of being a stranger among strangers.

Of *La Princesse de Clèves*, discussed in the prior chapter, Joan DeJean writes of "Lafayette's fidelity to the ideals of her century's most powerful female voices. These hyperbolic affirmations of female superiority, of woman's advancement beyond previous norms and thereby outside narrative, are the language of *préciosité*" (*Tender Geographies*, 267). Essential to DeJean's claims about seventeenth-century French female novelists and of the *roman* as "the estate of *écriture féminine*" is the unique set of privileges conferred by anonymity on the woman writer to "simultaneously assert her power and protect her person" (268, 246). DeJean reads the princess's final choice of philosophical solitude over conjugality in relation to the unpublished manuscript once attributed to Lafayette, *Le triomphe de l'indifférence*, a tale in which three women discuss the merits of a life without erotic attachments as "a happy indifference, whose peace or repose render it infinitely preferable to the bitter pains of love" [*une heureuse indifférence* (*la paix ou le repos dont il est accompagné le rend infiniment préférable aux amères douleurs de l'amour*)].[64] Similarly, the princess of Clèves, DeJean points out, chooses *repos* in her "decision to live apart from all the 'agitation' and the 'anxieties' of the world of *galanterie* in which men control all the plots" (*Tender Geographies*, 266). The princess's retreat, like Lafayette's disavowal of her own work, DeJean writes, "creates a narrative void that is also a repartition of territory and an outpouring of women's language" (267), an exchange of the "husband's estate for the female literary estate, a territory beyond male control."[65] What DeJean illuminates as the narrative void of anonymous writing, indifference, and *préciosité* is recapitulated in *Clarissa*. Richardson elaborates their connections but, what is more, reattaches them to the misogynistic violence they inspire—doing so with such narrative torque as to call the whole program of the *roman* into question.

It is crucial that Clarissa get rid of her name. Neither Clarissa Harlowe nor the Paragon Formerly Known as Clarissa Harlowe, she enjoys the fabled status of Nobody. In her fragmented papers composed immediately after the rape, she will not sign her name. "I am still, and I ever will be, Your true—Plague on it!" she closes to Anna Howe (5:303 [890]). In a scratched message to her father she writes, "I don't presume to think you should receive me—No, indeed—My name is—I don't know what my name is!" (5:304 [890]). In subsequent messages she reclaims what Starr calls "the ragged anatomy" of her name with embellishments such as "Your miserable Clarissa Harlowe" (6:107 [974]), "The unhappy Clarissa Harlowe" (6:111 [976]), "The unfortunate Clarissa Harlowe" (6:114 [978]), "Obliged servant, Clarissa Harlowe?" (7:71 [1177]).[66] In her anonymous, pseudonymous, metropolitan life, Clarissa's identity crisis marks a new dispensation of fiction. One episode, in particular, shows the upside.

On dragging Clarissa to prison for trumped-up debt charges, the arresting officer asks, "Is your name Clarissa Harlowe, madam?" to which she responds, "Yes, yes, indeed, ready to sink, my name *was* Clarissa Harlowe:—But it is now *Wretchedness*!" (6:250 [1052]). Clarissa's name is swallowed up as if by a figure in a morality play. She identifies only and entirely with a state of *Wretchedness*. While this collapse of identity cannot exactly be affirmed, Clarissa's renaming is consistent with her self-exposure as a rape victim, a disarming act of self-representation. Clarissa draws here on the unassailability of allegory: you cannot make *Wretchedness* any more wretched than itself. In not just claiming to feel wretched but in making herself the very emblem of Wretchedness, Clarissa forecloses the possibility of further degradation. Simply, there is no further. (As Gilbert Ryle states, "The vain man never feels vain.")[67] Clarissa Harlowe shakes off Virtue and dons its wreckage, a form with surprising perks.[68]

In analyzing Clarissa's turn toward allegory, critics have observed a shift in Richardson's project of the novel, what Claudia Brodsky describes as his "self-exposing representation of representation."[69] Elizabeth Heckendorn Cook describes how the text's "signifying system of allegory," which transforms Clarissa into a Christian martyr, displaces its former narrative values of verisimilitude, plausibility, and authenticity. In this account allegory supersedes psychological realism, alienating the reader and challenging the genre's epistemology of the transparent and "dictating heart."[70] How does the structure of character change under these new terms for fiction? After allegory, is character even possible? We know that after the rape Clarissa does away with a depth-model of character. As John Richetti writes, she occupies "an essentially social and political location in which one can claim to be exactly what one appears to be to others, and at the same time refuse to be defined by a turbulent interiority where unruly desires and impulses operate beyond full control of the will."[71] The values emphasized by Richetti, "scope, breadth, and comprehensiveness" over "mere depth . . . unstable and destructive," resonate with the postrape narrative that I am privileging, which dispenses with the terms of receptivity and sensibility otherwise so crucial to Richardson's story and to the subsequent course of Western fiction. Richetti aligns Clarissa's transparency with her refusal to be victimized: no depth means no violation. After virtue, other configurations become possible.

HAMPSTEAD, HIGHGATE, BREAKFAST, WRITE

Hiding in plain sight, Clarissa lives anonymously (she does not want to be traced by Lovelace) but also publicly (any other urban dweller might see her around). Noting London's role in the novel, Hilary Schor has observed "the energy and vibrancy of the city, the commercial spaces which the readers enter with some relief after the terrors of Clarissa's 'closet.' "[72] An energized urbanite suggests a new vision of the heroine—fearless, anonymous, itinerant—a figure who explores the streets of the city much more than she does the recesses of her heart. In this phase *Clarissa* shuts down the space for private feeling, ultimately rejecting a model of always violable personhood and making room for a metropolitan identity that challenges the purpose of the novel to investigate emotion. Whereas in the nineteenth-century novel, London is the setting for mysterious events—the unraveling of secret lives and unknown identities—London in *Clarissa* propels a different, strangely wholesome-looking narrative. Edward Copeland has written persuasively and in detail about Clarissa's active life in London. The city's well-regulated commercial sprawl, he argues, gives her the stability she's been looking for. "The language of commerce is the language of truth: in Clarissa's London, the coaches run on time."[73] A system based on money is much more transparent and benign than one premised on violent passions. Clarissa's London, according to Copeland, is "an imaginary world of stable signs and symbols." The city's infrastructure—the post, transportation, housing, and retail—runs efficiently and impersonally, unlike "the disorder of Lovelace's anarchic imagination" (68). But finally, tragically, Copeland argues, Clarissa's exit from London in a hearse down King Street expresses the city's inability to protect her. If the impersonal conveniences of urban living benefited her in exile, they ultimately let her down. He writes, "The map of London, its public landmarks, its churches, inns, and parks, the business of its streets *seem* to give the option of freedom to Clarissa. . . . But London, as part of its modern definition, supplies no knight in shining armour to help the heroine" (57). The city can shelter; it cannot intervene.

Copeland's grim summation of Clarissa's urban experiment ("a chilling vision of anomie—a world filled with people, and at the same time, a world despairingly empty" [69]) addresses the shortcomings of the city as an actor, but it overlooks the subjectivity that such a setting makes possible. Although London cannot keep Clarissa alive forever, it does for four hundred pages—long enough for her to organize her afterlife as a book. Clarissa's corpse may be driven back to the country and reinstated as the eternally virtuous daughter, but her summer in London stands out as her most memorable and radical incarnation. In her rented rooms in Covent Garden and in her constant roving in the city, Clarissa approaches the kind of cosmopolitanism that Amanda Anderson defines foremost as "reflective distance from one's original or primary cultural affiliation."[74] In the final installment of Clarissa's life urbanity fosters a cognitive and physical disengagement that becomes the condition for writing. Belford records her movements: "She ordered the coachman (whom she hired for the day) to drive any-whither, so it was into the Air: He accordingly drove her to Hampstead, and thence to Highgate. There at the Bowling-green House, she alighted, extremely ill, and having breakfasted, ordered the coachman to drive very slowly any-whither. He crept along to Muswell-hill, and put up at a public house there; where she employed herself two hours in writing. . . . And then she wrote on for three hours more" (7:199–200 [1246]). Extreme illness aside, Clarissa's regimen of outdoor air and indoor refreshment supports her extensive, concentrated labors. Any-whither that is not Harlowe Place, that is not home, makes a refuge for the writer. Hardly closeted, but visible, busy, unconcerned, she finishes her book. Not "Clarissa's London," as Copeland writes, but London's Clarissa commands our attention as a new direction for the novel.

Much earlier, when persecuted by her family to marry Solmes, Clarissa ruled out her friend's "*advice for me to escape to London*" (2:247 [334]) as her best shot at liberty. "But, alas! my dear, this, even *this* alternative, is not without difficulties, which, to a spirit so little enterprizing as mine, seem in a manner insuperable" (2:249 [335]). She ticks off several "[in]surmountable" objections: (1) inadequate time to prepare for the trip, (2) fear of capture and punishment, (3) lack of acquaintances in London ("I know nobody there"), (4) fear of London itself ("that great, wicked town"), and (5) fear for her reputation ("Who knows but I might pass for a kept mistress"). Her final residency as an anonymous ex-con, who wears the same nightgown every day and gives away her few possessions, speaks to their methodical overturning. In the most startling reversal, she tells everyone that she is raped and still single.

Clarissa's practice "not to keep her own Secret" but instead to publicize her rape scandalizes even Lovelace, who cannot imagine any incentive for making "our affair so generally known among the *Flippanti* of both sexes" (7:17 [1149]). But for Clarissa, the dishonored have no reason to hide. She explains to Anna Howe: "While *I* know it, I care not *who* knows it" (6:146 [996]). In declining to seek legal redress, Clarissa seeks to avoid the strain of public prosecution but not the shame of public exposure. "Not that I am solicitous, that my disgrace should be hidden from the world, or that it should not be generally known" (6:177–78 [1013]).[75] Clarissa feels that since she knows the worst of herself, everyone else may as well know it, too (and probably already does), but hers is a logic of insensibility that eludes nearly everyone else. In the letter to Lady Betty Lawrance, she reveals, "I was first robbed of my Senses; and then of my Honour. Why should I seek to conceal that disgrace from others, which I cannot hide from myself?" (6:126 [985]). To illustrate Clarissa's eccentricity, Belford repeats the line in a letter to Lovelace: "The disgrace she cannot hide from *herself*, as she says in her letter to Lady Betty, she is not solicitous to conceal from the *world*!" (6:288 [1073]). Immediately upon returning to the glove shop from jail, she announces to her landlady, "Oh Mrs Smith, said she, as soon as she saw her, did you not think I was run away?—You don't know what I have suffered since I saw you. I have been in prison!" Belford glosses the account, "But dost thou not observe, what a strange, what an uncommon openness of heart reigns in this Lady: *she had been in a prison*, she said, before a stranger in the shop, and before the maid-servant: and so, probably, she would have said, had there been twenty people in the shop" (6:287–88 [1072]).[76] Courting the shock of friends and neighbors, Clarissa owns up to her scandalized position and outs herself: "You'll observe, Mrs. Lovick (for you seemed this morning curious to know if I were not a wife), that I *never was married*.—You, Mr. Belford, no doubt, knew before, that I am no wife: And now I never will be one" (6:356 [1105]). In this last declaration, one hears not remorse but jubilation.[77]

The lady once tasked to report her tenderest feelings to her best friend now makes cheery gossip of her incarceration before stray shoppers. The chance and disinterested audience of a retail establishment enables a freedom of speech that prying, intimate correspondents never could. Disgrace has its privileges, namely freedom from the cultural illogic of simultaneous concealment and transparency demanded by female decorum. By refusing to keep her rape a secret, by refusing to keep any secrets, Clarissa assumes a certain control of her story. To say, as she does to Lovelace's relations, "I was robbed of my honor" disables others from accusing her of having none (she already said so herself) and of giving it up (she was robbed of it). When Clarissa later says that she was raped and jailed, she breaks her own taboos. Who could say worse of her than she has already and repeatedly said of herself? Clarissa after the rape achieves a kind of transparency, not about her thoughts and feelings but about her experiences—experiences that make even libertines blush.[78]

In publicizing her rape, Clarissa, as William Ray writes, "distributes the burden of her identity among a large segment of the population."[79] Ray refers to her selected friends, family, and supporters, but her openness with Londoners extends that population to the entire city. Clarissa has nothing to lose but something to gain from mass disclosure. Rachel Carnell observes that Clarissa's chattiness redefined who counted as the public in eighteenth-century London: "By thus publicizing the most intimate details of her private oppression, Clarissa expands the idea of the public sphere from periodical and coffee-house debates among propertied men to include gossip among neighbors and boarding-house keepers as well as epistolary exchanges between aristocratic women."[80] Like Belford, Sarah Fielding's character Bellario takes note of Clarissa's logorrhea: "All false Shame has [Richardson] exposed, by shewing the Beauties of an open and frank Heart in *Clarissa*'s charming Simplicity, when she tells Mrs. *Smith,* in a publick Shop, that she had been in Prison; and when in a Letter to Lady *Betty Laurance* she declares, that *the Disgrace she cannot hide from herself, she is not solicitous to conceal from the World.*"[81] All shame has turned to false shame, and dropping the pretense of modesty now merits public praise. Even more radical than the princess of Clèves's *aveux*, Clarissa is just out. The construct of *fausse sagesse* that animated prude discourse has no more purchase. Like the prude, Clarissa spoils the story and similarly could not care less.

An impersonal Clarissa evacuates a trifecta of interiority, secrecy, and privacy—perhaps flagging a return to an earlier conception of the self. Paula McDowell points out the anachronism of "the autonomous gendered self of modern liberal individualism" in the context of seventeenth- and early eighteenth-century writing.[82] The model of personhood advanced by certain female polemicists, McDowell argues, does not portray an autonomous or absolute or even gendered individual but a unified, collective, and "fluidly sexed" body (184)—a dispersed, connected, and fundamentally political being. This state is expressed in intriguingly material terms by one of McDowell's subjects, the prophet Jane Lead, who understood herself as "a configuration of states of being—a space across which psychic impulses flowed" (196). The counterbeing who emerges in McDowell's analysis challenges the idealization or even existence of autonomy. For example, of the printer and author Elinor James, McDowell writes, "James saw herself as subject to the state and on a continuum with all the other elements of the kingdom. Her social identity was not a matter of choice; indeed, it was not founded in subjectivity at all. James saw herself as born into a network of dependencies, and did not consciously differentiate herself from the other elements of that web" (183). McDowell's analysis offers a historical precedent for the desubjectivized woman writer, whose very claims to divine and political power are underwritten by her nonindividuation. Richardson makes something like the inverse demonstration in depicting the violence of individuation, or what it takes to make "a Clarissa." In her unmaking, Richardson offers some amends.

THE NEW FACE OF HEADLESSNESS

If drugged insensibility presents a dark corollary to the clearing of the mind necessary to Lockean indifference, then Clarissa's headlessness is something of a puzzle. "My head is gone," she writes to Lovelace after the composition of her mad papers. "I have wept away all my brain, I believe; for I can weep no more. Indeed I have had my full share. . . . What would I say!—I forget what I was going to say. . . . Alas! you have killed my head among you—I don't say who did it!—God forgive you all! . . . Let me hurry off my thoughts, lest I lose them again—Here I am sensible—And yet I am hardly sensible neither—But I know my head is not as it should be, for all that" (5:309–11 [894–95]). Clarissa describes her attention deficit not, as she did earlier, as a derangement of the contents of her mind ("O my dear, what a poor, passive machine is the body when the mind is disordered!" [2:188 (303)]) but as its missing container: "My head is gone" and, with it, "all my brain," killed by those "among you." Against Lovelace's assessment that she has lost her wits—is no more "a regular mind" (5:309 [894])—Clarissa self-diagnoses as having a "head [that] will not hold" (5:313 [896]). If Clarissa's head is now missing (or exploded), its absence testifies to its earlier substance: a surfeit of tears that wept themselves clean. Swelled to capacity—"I will not oppress you, my dearest friend, with further reflections of this sort. I will take them all into myself. Surely I have a mind that has room for them" (2:246 [333])—Clarissa's mind switches from full to empty, a head that will hold no more, that has had its "full share." This change depletes a model of the mind as an opaque vessel full of motives or intentions. A missing head, like a transparent one, does not hold or hide. Where an earlier Clarissa followed the script of internalization—"I have cleared *them* of blame, and taken it all upon *myself*!" "My blame was indeed turned inward" (2:338 [382], 3:12 [391])—the postrape, busy, writing Clarissa has no time for such melancholic containment: "I believe I do amiss in writing so much, and taking too much upon me: But an active mind, tho' clouded by bodily illness, cannot be idle," she breezily tells her friend, reporting a physical fragility that seems to assist rather than inhibit her working life (7:235 [1265]). The once insensible that could not "move hand or foot," who was "as destitute of will, as she always seemed of desire," is now pleasantly in motion, endlessly occupied.

As counterintuitive as it may seem to compare a canonical Western novel to a theory of East Asian theater, I am compelled to think of Richardson's eighteenth-century experiment through Roland Barthes's conception of

Bunraku. In his essay about Japanese puppetry Barthes describes the function of Western theater as "essentially to reveal what is reputed to be secret ('feelings', 'situations', 'conflicts') while concealing the very artifice of the process of revelation."[83] Such a description easily applies to the machinery of the psychological novel with its realistic unfolding of human desires. Bunraku, Barthes writes, dissolves "the driving link between character and actor which is always conceived by us as the expressive channel of an interiority" (173). Disconnected from the operations of an expressive interior, the subject of Bunraku is defined by its features, interactions, and movements. *Clarissa* in this analogy works both sides: it stages secret feelings like Western theater, but instead of concealing its "interiority effects," the novel, like Bunraku, dismantles the apparatus.[84] Its elaborate narrative mechanics to search and then expose Clarissa's heart drive the novel forward until the whole machine breaks apart, at which point another concept of the subject emerges. Barthes writes that the face of the Bunraku puppet master "is offered to the spectator for reading, but what is so carefully and so preciously given to be read is that there is nothing to be read." Moreover, he writes, "we are scarcely able to comprehend [this exemption from meaning] since for us to attach meaning is to conceal or oppose it, never to absent it" (173). Clarissa, I am arguing, is similarly incomprehensible—even more so because Richardson baits us to search for the truth of her feelings before vacating the conceit altogether. The difficulty of reading Clarissa (including her spectacularly blinding person, even as a "lovely corpse") has to do with her strange exemption from meaning, the way she neither conceals nor opposes nor possesses the desires imputed to her—there is just nothing to be read (8:14 [1367]). Barthes writes, "What is expelled from the stage is hysteria, that is theatre itself, and what is put in its place is the action necessary for the production of the spectacle—work is substituted for interiority" (173–74). Suddenly Richardson's *History of a Young Lady*, with its seemingly immanent structures of suppressed erotics, replaces hysteria with facts. Appending Lovelace's famous report, "And now, Belford, I can go no farther. The affair is over. Clarissa lives," is the rest of the story in which Clarissa lives, works, talks, moves, and *then* dies (5:291 [883]).

If *Clarissa*'s new narrative economy does not run on secrets and lies (the ruling passion to "unlock and open my Charmer's heart" [4:146 (620)]), then what does it propose as an alternative source of energy? We return to the experience of reading Richardson's heroine as an encounter with an unyielding surface and to Barbauld's defense of such hardness. Barbauld's praise of Clarissa's moral and formal stasis honored an interpretation in which there is no "wonderful recognition" of who a character really is. Whatever is to be known about her, we've known (and she's known) all along. We recall that for Barbauld, such lack of personal development is not to be regretted but rather revered as a formal value. Not tragic senselessness but vibrant insensibility sheers away from the novel's own construct of psychological volatility—what, according to the subject of my next chapter, Oliver Goldsmith, established the cursed mandate "of every modern novel" to incite and gratify prurience. Goldsmith would try to reset its program of narrative pleasure, but he would only succeed in a form that Richardson probably never dreamed of tackling: comedy.

CHAPTER 3

The Man of No Feeling

THE INSENSIBLE WHO LOOMED OVER the eighteenth century in Britain was Charles I, whose striking impassivity during his public trial and subsequent execution on 30 January 1649, outside the Banqueting House in Whitehall, pressed into cultural memory an Enlightenment primal scene that blended infinite suffering with palpable contempt.[1] William Harris's observation of "the equanimity or insensibility of Charles before, at, and after his tryal" in his influential 1758 biography flagged sovereign unfeeling as a historical problem: "Whether he had much *sensibility of temper*, may, perhaps justly be made a question."[2] For eighteenth-century Britons, the meaning of the civil war remained open, sovereignty having been destabilized yet again by (Charles's son) James II's forced abdication in 1688. While the Glorious Revolution reset the terms of monarchical power, its fragility had been seismically introduced by Charles's trial, which shut down the principle of divine right and, with it, the untouchable status of the king. Yet, as Harris documented, the myth of Charles's imperviousness, "the unmovedness of his mind," continued to captivate the public imagination with its split signification of regal transcendence and sheer "want of feeling." Noting several instances "which seem to show [the king] not overstocked with compassion at the misfortunes of others, or touched with their calamities," Harris quotes the following remembrance: "He was seldom, in the times of war, seen to be sorrowful for the slaughter of his people or soldiers, or indeed anything else. . . . Whether by nature or custom his heart was hardened, I leave others to judge."[3] In one particularly grievous scene of suffering, Charles "was content to be a spectator of their calamities" and "rejoiced in their sad affliction" (67–68).

Simultaneously "implacable Enemy to the Commonwealth of England" and its gentle, slaughtered sovereign, Charles would appear to originate every riddling aspect of the Bartleby problem discussed so far, from Hobbes's unnerving exemption from calamity to Smith's stoic ideal to Clarissa's passive-aggressive martyrdom.[4] Like the slide from neutral to cruel that obtains in contempt, Charles's shining impassivity shades into sadistic pleasure—a rejoicing in others' affliction. Insensibility's surprising incitements thus return us to this ultimate historical fiction—a series of encounters (in prison, before the court, on the scaffold) continuously reinterpreted for modern publics. The king's landmark unfeeling—the riddle of his "unmoving" mind and body—recurs, as we have seen, throughout modern literature. The Bartleby phenomenon, as I argued earlier, derives conceptually from a prime mover, which sets everything in motion by not being subject to motion itself. The fixed axis of an ever-fluctuating world, the insensible acts from the high seat of inaction.

Sovereign unfeeling, I am arguing, is a primary case of the oscillation between tranquility and contempt that defines insensibility. In theorizations of monarchy at issue in the English civil war, the sovereign formalized the ambiguity between paternal care and unconscionable harm embedded in the very idea of the state. The early modern ruler's yoking of heteronomy (wholly constituted by his subjects) to absolute power (master of all their motions) exemplified the meeting point of susceptibility and imperviousness that inheres in insensibility. A monarch may represent an inhuman godhead,[5] according to James I, but he exists only to show fealty to others: "bounde to care for all his subiects," to take on "all the toyle, and paine, that the Father can take for his children," even at "the hazarde of his owne person."[6] A figure of limitless compassion *and* obliterating self-erasure, the sovereign must "think all his earthly felicitie and happinesse grounded vpon your weale, caring more for himselfe for your sake then for his owne, thinking himself onely ordained for your weale" (32).[7]

Accused of corrupting his position (so that subjects existed only for *his* weale), Charles responded by claiming transcendence of all earthly matters, seizing on the trope of immobility to do so. An "Explanation of the Embleme" accompanies the frontispiece of his spiritual autobiography, *Eikon Basilike* (fig. 2), published days after his execution:

> Though clogg'd with *weights* of miseries,
> *Palm*-like deprrss'd [*sic*], I higher rise.
> And as th' *unmoved Rock* out-braves
> The boyst'rous *winds*, and raging *waves*;
> So *triumph* I.[8]

According to this key, only that which is "unmoved" can ascend—a law illustrated by the motto "Immota, Trivmphans" ("Unmoved, Triumphant"), which appears on a scroll decorating a Gibraltar-like crag in a swirling sea. At his trial, similar metaphors were leveled against Charles, portraying him not as a triumphant divine but as a "hard-hearted man": less pliant than stone, more chilling than ice, as rigid as diamonds.[9]

FIGURE 2. Frontispiece from *Eikon Basilike: The Povrtraictvre of His Sacred Majestie in His Solitudes and Svfferings* (1649). Courtesy of the Beinecke Library, Yale University.

Charles I is significant to this study not only as an example of revolutionary sangfroid but, more pointedly, because his trial altered the structural position of nonresponsiveness (the seat of law) into an affective disposition (contempt). We could say that insensibility was born in this moment of challenged sovereignty, when immobility became a problem of feeling or intention—a personal deficiency that somehow retained its political charge. At Charles's sentencing, the court dangled the option to be "a repentant king," pardonable by God and saved from death (*Cobbett's*, 1016). In reply the sovereign showed no signs of regret and, all the way to the scaffold, betrayed no emotion at all: "without the least sign in his countenance of any discomposure of mind."[10] As an origins story, Charles's unfeeling helps to explain the bafflingly high stakes of the Bartleby problem, what renders a single case of dispassion a matter of life or death—for everyone. We can see how an entire theological and political order might hang on the insensible's no-show of feeling. Thus, when human rights lawyer Geoffrey Robertson rewrites Charles I as a sociopathic war criminal "entirely lacking in remorse," with a conscience "not troubled by any of the bloodshed of the wars," we can appreciate how insensibility has long united the affairs of the heart with those of the state.[11]

What, this chapter asks, does sovereign insensibility have to do with laughter, that "passion," as Hobbes writes, "which hath no name"? The flat world of eighteenth-century comedy, in which manners are tested across characters, would seem inhospitable to sovereign exemption. But if, as recent theorists have formulated,[12] laughter is an event that confounds the funny with the unfunny, the singular with the social, the coherent with the crackbrained, then sovereign laughter returns us to what is truly mirthless about the still Hobbesian relation between power and humor. This chapter takes up two seemingly disparate areas of inquiry: Charles I and Oliver Goldsmith, the latter an equivocal figure of sentimental literature committed both to monarchy and to comedy. Sovereign contempt, I will argue, finds an unlikely afterlife in the eighteenth-century "man of feeling" and "good-natured man," closing the loop once again between extreme sensibility and gross unfeeling. In this study of masculine character (for Goldsmith, an explicit redirection from Richardson's legacy), I analyze the insensible's classic disdain of death—not from the angle of Stoic endurance but through the eighteenth-century sympathizer's morbid imagination.[13] The version of insensibility that emerges here proves to be fundamentally theatrical, constructed by affect, gesture, and speech.

Hard-pressed to handle its performative negations, fiction heads back to the stage and, specifically, to comedy, where Goldsmith reanimates its diabolical figure of laughter and misrule, Puck.

SOVEREIGN LAUGHTER

Numerous accounts of his unprecedented trial feature Charles's affective responses: his "stern" demeanor or "countenance not at all moved," abrupt laughter, haughty smile, and bold gazes (*Cobbett's*, 995, 1072–74). Laced into the several charges brought against him were insensibility's signature affects of "contumacy" and "contempt"—indicators of a general heedlessness that could conduce to warmongering (1079, 1081). Lengthy indictments delivered by John Bradshaw, Lord President of the High Court of Justice (a self-selected body drawn from the House of Commons—and not, as Charles repeatedly pointed out, from the House of Lords), portrayed "the prisoner" as emotionally defective: "it had been much to be wished that God had put [real peace] into your heart" (1008). If not cruelty, Bradshaw suggested, then some inexplicable intent was to blame for Charles's tyranny. He reprimanded the king: "As you were told the other day, actions must expound intentions; yet actions have been clean contrary [to your professed intentions]. And truly, Sir, it doth appear plainly enough to them, that you have gone upon very erroneous principles: The kingdom hath felt it to their smart . . . for, Sir, you have held yourself, and let fall such language, as if you had been no way subject to the Law, or that the law had not been your superior" (1008–9). Confused by a case in which motive, speech, and action were so out of joint, Bradshaw hung on to the reasoning that whoever believes he is above or unreachable by the law must do harm. Directed by this "very erroneous principle," such a ruler will make his subjects suffer ("smart") for his own immunity.

Where the king's incidental speech (the language he "let fall") imparted contempt, it was his silence that bespoke contumacy. Prosecutor John Cook interpreted his "refusal to plead" as the legal equivalent "to a standing mute, and tacit confession of the charge" (1095). Charles's nonresponsiveness thus became the legal basis for his culpability. As Cook successfully argued, "If a prisoner shall stand as contumacious in contempt, and shall not put in an issuable plea, Guilty or not Guilty of the Charge given against him, whereby he may come to a fair trial; that, as by an implicit confession, it may be taken *pro confesso*" (1096). Contumacy is a sign of both guilt and, as Jacques

Derrida writes, sovereign power: "The sovereign does not respond, he is the one who does not have to, who always has the right not to, respond, in particular not to be responsible for his acts. He is above the law, and has the right to suspend the law, he does not have to respond before a representative chamber or before judges, he grants pardon or not after the law has passed. The sovereign has the right not to respond, he has the right to the silence of that dissymmetry. He has the right to a certain irresponsibility."[14] In other words, the same contradictions that infuriated the High Court underwrite sovereign power: an irresponsibility that attends ultimate responsibility, a nonresponsiveness that purports to answer for all, silence that permits speech.

Robertson's account of Charles's trial as the first modern war crimes tribunal reads the king's courtroom tics as symptoms of pathological unfeeling.[15] Particularly intolerable was the sign of what Hobbes called "that distortion of the countenance that we call LAUGHTER" (*EL* 31). Robertson writes, "There is a limit to body language for indifference but Charles did his best—rolling his eyes at the gallery, outstaring the judges, getting up to look behind him at the guards and spectators. At the description 'tyrant, traitor, murderer . . . ' he laughed loudly, as if trying to laugh the charge out of court. It was not a predictable response and seemed to rattle Bradshaw" (155). What Robertson paints as the loud, dismissive laughter of the king ("he scoffed loudly" [185]) is recorded by trial records in more riddling form:

> LD. PRESIDENT. Sir, the Charge hath called you *Tyrant*, a *Traitor*, a *Murderer*, and a *Public Enemy* to the Commonwealth of England. Sir, it had been well if that any of all these terms might rightly and justly have been spared, if any one of them at all.
>
> KING. Ha! (*Cobbett's*, 1014)

This monosyllabic mark encapsulates sovereign laughter.

The occasion for so much of Hobbes's writing, the civil war shapes even the philosopher's conception of laughter. According to Hobbes's notorious definition, "laughter is nothing else but a sudden glory arising from sudden conception of some eminency in ourselves, by comparison with the infirmities of others, or with our own formerly" (*EL* 32). The phenomenon is distilled in *Leviathan*: "*Sudden Glory*, is the passion which maketh those *Grimaces* called LAUGHTER; and is caused either by some sudden act of their own, that pleaseth them; or by the apprehension of some deformed thing in another, by comparison whereof they suddenly applaud themselves" (*L* 1.6: 88). In drawing out its fundamental aggression, Hobbes unknowingly launched a modern controversy around humor, giving rise to a "superiority theory" of laughter, in contrast to models that feature relief or incongruity. Addison paid it explicit homage in an influential number of *The Spectator*, describing laughter as a "little Triumph of the Understanding" and dwelling on its "secret Elation and Pride of Heart."[16] Yet Addison curiously missed Hobbes's point when he distinguished "Men of a gross Taste," who laugh at idiots and jesters, from "Men of superior Sense and Knowledge," who "do not find their Risibility affected by such ordinary Objects." Consistent with *The Spectator*'s modeling of genteel play, Addison's distinction was remarkably out of tune with Hobbes's essential egalitarianism—his organizing view that, in a world in which we must constantly assess our own powers, interior life cannot be understood apart from those "ordinary" calibrations. For Hobbes the point is not that better people ("of superior Sense and Knowledge") engage in polite forms of laughter. The point is that the passion itself (whatever laughter *is*) signals a flash of insight into your situation—like suddenly realizing that you possess more (because your companion's ice cream has fallen to the floor) or that you are weak (because you dropped your own scoop without even noticing it). "What joy, what we think, and wherein we triumph when we laugh" or what makes us so "fall out with ourselves" when we cry are moments of cognition and not—as Addison and, later, Francis Hutcheson would suggest—indicators of character (*EL* 31–32).

Addison and Hutcheson aimed to restore the place of wit to a more benign theory of humor, refuting Hobbes's explicit polemic that "there lieth no wit or jest at all" when "men laugh at mischances and indecencies" (*EL* 41). For starters, Addison argued, some people like to be laughed at—like "honest Gentlemen that are always exposed to the Wit and Raillery of their Well-wishers and Companions; that are pelted by Men, Women, and Children, Friends and Foes, and, in a word, stand as Butts." In Hutcheson's view laughing *with* someone entails parity and admiration, not exultation—an experience confined to the subspecies of "Ridicule."[17] The comedian, or self-knowing "person who raises the laugh," he wrote, understands "the oddness and impropriety of his own allusion as well as any in company; nay, laughs at it himself" (10). As part of a broader campaign to expose the earlier philosopher's "palpable absurdity" and "ill-natured nonsense," Hutcheson ridiculed Hobbes's theory of laughter, inverting affects in its scenario (6). "If, we observe an object in pain while we are at ease," quipped Hutcheson, "we are in greater danger of weeping than laughter: and yet here is occasion for Hobbes's sudden joy" (11).

Unwittingly, Hutcheson illuminated the dialectical nature of Hobbes's taxonomy—what makes WEEPING, as in the entry that follows LAUGHTER, "another distortion of the face with tears" (*EL* 32). Whereas laughing is the sign of sudden glory, or awareness of advantage, crying signifies the apprehension of infirmity. In this "sudden falling out with ourselves, or sudden conception of defect," the weeper not only perceives his own weakness but, more bitterly, its ongoingness (*EL* 32). Only time separates the funny from the sad, since in laughing I may triumph over your weakness *or* my own—so long as it belongs to the past ("our own self formerly"). "Men laugh at the follies of themselves past, when they come suddenly to remembrance, except they bring with them any present dishonour" (*EL* 32). In other words, if my perception of personal defect involves having to acknowledge current inferiority, then what I feel is not joy but shame, the passion that is the "sign of infirmity, which is dishonor." The haziness between joy and shame, glory and remorse, ability and deformity, laughing and crying does not reflect cynicism (as Hutcheson criticized) but rather an insistence that emotions are situations, not constitutions. The passions, Hobbes continually clarified, do not arise so much from our biological natures as they do from the relations of power in which we subsist day to day. Children, for example, cry a lot because they are frequently reminded of "their too much weakness to make themselves masters of all they look for" (*EL* 32). Women cry more than men not because they are innately sad but because they must "measure their power by the power and love of others that protect them" (32). In Hobbes's philosophy, as this book has emphasized, all passions are responses to circumstances, and all circumstances are pictures of power. As Daniel Gross writes of a "secret history of emotions" (here Aristotelian anger): the passions are "constituted not in the biology nor even in the dignity all humans are supposed to share equally, but rather in relationships of inequity." Hobbes's project in *Leviathan*, Gross succinctly captures, was to illustrate how such inequities could "be mobilized for the sake of peace."[18]

At the trial of Charles I—for Hobbes, the most consequential subject of human history—the king's open contempt, added to his long-standing disregard (he had dissolved Parliament thrice), doomed his bedside manner. Not only did he stand guilty *pro confesso* by refusing to plead, but he also knocked the solicitor about with his cane and conspicuously failed to remove his hat ("The Prisoner all the time having kept on his hat, departed, without shewing any the least respect to the Court" [*Cobbett's*, 1073]). The keeper of ancient laws of hereditary descent, Charles explained that he could not acknowledge this body's "new" and "strange" authority (1091). To the charge that he "hath traitorously and maliciously levied War against the present parliament, and the people therein represented" (1071), his response was not to answer but to ask again and again why and how he had been brought there. Such a Bartlebyan reply, unnerving in its obliquity, was epitomized by his often quoted "I would know by what power I am called hither."[19] Spinning his criminal hearing as the Parliamentarians' own bid for authority, Charles stated, "For me to acknowledge a new Court that I never heard of before, I that am your king, that should be an example to all the people of England for to uphold justice, to maintain the old laws; indeed I know not how to do it" (1095).

Laughter asserts superiority in the face of powerlessness. Charles's "Ha!" was a form of poker-faced surrender that still managed to insinuate a last laugh. Declared in "Contempt and Default," Charles conceded, "I am no sceptic to deny the Power that you have; I know that you have Power enough" (1008). Sociologist Norbert Elias observes the disarming nature of laughter: you cannot giggle and fight at the same time. Elias writes, "Laughter, even though it might be hostile and aggressive, indicates to the beholder that the person who laughs is not in a state ready for physical attack. If you are in danger of being physically assaulted, make the attacker laugh (if you can)" ("Essay on Laughter," 288).[20] Hardly catching, Charles's "Ha!" and his Mona Lisa–like smile imparted a singular incredulity.[21] Exasperated by the king's unfeeling, the court likened his crimes to Caligula's, emphasized his eternal damnation and, finally, declared him "not to be heard" (1014–17).

Contempt disavows impotence, a demonstration theatrically produced at the king's execution. By the eighteenth century, Charles's royal bearing on the scaffold was a narrative cliché. As Clarendon writes in his *History of the Rebellion*, "the saint-like behaviour of that blessed martyr, and his Christian courage and patience at his death; are all particulars so well known, and have been so much enlarged upon . . . that the farther mentioning it in this place would but afflict and grieve the reader, and make the relation itself odious."[22] Yet Britons continued to mine the details of the scene (consider the still popular reenactments by the United Kingdom's largest historical society, The Sealed Knot), exalting Charles's impassivity. His every gesture seemed a testament to divine serenity: the calmness with which he ate his last "bit of bread, and drank a Glasse of Claret" (*England's Black Tribunall*, 33); the quiet dignity of his final address ("my Charity commands me, not only to forgive particular men, but my Charity commands me to endeavor to the last gasp the Peace of the Kingdom" [35–36]); and the lamblike way with which he "laid his neck upon the Block,"[23] tucked "his hair under his Cap," and bid the executioner to "*set it fast*" (39)—details apotheosized by Marvell's outrun sovereign, who "bowed his comely head / Down as upon a bed." The claret is telling. Like the extra shirt he reputedly wore to inhibit any effects of winter's chill, the precautionary drink would have muffled the signs of even involuntary, physical susceptibility, "which some observers will imagine proceeds from fear" (Harris, *An Historical and Critical Account*, 414). In orchestrating his own nonresponsiveness, Charles would continue to deny the existence of any power to move him. Harris's account, despite faulting the king politically, construed his "insensibility" as "remarkable" "patience" and "great equanimity" (409–11).[24]

We can trace the contours of the martyred king in Adam Smith's model of moral sentiments, who is never seen "breaking out into a passion, or uttering a reproachful or revengeful word against any that were his adversaries" (*TMS* 1.2.1.12: 37). Smith sketches here a subject who, "under the severest tortures allows no weakness to escape him, vents no groan, gives way to no passion which we do not entirely enter into" (37). Rescripted as Christlike self-regulation, what was opaque contempt became an appropriable virtue, fit for a market society. Smith's sympathetic showman of unfeeling mirrors and accommodates general, physical insensibility—the fact that different bodies cannot experience the same sensation: "The little sympathy which we feel with bodily pain is the foundation of the propriety of constancy and patience in enduring it" (37). Smith's tortured subject, having internalized a universal indifference to physical suffering, is able to curb his own instinct to express pain—if not, more disturbingly, to eliminate the pain itself. Thus, in what Richard Halpern has recently called "the real 'Adam Smith problem,'" the Smithian man of feeling is oddly vacant, even "self-annihilating," imbibing the feelings he is meant to have or, in Halpern's view, that the market selects for him.[25] As David Marshall writes in his important essay about Smith's theatricalization of interiority, one enters into a spectatorial relation with oneself as well as with others: "Smith's theory presupposes a certain instability of self; it depends upon an eclipsing of identity, a transfer of persons in which one leaves oneself behind."[26] The extraordinary "firmness" that allows Smith's silent sufferer "to keep time with our [general] indifference and insensibility" replaces the primacy of bodily sensation—of passion and action—with social instinct. Such a "magnanimous effort" entails an elaborate production of apathy. As in Charles's stagecraft, what redeems insensibility for Smith is its performance.

As I discussed in my introduction, a heroic simulation of indifference is not to be confused with its noxious, "mean-spirited" actuality, in which nonresponsiveness (or submission "to insults, without attempting either to repel or to revenge them") entirely disables affective circulation (*TMS* 1.2.1: 42). Stoic firmness indicates the suppression, not the absence, of emotion. What the Bartleby problem upsettingly points out is that they look exactly the same: endurance being indistinguishable from contempt. Charles's exertions to ensure that "no outward perturbation could be discerned" inverted an inside-out trajectory of emotions—and who could tell the difference?[27] In the prude fictions examined earlier, regal manipulation of affect becomes ripe for travesty, shading easily into ludicrous deception. Here, too, a stoic Charles became paired with a hypocritical Cromwell, the two faces of insensibility that emerged in the long postwar meditation on what makes a good man or a bad one: Cromwell "had an absolute command over all the Passions and Affections of his own Mind; could weep when he saw his Friend in Tears, yet without any Grief; he would seem to hug in his Bosom, and shew a kind of Civility to the Man whom he hated."[28] In contrast to Charles's "Royal Courage" and dignified immobility appeared the "wantonness, cruelty, or hatred" of the Parliamentarians, which drove them to hideous action (*Elenchus motuum*, 153, 151). Once again, allegory splits the insensible, enacting a formal version of Smith's efforts to distinguish between fortitude and callousness—the one lubricating the machine of political economy, the other blithely allowing its gears to crumble.

THE FEEL OF NOT TO FEEL

At work in the rewriting of Charles's impassivity into heroic calm is the propulsive nature of narrative, which turns anything to motion, to story. What might appear to shut down circulation (of affect, language) becomes a blank canvas for more. Smith, in particular, showcases a core contradiction between ontological "indifference and insensibility" and an overriding theory of mind. Like Addison's much-discussed faculty of imagination (with its "diffusive kind of Touch" that "spreads itself over an infinite multitude of bodies, comprehends the largest figures, and brings into our reach some of the most remote parts of the universe"),[29] sympathetic cognition finds its way into every nook and cranny of the subject—even the dead's. Of the murdered, Smith writes:

> As we put ourselves in his situation, as we enter, as it were, into his body, and in our imaginations, in some measure, animate anew the deformed and mangled carcass of the slain, when we bring home in this manner his case to our own bosoms, we feel upon this, as upon many other occasions, an emotion which the person principally concerned is incapable of feeling, and which yet we feel by an illusive sympathy with him. . . . We feel that resentment which we imagine he ought to feel, and which he would feel, if in his cold and lifeless body there remained any consciousness of what passes upon earth. His blood, we think, calls aloud for vengeance. The very ashes of the dead seem to be disturbed. (*TMS* 2.1.2.5: 83)

Regicide might be seen to lurk behind Smith's account of "the deformed and mangled carcass of the slain." In this lurid scenario sympathetic projection peaks when we contemplate someone "incapable of feeling." Here, however, that subject is born of a violent act of injustice—so unholy that we imagine it waking the dead to vengeance, stirring up the blood and ash so evocative of war.

Following the "bloodless" revolution of 1688, Aphra Behn returned readers to the "frightful spectacles of a mangled king" in *Oroonoko: or, The Royal Slave*, whose hero, as Laura Brown has definitively argued, so closely tracks Charles I.[30] As Brown writes, "For Behn and others, the colonies stage an historical anachronism, the repetition of the English revolution, and the political endpoint of Behn's narrative is the reenactment of the most traumatic event of the revolution, the execution of Charles I" (57). In delivering a "True History" that influentially entwined the subject of the slave with that of the sovereign, Behn disavowed "Fancy" and "Invention," putting herself forward as eyewitness and spokeswoman for her fictionalized African prince. But the narrator's pointed absentia during Oroonoko's grisly execution renders his death scene an act of pure imagination.[31] The blow-by-blow details of his dismemberment ("they cut off his Ears and his Nose, and burn'd them . . . then they hack'd off one of his Arms, and still he bore up and held his Pipe; but at the cutting off the other Arm, his Head sunk") do not record perception or memory or even sympathetic identification. Each macabre detail—told with what Ramesh Mallipeddi calls the text's "excessive and hyperbolic intensity,"[32] like the pipe that his earless, noseless head "still smoak'd on"—is curated by the self-appointed authority on "every Circumstance of [Oroonoko's] Life." Claiming editorial privilege, Behn asserts her rights to "omit, for Brevity's Sake, a thousand little Accidents of his Life, which, however pleasant to us, where History was scarce, and Adventures very rare; yet might prove tedious and heavy to my Reader" (2). The immensely popular 1696 theatrical version of *Oroonoko* by Thomas Southerne, which took copious creative license with Behn's plot, needed no such overtures. But Behn, writing in the early life of the English novel, found herself advancing the criterion of true *enough*: "there being enough of Reality to support it, and to render it diverting" (2).

The popularity of the staged *Oroonoko*, over and above the novel, suggests that sovereign insensibility is primarily a theatrical production, embedded in the public spectacle of regicide.[33] If Behn's narrative did not quite justify Samuel Johnson's panic that novels might "take possession of the memory by a kind of violence, and produce effects almost without the intervention of the will,"[34] it nonetheless purported to abrade the difference between what you once saw and now remember and what your novelized mind imagines to have been. As Jonathan Lamb writes of "the evolution of sympathy," these texts jumble "the categories of miracle, passion, person, fiction, and reality," so that a "preposterous realism . . . reverses the relation of what is to what was, and what is true to what is imagined." Such narratives, Lamb writes, replace the model of "empirical facts shaping a consciousness capable of recognizing various representations as probable" to "a sequence that is much less stable and which tells a tale not of rational conduct but of our enslavement to our feelings."[35]

For Johnson, fiction hijacks the understanding, implanting false memories by simulating a virtual reality. Most vulnerable to its epistemological dangers are the young, for whom "nothing indecent should be suffered to approach their eyes or ears." Behn's text bends this logic, calling attention to and also compensating for the lack of real spectacle in the novel, or what Rebecca Tierney-Hynes, writing on Behn's "narrated performances," calls "the circulation of spectacular bodies on [the] mental stage" of fiction.[36] In Oroonoko's unwitnessed but extravagantly narrated death scene, fiction fills in for the inadequacies of sense perception, supplying what, even for this self-proclaiming "Eye-Witness," is unbearable to see, to hear, to smell: "the Sight was ghashly [*sic*]: His Discourse was sad; and the earthy Smell about him so strong, that I was perswaded to leave" (2, 235). Narrative goes where the senses fear to tread, preparing for consciousness those experiences that still seem shockingly unmediated, that are *real enough*. Mallipeddi writes that at a time when "the interface between narrative and dramatic forms was being renegotiated by the emergence of a small but powerful print culture," narrative spectacle was still distinguished by the determining "subjectivity of the narrator" (29). The teller of *Oroonoko* conveys the unsightly *as* unsightly but can still engulf it in language, give it a name: "I must call *Oroonoko Caesar*." ("'Bartleby,' I roared.")

A graphic scene of execution that appears in part 5 of *The Theory of Moral Sentiments* characterizes the insensibility of "savages and barbarians" (beings hardened to distress) as nothing short of "heroic and unconquerable firmness" (*TMS* 5.2.9–10: 240–42). Sentenced to die as a prisoner of war, a savage hears his fate "without expressing any emotion, and afterwards submits to the most dreadful torments, without ever bemoaning himself, or discovering any other passion but contempt of his enemies"; he even goes so far as to perform his own original composition, "the song of death" (*TMS* 5.2.9: 241). Such demonstrations of "the highest contempt of death and pain," "greatest insensibility," and "most complete indifference" may be quintessential traits of the sovereign but, according to Smith and to *Oroonoko*, not a white one (*TMS* 5.2.9: 240–41). "Their magnanimity and self-command, in this respect, are almost beyond the conception of Europeans," for whom such exertions are simply not required (*TMS* 5.2.9–10: 240, 242). Where the barbaric spectators of a savage's execution ("he is hung by the shoulders over a slow fire," "scorched and burnt, and lacerated in all the most tender and sensible parts of his body for several hours") "express the same insensibility" as the prisoner (smoking, laughing, having fun), "a humane and polished people" would presumably disappear, shield their eyes, black out (*TMS* 5.2.9–10: 241, 242).

The softening powers of sentimental narrative can be found in the fifth volume of Hume's *History of England*, which portrays Charles I as "firm and intrepid," "possessing the utmost perspicuity and justness both of thought and expression." In Hume's variation the sovereign does not haughtily refuse to answer but only gently demurs ("With great temper and dignity, he declined").[37] Once perverse, now kindly, Charles is contemptuous only of evil: "Mild and equable, he rose into no passion. . . . His soul, without effort or affectation, seemed only to remain in the situation familiar to it, and to look down with contempt on all the efforts of human malice and iniquity" (537). Where previous accounts emphasized his solipsistic contempt, Hume depicts a doomsday serenity that provokes "contagious sympathy" in the public, manifesting itself in fervent prayers, endless tears, premature childbirth, and even sudden death.[38] A century after the fact, Hume confidently reports, "It is impossible to describe the grief, indignation, and astonishment, which took place, not only among the spectators, who were overwhelmed with a flood of sorrow, but throughout the whole nation" (540–41).[39] "Sympathy," argues Mary Fairclough in her study *The Romantic Crowd*, "is not a passion, a feeling or an opinion in its own right, but rather . . . a medium for the transmission of energies, ideas and emotions within a collective."[40] Like the vacant center of a tidal wave, the insensible initiates the turbulence that surges through a population, making a nation feel itself as whole, as affected by the same thing, together. Or, to try a less scenic metaphor, Hume's narrative, like many of its contemporaneous fictions, uses the insensible like a CPR mannequin: open-mouthed, wall-eyed, its hollow torso primed for inspiration. Henry Mackenzie's *Man of Feeling* (1771) ends with a contemplation of its hero's cadaver:

> I entered the room where his body lay; I approached it with reverence, not fear: I looked; the recollection of the past crowded upon me. I saw that form which, but a little before, was animated with a soul which did honour to humanity, stretched without sense or feeling before me. 'Tis a connection we cannot easily forget:—I took his hand in mine; I repeated his name involuntarily;—I felt a pulse in every vein at the sound. I looked earnestly in his face; his eye was closed, his lip pale and motionless. There is an enthusiasm in sorrow that forgets impossibility; I wondered that it was so. The sight drew a prayer from my heart: it was the voice of frailty and of man![41]

As critics of sentimental literature have remarked, men of feeling thrive on senseless (often female) persons.[42] Their plaintive, universalizing effusions ("the voice of frailty and of man!") echo best through the hollow chambers of a fresh cadaver. "Humanity" is produced here, in the impossible pulse-check of the insensible—a gesture that gathers all temporalities (recollection, encounter, prayer) in one breathless moment of ecstatic sorrow.

The lawyer's "Ah Bartleby! Ah humanity!" that closes Melville's story repurposes the topos of rapturous *memento mori*. Having related his clerk's past employment in a Dead Letter Office, the lawyer muses:

> When I think over this rumor, I cannot adequately express the emotions which seize me. Dead letters! does it not sound like dead men? Conceive a man by nature and misfortune prone to a pallid hopelessness, can any business seem more fitted to heighten it than that of continually handling these dead letters, and assorting them for the flames? For by the cart-load they are annually burned. Sometimes from out the folded paper the pale clerk takes a ring:—the finger it was meant for, perhaps, moulders in the grave; a bank-note sent in swiftest charity:—he whom it would relieve, nor eats nor hungers any more; pardon for those who died despairing; hope for those who died unhoping; good tidings for those who died stifled by unrelieved calamities. On errands of life, these letters speed to death.[43]

Like Mackenzie's narrator, whose flights of feeling are let loose by Harley's "pale," "closed," and "motionless" form, Melville's lawyer uses the low-pulsed neutrality of the scrivener to conjure a landscape of suffering (loneliness, hunger, despair, heartbreak) through which he can "express the emotions which seize" him. Here, the lawyer's daydream (of a ringless, mouldering finger) casts Bartleby as steward of annihilation and keeper of counterfactual lives. The clerk's activity ("continually handling these dead letters, and assorting them for the flames") consists in methodically eliminating the traces of inaction, aborted communiqués of relief, intimacy, nourishment, and support—all evidence of uncircumvented suffering. Pushing long-stalled errands of life down an infernal line, Bartleby sends their sentiments into oblivion. But the clerk—through his motions of carting and picking, with his "pallidly neat, pitiably respectable, incurably forlorn" body (19)—becomes himself an archive of missed connections, the ring-bearer of untold loves. Embodiment of potentiality (like Bartleby's metonymically "closed desk, the key in open sight left in the lock" [28]), the insensible initiates waves of feeling not merely because he is so blank that I have to project my own passions onto his moonlike face and cadaverous form but, more mystifyingly, because he contains prenarrative life, which is to say, nonexistence. What I project upon, sympathize with, and obsess over in the insensible's bafflingly alive state is its "nothingness or non-being," the residue of which Descartes tantalizingly suggests can be found in our own makeup (*M* 100). Moreover, it is not "humanity's" nonbeing that primarily moves me. The insensible allows me to sympathize with my own.

Observing how "we sympathize even with the dead," Adam Smith claims that our ability to reconstruct someone else's situation is so powerfully instinctive that in the case of the departed, we imagine not only the physiological reasons for the person's death (illness or accident) but the feeling of deadness itself: what it is like "to be deprived of the light of the sun; to be shut out from life and conversation; to be laid in the cold grave, a prey to corruption and the reptiles of the earth; to be no more thought of in this world, but to be obliterated, in a little time, from the affections, and almost from the memory, of their dearest friends and relations" (*TMS* 1.1.1.13: 16). The ratcheting in this passage from physical (dark, cold, reptiles) to social (no more conversation) to emotional (unloved, unremembered) showcases sympathy's range—its searching device for every corner of subjectivity. When we feel sorry for the dead, Smith explains, we are "joining to the change which has been produced upon them, our own consciousness of that change, from our putting ourselves in their situation, and from our lodging, if I may be allowed to say so, our own living souls in their inanimated bodies, and thence conceiving what would be our emotions in this case" (*TMS* 1.1.1.13: 16). Sympathy is viral—not merely in its contagiousness but, more specifically, in its dependence on a host or a foreign body that can be turned into a lodging for the subject's voracious energies. By this analogy, it makes sense that the host body would have no feelings of its own. (As Rae Greiner puts it, "Others needn't feel anything for us to sympathize with them.")[44] It is ideal that the dead do not experience our anguish for them. In fact, their unfeeling supports our sorrow: "That our sympathy can afford them no consolation seems to be an addition to their calamity; and to think that all we can do is unavailing, and that, what alleviates all other distress, the regret, the love, and the lamentations of their friends, can yield no comfort to them, serves only to exasperate our sense of their misery" (*TMS* 1.1.1.13: 16). Like the pathos induced by dead letters, sympathy bears an inverse relation to efficiency. The deceased cannot be moved, yet their rigid surfaces send my love rebounding, proliferating with even greater force. Whereas in mourning I feel for a particular object, here I feel for the condition of nonbeing itself—the missing out on any chance to be moved, ever again.[45] What could be sadder? Yet this thought only heightens my powers of cognition, victorious now over death because even *its* situation can be inhabited, down to its dirt, worms, and eternal forgottenness. So, in my extreme sensitivity to death, I become insensible to it.

Smith's postmortem narrative follows a certain trajectory, taking us from material decomposition to historical obliteration "in a little time" and thus suggesting an orientation toward the future that is inseparable from sympathetic projection. Such thinking encompasses "the foresight of our own dissolution," a cognitive reach that sets adult human consciousness apart from that of babies and animals (*TMS* 1.1.1.13: 16). Insensibility appears here as the blissful absence of anxiety—a counterpoint to Hobbes's "perpetuall solicitude of the time to come" that attends all desires. According to Hobbes, "man, which looks too far before him, in the care of future time, hath his heart all the day long, gnawed on by feare of death, poverty, or other calamity; and has no repose, nor pause of his anxiety, but in sleep" (*L* 1.12: 166). Locke repurposed Hobbes's account in his description of a "topping *uneasiness*" that we experience in the absence of the desired object (*EHU* 2.21.24: 256, 251). For Smith, "the most complete image of misery and distress" of this kind belongs to the mother of a sick baby, whose agonies are compounded in her mind by "her own terrors for the unknown consequences of its disorder" (*TMS* 1.1.1.12: 15). Smith observes that "the infant, however, feels only the uneasiness of the present instant, which can never be great. With regard to the future, it is perfectly secure, and in its thoughtlessness and want of foresight, possesses an antidote against fear and anxiety, the great tormentors of the human breast from which reason and philosophy will, in vain, attempt to defend it, when it grows up to a man" (*TMS* 1.1.1.12: 15–16). Feelings experienced only in the here and now are negligible compared to those projected into the void of the future. It is uncertainty that opens up the complex grammar of fear, casting its tangled lines of conditional, subjunctive, and imperfect thoughts into the dark reaches of consciousness. Without "care of future time," the insensible, though he might suffer, is immune.

VAINGLORIOUS MEN

It is not hard to argue that the central condition and concern of sentimental narrative is, by modern accounts, insensibility. One commonplace about the genre is that it expresses a dystopic, even misanthropic, vision of human life. Defined, in John Mullan's touchstone study, by its commitment "to the resources of a language of feeling for the purpose of representing necessary social bonds," sentimentalism is a discourse that sets out to fail, demonstrating both the inadequacy of people's emotions and the broken state of their relations.[46] Flipped into a culture of pervasive unfeeling, Britons are especially marked. From Burke's praise of the "cold sluggishness of our national character" to Smollett's condemnation of "this Land of Indifference and Phlegm," a group portrait emerges of a blocked people, whose flow of feeling has been obstructed, resulting in clogged and defensive sensibilities.[47] As Croaker says in Goldsmith's *Good Natur'd Man* (1768): "Sleeping and eating, sleeping and eating is the only work from morning till night in my house. My insensible crew could sleep, tho' rock'd by an earthquake; and fry beef steaks at a volcano."[48] Harkening back to a humoral classification of emotions, English phlegmatic reserve and dogged insusceptibility would appear to align with depression: a "dull, sad, sowre, lumpish" disposition that tends to solitude and a "heavinesse of the heart" in Burton's terms, or what George Cheyne named in 1733 as that nervous distemper of listlessness and anxiety, "the English Malady."[49]

Discourses of sympathy wade through this alternately anxious and lumpish terrain even as they reach for a way out. As Sean Gaston observes, the period's "continual need to imagine, idealize, and describe what is lacking suggests that we need to re-examine the eighteenth century as a century in *search of* sympathy" (145–46).[50] This search comes to provide a boilerplate for much of the period's fiction, in which unresolvable tensions between sentiment and sociability generate what Mullan calls tales of "a simple soul in an unsentimental world" or exiles "who have had to retreat from a world which maligns or abuses their feelings."[51] Mullan cites Richardson's *Clarissa* as one example (unique for "its identification of the family as the very realm of violence and conflict" [34]), but he singles out the importance of Goldsmith's *Vicar of Wakefield* (1766), a novel as underread today as it was revered in the nineteenth century as "the bible of moral sentiment."[52] The remainder of this chapter takes up a discussion of Goldsmith, focusing on *The Vicar of Wakefield* and *She Stoops to Conquer*, in order to connect sentimental literature's man of feeling or "good-natured man" back to the figure of the sovereign animated by Charles I. This unlikely provenance, I argue, illustrates the generative role of comedy in the history of insensibility and its disruptions to the Richardsonian novel.

Occupying an uncertain position in a tradition of sentimental literature (and often simply omitted from its study), *The Vicar of Wakefield* showcases a depleted man of feeling in a landscape of nationalized insensibility.[53] Seen against the Irish writer's oeuvre, this subject forms one piece of a mosaic of hard-heartedness: from the "absolute frigidity" of the Chinese philosopher in the *Citizen of the World* (1760) to "trade's unfeeling train" in "The Deserted Village" (1770) to the contemptuous "indifference" of Grub Street at large.[54] Nigel Wood diagnoses Goldsmith's characters (including "the indigent giver" and "the *idiot savant*") as "peculiar forms of *anomie*," expressive of an Anglo-Irish malady rooted in displacement.[55] Writing on *She Stoops to Conquer*, Wood says, "The sentimental is here portrayed as part of what we would now term a bipolar disorder, namely an inability to find some coherence in one's personality" (65). In the case of *Vicar* emotional disorder is tacked onto narrative incoherence, a journey through a fictional no-man's-land between satire and sentiment.[56] Contemporaries faulted the unbelievably good hero, Doctor Primrose, whom Goldsmith quickly defended: "In this age of opulence and refinement whom can such a character please?"[57]

The leading man of the novel is not actually Primrose, however, but the "exquisitely sensible" Sir William Thornhill, the story's *deus ex machina*, who continues to draw charges of narrative failure. Sir William, slumming as the penniless Mr. Burchell, witnesses and eventually remediates the Primroses' battery of misfortunes. Early on, Burchell offers this diagnostic (auto)biography of Thornhill:

> Physicians tell us of a disorder in which the whole body is so exquisitely sensible that the slightest touch gives pain. What some have suffered in their persons, this gentleman felt in his mind: the slightest distress, whether real or fictitious, touched him to the quick, and his soul laboured under a sickly sensibility of the miseries of others. Thus disposed to relieve, it will be easily conjectured, he found numbers disposed to solicit: his profusions began to impair his fortune, but not his good-nature; that, indeed, was seen to increase as the other seemed to decay: he grew improvident as he grew poor; and though he talked like a man of sense, his actions were those of a fool. Still, however, being surrounded with importunity, and no longer able to satisfy every request that was made him, instead of *money* he gave *promises*. They were all he had to bestow, and he had not resolution enough to give any man pain by a denial. By this he drew round him crowds of dependants, whom he was sure to disappoint; yet wished to relieve. These hung upon him for a time, and left him with merited reproaches and contempt. But in proportion as he became contemptible to others, he became despicable to himself. (4:29–30)

A former man of feeling ("he carried benevolence to an excess *when young*; for his passions were *then* strong" [4:29]), Sir William has already learned the art of nonresponsiveness when we meet him. Removed from the undeniable pull of familiar objects, he reprioritizes self-preservation, newly "resolved to respect himself" and shore up his fortunes while wandering the Continent. A whimsical if disillusioned itinerant, only thirty-years old, Sir William becomes a "humourist," who takes pleasure in "eccentric virtues" much like Mr. Bennet of *Pride and Prejudice* (4:30). R. F. Brissenden, in his classic study of sentimental literature, calls Thornhill a "melancholy man of feeling," the text's "symbol of alienation," or the "dispossessed conscience of a sick society," which belies this sentimental comedy.[58] For Brissenden, the "radical disquiet" represented by Thornhill contributes to the dark tenor of Goldsmith's work, including his popular "The Traveller, or, a Prospect of Society" (1764) and "The Deserted Village." Yet, where the personae of these poems (loners, wanderers, and hermits) are conspicuously solitary ("My fortune leads to traverse realms alone / And find no spot of all the world my own"), the man of feeling, like the stock figure of the prude, is aggressively social. Sir William returns to his village, and not only won't he leave the Primroses alone (even after they try to shake him), but he keeps at the hard business of comedy.

I have claimed elsewhere that Goldsmith's novel reprises Hobbes's world without a sovereign—a grim scene of abandonment that is flagged in the very meaning of *vicar* as substitute or proxy.[59] Elaborating the explicit monarchism in Goldsmith's work, especially in *Vicar*, I argue that the fundamentally dystopic outlook that drives sentimental narrative records the collapse of a political covenant, a pact not between subjects and their ruler but among subjects themselves (as in *Leviathan*: a "Covenant, every one, with every one" [1.18: 88]). In his prison speech endorsing "monarchy, sacred monarchy," Primrose laments the state of "false compact" that has resulted in systemic injustice, including a corrupted legal system, unchecked avarice, and mass incarceration of the poor (150). For Primrose, as for Hobbes, the end of monarchy meant the dissolution of the only structure that could hold subjects accountable to each other. Hobbes writes that in such conditions, "he that performeth first, has no assurance the other will performe after; because the bonds of words are too weak to bridle mens ambition, avarice, anger, and other Passions, without the feare of some cöercive Power." For Hobbes, only the sovereign can solder intention to speech to action: "*He upholdeth all things by the Word of his Power*, that is, by the Power of his Word; that is, by his Power," he writes in a riff on the Epistle to the Hebrews (*L* 3.36: 652). Without a unifying covenant, individuals have no standing to make a promise or to have their promises believed. The enfeebled Sir William, drained of funds by his own charity, dispenses empty "promises," which "were all he had to bestow."

We return to the problem of intention that marked the trial of sovereign insensibility, expressed by Bradshaw's remonstrance to Charles that "actions must expound intentions." Tyranny, in Bradshaw's logic, had resulted from a perverse glitch in the relays among motive, speech, and action—obscuring but also indicating the "very erroneous principles" that had led Charles to commit violence against his own subjects. That glitch is systemic in *Vicar*'s state of "false compact," in which subjects' relations to each other have dissolved (or, in Goldsmith's consistently class-based terms, "the natural ties that bind the rich and the poor together are broken" [*Vicar*, 101]). The affective medium of society (already "dull, sad, sowre, lumpish" to begin with) is shot through with mistrust. People cannot believe each other's words; speech no longer corresponds to action. The sovereign, who alone secured the social ties of commonwealth, is not dead, but he's battered, broke, backpacking somewhere in Europe.

The Vicar of Wakefield rescripts the supersession of sovereign power by a market economy as the story of a lost figure of benevolence, a spent man of feeling just trying to find his way back. The depression of the good-natured man is an index of political-economic displacement. Capitalism may replace the need for a sovereign, but it can't get rid of his feelings—the emotional confusion that, in Wood's analysis, lands him in the *DSM V*. In *Vicar* Sir William recants, gets ahead of his own disorder by turning himself into an object of public derision and then vaccinating with a shot of self-disdain. Declared "contemptible to the world," Mr. Honeywood in *The Good Natur'd Man* similarly embraces the charge, owning his own loathsomeness.[60] Modernity's wistful sovereign experiences a dysphoric misalignment, captured by Honeywood's insight that he possesses "the wish but not the power to serve" (27). Olivia restates his error: "he only mistook the desire for the power of serving us" (70).

A terminated covenant vacates the power to serve. To misinterpret one's wish to assist as the capacity to do so signals a deflated sphere of good intentions, what makes promises void from their inception, pledges always empty, the "exquisitely sensible" king "the voluntary slave of all" (*Good Natur'd Man*, 80). Hobbes calls the mistaking of desire for power *vainglory*:

Where glory arises from the idea that one has more power than another, and false glory when "one may think well of himself, and yet be deceived," vainglory is a singular habit of misperception, a "fiction . . . of actions done by ourselves, which never were done" and therefore "begetteth no appetite nor endeavour to any further attempt."[61] Vainglorious people are imaginative creatures, lovers of literature even: "as when a man imagineth himself to do the actions whereof he readeth in some romant, or to be like unto some other man whose acts he admireth. And this is called VAIN GLORY: and is exemplified in the fable by the fly sitting on the axletree, and saying to himself, What a dust do I raise!" (*EL* 37).[62] Forever at play (in "imitation of others, counterfeiting attention to things they understand not"), the vainglorious do not originate the actions they affect to. Moreover, the delusional fly is less to blame than the fictions of action (fables, romances) that fuel his "dreams, and other little stories."[63] Sentimental fictions reinvest quixotism with moral innocence, reinterpreting vainglory as "splendid error," or the unfortunate confusion of "injustice" for "charity," "weakness" for "benevolence," "credulity" for "friendship" (*Good Natur'd Man*, 80).

Hobbes advances that the moment when individuals have to fend for themselves, the commonwealth has stopped working. Once the sovereign ceases to protect his members, they no longer owe him obedience ("The end of Obedience is Protection" [*L* 2.21: 344]). *The Vicar of Wakefield* assumes the death of that relation. Subjects are not merely unprotected but aggressively hounded, imprisoned, molested, and humiliated. Only the Odyssean king come back in disguise, "whose virtues and singularities scarce any were strangers," can reinstate safety (168). Primrose recounts, "The poor Mr. Burchell was in reality a man of large fortune and great interest, to whom senates listened with applause, and whom party heard with conviction; who was the friend of his country, but loyal to his king" (168). A sovereign agent, Thornhill issues commandments in the very idiom of royalty. To his guilty nephew, now kneeling and "implor[ing] compassion," he pronounces, "Thy vices, crimes, and ingratitude . . . deserve no tenderness; yet thou shalt not be entirely forsaken, a bare competence shall be supplied, to support the wants of life, but not its follies" (179–80). By the time Sir William scoops up his "heavenly beauty" and dispenses cash gifts all around, he has sprinkled princely glitter over the plot, liberating and enriching one son, transforming a daughter from prostitute to wife (that fake marriage license was real!), and turning the other into a lady ("Lady Thornhill")—not to mention rendering "almost instantaneous relief" to the vicar's burnt arm with his surprising pharmaceutical skills (181). When, at the end of the day, Primrose gives himself a moment to pour "out my heart in gratitude to the giver of joy as well as of sorrow," he would appear to be giving thanks to Sir William as much as to God, indistinguishable as they are. But in Goldsmith's attempt to revive sovereign power through novelistic character, two problems arose: no one believed it, and it wasn't funny.

The insensible obstructs narrative felicity. Thornhill's clunky, kingly shape seems out of place in a novel. Vivasvan Soni reads *Vicar* as a Christian trial narrative that endlessly defers deliverance: "The ease and rapidity with which the felicitous matrimonial arrangements are made, with Sir William Thornhill playing the benevolent god, suggests that the labor of the narrative has been in vain, since it has not significantly impacted the protagonists' possibilities for happiness and can be set aside in a moment." For Soni, *Vicar*'s resolution, a triple-marriage plot in which Thornhill actively participates, cancels narrative meaning, reinforcing the "theological structure of a reward beyond."[64] John Bender's critique of *Vicar* likewise targets Sir William as a *figuration* of power, expressive of the author's monarchism. Goldsmith's political nostalgia—his participation in popular hopes that George III would be "an enlightened monarch"[65]—committed him to the passé construct of fictional character. This attachment, Bender ingeniously argues, kept Goldsmith from alighting on narrative's greatest expression of modern state power: free indirect discourse. Thus, instead of approaching Austenian style, *The Vicar of Wakefield* keeps rolling back into allegory: in Thornhill's "embracing, neutral, guarding force" we see an "incongruous attribution of regulative omniscience to personal agents" such that, in the end, "overdetermined personifications of authority crowd the whole text." E. P. Thompson, in the essay about eighteenth-century society quoted by Bender, writes of popular visions of a "patriot king," whose impartiality would absorb the impersonal workings of a bureaucratic state in league with the self-regulation of a free market. In Bender's analysis Goldsmith's investment in the good-natured sovereign or patriot king prevented him from grasping the "textual ideology" that would capture such forces (143). Crucial here is Bender's positioning of Goldsmith on the cusp of Austenian narration, as just on the other side of the liberation from personhood made possible by free indirect style. But for Goldsmith, still in search of an alternative to market society, still attached to the person of the sovereign, the novel offered no redemption. For one thing, it was inhospitable to the atavistic, liberatory potential of laughter.

LUMPKIN'S PUCK

A decade after writing *Vicar*, in his "Essay on the Theatre; or, A Comparison Between Sentimental and Laughing Comedy," Goldsmith claimed that while the middle class possessed fine feelings, it had no sense of humor (*CW* 3:209–13). Accordingly, its preferred genre, the sentimental comedy, was a vehicle for bourgeois distress. Its vogue reflected the unfortunate novelization of the theater and, as such, had "banish[ed] Humour from the Stage" and "deprived [us] of the art of Laughing" (213). Taking an implicit dig at his own *Vicar* (whose manuscript was famously fished out by Johnson to pay Goldsmith's back-rent), the writer denounced sentimental comedy as a pedestrian form, "insipid[ly]" undramatic and incurably accommodating: "almost all the characters are good. . . . If they happen to have faults or foibles, the spectator is taught, not only to pardon, but to applaud them, in consideration of the goodness of their hearts." Unable to resist, Goldsmith added that the future of the genre was secure: "Those abilities that can hammer out a novel, are fully sufficient for the production of a sentimental comedy" (400–401). Easy to write, risk-free fictions would always find an audience.

Goldsmith embeds another jibe at the novelist in *The Life of Richard Nash* (1762), contemporaneous with the probable writing of *The Vicar of Wakefield*:

> Were I upon the present occasion to hold the pen of a novelist, I could fill a volume with little anecdotes, which contain neither pleasure nor instruction; with histories of professing lovers, and poor believing girls deceived by such professions. But such adventures are easily written, and as easily atchieved [*sic*]. The plan even of [a] fictitious novel is quite exhausted; but truth, which I have followed here, and ever design to follow, presents in the affair of love scarce any variety. The manner in which one reputation is lost, exactly resembles that by which another is taken away. The gentleman begins at timid distance, grows more bold, becomes rude, till the lady is married or undone; such is the substance of every modern novel. (*CW* 3:321–22)

In just fourteen years since the first volume of *Clarissa* appeared, Goldsmith insinuates that Richardsonian plots had taken up all the air, stifling every other configuration of story. What's worse, they were boring—the sameness of their formulae having overtaken any intent to instruct and delight. A moratorium on its stock figures of "professing lovers and poor believing girls" might start the work of narrative rehabilitation. In his own dramatic writing,

Norma Clarke observes, Goldsmith may have drawn on erotic conventions, "but there is no serious love interest in any of his writings, no love scenes and no bawdy. None of his heroes are lovers."[66] Forced by genre to attempt such a scene, Goldsmith falters in the final pages of *Vicar*, leaving a whiff of authorial embarrassment. Turning to Sophia Primrose, who has just refused the hand of a rake, Sir William pronounces, "'If that be the case then,' cried he, 'if you will not have him—I think I must have you myself.' And so saying, he caught her to his breast with ardour" (181).

Lisa Freeman discerns a double impulse in eighteenth-century sentimental comedies "to accommodate the social and economic merits of the new middling classes" and "to satisfy an ideology of patriarchal benevolence," where the distribution of property and posterity are (as in bawdier "laughing" comedies) still at stake.[67] Softening the staple conflict between parents and children over marital choice, "sentimental comedies reform comedic plots, taming intrigue and transforming generational conflict into generational respect by substituting displays of 'good breeding' for contests of wit" (196). That substitution, in Goldsmith's critique, had killed the form. Too nice to be funny, sentimental fiction ventured nothing. Where, in Lauren Berlant and Sianne Ngai's assessment, comedy "risk[s] transgression, flirt[s] with displeasure, or just confus[es] things in a way that both intensifies and impedes the pleasure,"[68] sentimental comedy, like its good-natured man, tried too hard to please. At the start of the twentieth century, Henri Bergson's *Le rire* would expand memorably on the opposition between sensibility and humor posited by Goldsmith. "Laughter," declares Bergson, "has no greater foe than emotion"; it calls for an "absence of feeling," or, at least, a "momentary anesthesia of the heart."[69] Bergson went on: sentimental people with "highly emotional souls, in tune and unison with life," cannot understand humor. While laughter is social ("Our laughter is always the laughter of the group"), it must be out of sync. Bergson's scene of insensibility spotlights hearing: if we "stop our ears" at a dance, then all the dancers will look funny, allowing us to enjoy the spectacle of their gesticulating bodies (4). Without "the accompanying music of sentiment," most actions appear ridiculous. Like a reformed Sir William Thornhill, the humorist knows that it takes a certain desensitization (stopping your ears to the wants of others) to grasp the big picture. But where Sir William eventually removes his noise-canceling headphones, aiming this time for selective attunement, the humorist keeps them planted on his head. Indeed—as

Goldsmith finally realized in *She Stoops to Conquer*—the truly funny person plops himself in a soundproof booth, where he can laugh at everyone, high above the dance floor:

> TONY. [*From a reverie.*] Ecod, I have hit it. Its [*sic*] here. (195)

In *She Stoops to Conquer*, what Covent Garden manager George Colman called "one of the most eccentric productions that had ever been put on the stage,"[70] Goldsmith wrested a rarefied insensible from the exhausted literature of sensibility: as if Clarissa Harlowe were not a lady but a ladybug that had shed its carapace and then died from exposure, but then, from out of nowhere, its exoskeleton crawled back, dusted off its wings, and danced away with new, impossible life. Clarissa Harlowe had it all, lost it all, and, post-*Wretchedness*, carried on with shimmering transparency. "Below resentment," a "poor contemptible booby, that would but disgrace correction," Tony Lumpkin also reconfigures contempt—another insensible who, like the eponymous hero of *The Prude*, is "past Insults" and, therefore, free to live (or die) in his own way. (The actor John Quick was said to perform Lumpkin "exceedingly well" but "with rather too much grimace"—meaning perhaps with too much effort, affect [*CW* 5:92]; see fig. 3.) Beyond the social pale, Goldsmith's insensible walks on air; he is "Humour, my dear, nothing but humour" (108).

Having dropped its original title, *The Novel*, while retaining its subtitle, *The Mistakes of a Night*, *She Stoops to Conquer* aimed—and, by many accounts, succeeded—at redeeming comedy from narrative's treacly sensibilities.[71] To this end Goldsmith turned to theater's ready-made insensible, the demonic fairy Puck, or Robin Goodfellow, an ancient folk figure turned into a "Petulant and Malapert," "Malicious and abusive," "bold and impudent" icon, according to a 1680 text dedicated "to Robbin Goodfellow."[72] Lumpkin—that inimitable "unfeeling monster," "graceless varlet," and "insensible cub" (2.1.574, 5.2.128, 4.1.379)—takes his cue from Shakespeare's "mad spirit" of nocturnal misrule, who "mislead[s] night-wanderers, laughing at their harm" in *A Midsummer Night's Dream* (3.2; 2.1). But it is Lumpkin's more immediate lineage that, as I will argue, completes the picture of his insensibility: a politicized, early modern version of Robin Goodfellow, who combines Hobbesian extremity with lawless play. One 1673 character sketch delineates the qualities Lumpkin will inherit: Puck is disgraceful ("the *stain* of a good Family"), illiterate ("A *wilde unback'd Colt*, whose *brains* are not

FIGURE 3. The actor John Quick as Tony Lumpkin in *She Stoops to Conquer*, engraved by P. Audinet (1808). Courtesy of the Rare Book and Manuscript Library, University of Illinois at Urbana-Champaign.

half *codled*"), cheerfully delinquent (always singing and whistling with "three or four wilde *Companions* [and] half a dozen bottles of *Burgundy*"), and a man-child ("effeminated by the childish *Toyings* of a rampant imagination" and by "his *Mothers indulgence*").[73] Less apparent is his amorality, the indelible stamp of "that *unlucky Author*," Thomas Hobbes. With his "two leaves of *Leviathan*," this Goodfellow rebukes "*Spirits*" and "*Immaterial Essence*," while "boast[ing] aloud that he holds his *Gospel* from the *Apostle of Malmsbury*" (5). Puck returns contempt (his "*pert* and *pragmatique* scorn") to its heretical roots. And although "he will not confess himself *Atheist*," "he is so refractory to *Divinity* that Morality it self cannot hold him, [and] he affirms humane Nature knows no such things as *principles* of Good and evil" (4–5). Whether Goldsmith meant to deploy this Hobbesian incarnation of Robin Goodfellow is less important than the fact that Shakespeare's Puck had already changed, absorbed by the combativeness of the prior century's print culture, which relied on a deep repertoire of scapegoats and villains.

Where Sir William Thornhill had to be cringingly assimilated into the sentimental novel, the "*Arch Devil*" Puck retains comedy's edge. Lumpkin's emphatic nonconjugality—he is "no friend to the ladies"—allows Goldsmith to pull off an illicit double courtship plot while avoiding "the whining end of a modern novel" (82, 87–88):

> TONY. I beg you'll keep your distance. I want no nearer relationship; . . .
> MISS NEVILLE. I'm sure [he] would wish to see me married to anybody but himself.

Not quite the "cloying endgame" that Michael Griffin discerns, the conclusion of *She Stoops to Conquer* stages what Berlant and Ngai call comedy's pleasurable "self-violation" or what Simon Critchley describes as the "anti-rite" of the joke:[74]

> TONY. (*taking Miss Neville's hand.*) Witness all men by these presents, that I, Anthony Lumpkin, Esquire, of BLANK place, refuse you, Constantia Neville, spinster, of no place at all, for my true and lawful wife. (215)

The blanks fired by comedy's spirit of refusal abide by the strange physics of insensibility, the ascension of an unmoving object: *IMMOTA, TRIVMPHANS*. Demonstrating life's stuckness, Puck stages a commotion that goes nowhere:

Up and down, up and down,
I will lead them up and down.
I am feared in field and town.
Goblin, lead them up and down.
(*A Midsummer Night's Dream*, 3.2)

"Riddle me this then," taunts Lumpkin, "What's that goes round the house, and round the house, and never touches the house" (203). Through the mud in Feather Bed Lane, over the rattling stones of Up-and-Down Hill, past the gibbet on Heavy Tree Heath, landing in the horse-pond at the bottom of the garden, Lumpkin takes the insufferably "straight forward" narrative of courtship for a circular ride. Its participants are predictably slow to the joke. "Ha, ha, ha, I understand," Hastings finally cracks it. "You took them in a round, while they supposed themselves to be going forward. And so you have brought them home again" (203).

In Tony Lumpkin, Goldsmith returns Puck to his comedic roots and rustic setting, but the "prophane" and "fantastick *Buffoonry*" of Robin Goodfellow had long belonged to an undomesticated Londonized figure, who paraded his "Magick" of "strange Beasts" into the "*Phanatique Theatre*" and "*Hot-House*" of urban space. Like Sir William, this Puck "playes *Rex* where ever he comes, and makes as much hurry as *Robin Goodfellow* of old amongst our *Granams Milk-bouls*" ("Character," 5). No benign country scamp, the new Goodfellow is a "State-Quack" ("Will with a Whisp," 4), who "preten[ds] great skill in curing the *Tetters* and *Ring-worms* of *State*" and "thin[ks] Government and Religion fit objects" for his folly ("Character," 5–6). His "Jests and loud *laughter*," his singular "practice of *Fooling*" evoke the mirthlessness of Charles's "Ha!": he would "forfeit his neck to the *Gibbet*, or his shoulders to the *Batoon* rather than lose the driest of his idle *Quibbles*" ("Character," 6).

Puck had long been an expediter of sovereign power, presiding over comedy's mission to confuse and then correct: "this their jangling I esteem a sport," but "If you pardon, we will mend" (*A Midsummer Night's Dream*, 3.2, 5.1). A figure of what Louise Geddes, in her study of the early modern clown, calls "limited autonomy," Puck also represents rogue potential.[75] As Tim Reid writes, "Clowns live proximate to power. It's how they do."[76] In proximity to or as extension of legitimate rule, Puck occupies that inscrutable margin of potentiality that is home to the insensible. "This is thy negligence," accuses Oberon. "Still thou mistak'st, / Or else committ'st thy knaveries willfully" (3.2).

On a long leash to do his ruler's bidding, Puck is given only one directive: to do no harm. Winifried Schleiner, writing on Puck's rich multicultural origins, argues that while Shakespeare's character claims a long "nefarious and devilish ancestry," "the novelty of his achievement" was to delineate a subject who "intend[s] to torment but not to hurt."[77] Similarly, Haldeen Braddy, comparing Puck to a figure from Jean Froissart's medieval *Chronicles*, returns to the injunction to " 'do no hurt to any person in this house.' "[78] As the sixteenth-century celebrity clown Richard Tarlton jingles:

> Feare not me man, I am but Dick Tarlton that coulde quaint it in the Court, and clowne it on the stage: that had a quart of wine for my friend, and a sword for my foe: who hurt none beeing alive, and will not prejudice any being dead, for although thou see me here in the likenes of a spirite, yet thinke mee to bee one of those Familiares Lares that were rather pleasantly disposed than indued with any hurtfull influence, as Hob Thrust, Robin Goodfellowe and such like spirites . . . famozed in everie old wives Chronicle for their mad merry pranckes.[79]

Tarlton's claim to harmlessness rests here on a distinction between the pleasant clown[80] and the crazed, equivocal Robin Goodfellow. ("A man or Divell? Or what so ere thou art," asks a 1606 comedy in which Robin appears, laughing in his "hellish shape.")[81] After *Midsummer*, invocations of Robin Goodfellow and Puck signal the attempt to fall on the right side of "hurtfull influence," to claim, in other words, the prerogative of pure antic. Thus, Puck's very directive to do no harm speaks precisely to his capacity for destruction.[82] "Never fear me. Ecod!" trails Goldsmith's "unaccountable creature," "with cunning and malice enough to make himself merry with all our embarrassments" not to mention a propensity for real violence: "O lud! He has almost cracked my head" (164, 168, 193, 153).

During the anti-Catholic hysteria surrounding the Popish Plot, a beastly Robin Goodfellow resurfaced with a vengeance. In "The Bare-Faced Tories: A New Song. *To the TUNE* of Robbin-Goodfellow" (1682), lawless devils "learn to kill and slay, / And put our bloody Hands in use."[83] Far from boozy entertainers, who "quaint it in the Court, and clowne it on the stage," the Pucks entering the eighteenth century were figures of pure horror:

> Their Throats in pieces we will tear,
> We'll stab them to the Heart
> . . . .

> tear 'em Limb from Limb,
> And make brave Candles of their Greese,
> When we on their streams of blood can swim,
> Then surely we shall rest in peace.

Yet these gory acts were also construed as crimes of print: "playing of Tricks with thy Pen, and scraping with thy Cloven Feet, appearing in several Printed Shapes, Forms, and Disguises, to the no small affright of many people."[84] Where Shakespeare's sprite endearingly if enigmatically sweeps the stage ("I am sent with broom before, / To sweep the dust behind the door"), a reborn "Robbin Good-Fellow [is found] tweaking ever body by the Nose, and with thy Invisible Broom, sweeping the Dirt and Dung into every bodies Face" ("Will of the Whisp," 1).

What Goldsmith inherited with Puck was not just theatrical insensibility but a comic typology steeped in fear, corroborating Gaston's claim that the roots of eighteenth-century sensibility lay in political violence. Tony Lumpkin, half-child ("an awkward booby, reared up, and spoiled at his mother's apron-string") and half-fiend ("a sweet, pleasant—damned mischievous son of a whore" (121, 125), reprises a culture's campaign to make power safe again, to neutralize a figure of misrule and social injury. Goldsmith, working the revolving door between eighteenth-century "stage and page," reimagines a sovereign agent who may torment but does not harm. Sprites, fairies, clowns, kings—all figures of Bartlebyan exemption—belong, as Marjorie Garber writes (glossing Oberon's claim that "we are spirits of another sort" [3.2]), to "an alternate clan, race, or society"—an Oz of insensibility.[85]

Lisa Freeman has argued that in the anxious-making business of character—a concept that "raised the frightening possibility either that there was no true 'inside' or that if there were, we have no 'real' access to it"—eighteenth-century theater went about its work differently than did the novel (27). Where prose forms tried "to resolve or at least to compensate for" those problems by stabilizing individual identity, theater reveled in the discombobulating efforts of social interpretation. In other words, the novel's earnest pursuit and "discourse of 'the subject' " flounder on the stage, where, for Freeman, a very different set of protocols resist a metafictional "rise" of psychological realism (7). "On the stage," she explains, "there was no public/private split; there was only public space and public displays" (27). A purely exteriorized medium, the theater could exploit character-*effects* arising from "staged contests between interpretable surfaces" or "actions, words, figure, and reputation" (27). Emily

Hodgson Anderson, drawing out the performative aspects of eighteenth-century novels, makes the related and dazzling point that "masks create dimensionality; they produce the very inwardness that they obscure."[86] What the theater knows is that depth is an effect of surface or, in Anderson's analysis, that the novel's explorations of buried subjectivity are inseparable from the "costumes and vizards" of eighteenth-century performance. Theatrical flatness, she argues, makes conceptual layering possible, the "dimensionality" that animates tropes of authenticity, sincerity, and selfhood. To extrapolate, what *Vicar* needed was not a Thornhill but a Lumpkin. But Goldsmith, in his short but prolific life on Grub Street, made no second attempt at the feel-good form of the novel.

Drawing on the influential theories of historians J. G. A. Pocock and Lawrence Klein, Freeman depicts "the socioeconomic order of sentimental comedy" as the endless circulation of a newly commercialized society, in which the basis of value had irrevocably shifted from land-generated wealth to the exchange of mobile forms of property (201, 203). Under modernity, good nature (or what Freeman analyzes as "good breeding") functions like money as "both the end and the means of social intercourse because it underwrites all transactions and exchanges" (202). In other words, sensibility does not just buy things (commodities, relations), but it makes the whole system of buying and selling possible. As such, it becomes an end in itself, or in Freeman's terms, it acts as "credibility" as well as "credit" (202). We can see, then, how Goldsmith's revival of uncouth insensibility draws from a residual model of relations in both political-economic and literary domains, explaining his misfit in a tradition of sentimental literature. The animal laughter of Tony Lumpkin, erupting from the Three Pigeons with "a mallet in his hand," attempts to restore a noncommercial order, as well as a lost art of comedy. This is why *She Stoops to Conquer* could not be the novel that Goldsmith had initially envisioned. Comedy, as all Pucks know, belongs to an older dispensation, not to a novelized world of endless motion but to the terra firma of estate and of state, what compels all lovers to return to Theseus's palace and to Athens after a night of mistakes in the woods.

Speaking at the anniversary of the *People's Paper*, Marx said, "In the signs that bewilder the middle class, the aristocracy and the poor prophets of regression, we do recognise our brave friend, Robin Goodfellow, the old mole that can work in the earth so fast, that worthy pioneer—the Revolution."[87] Tapping into the manic rather than depressive strain of English "lumpishness,"

Goldsmith hit on "a good-natured creature" who could rework the narrative ground—who, in Elias's description of comedy, "confuses desire and aggression" and so unleashes energies within a form that looks deceptively the same ("Essay on Laughter," 239). For Goldsmith, the novel was scorched earth, purged of aesthetic or even social possibility. His insensible savior belonged not to Grub Street or even Buckingham Palace but to Covent Garden, in the still-salvageable ground of English theater. Unimaginable by Goldsmith was the infusion of sovereign laughter back into the novel form—not through the character of a lover or a weeper but through narration itself, that is to say, through Jane Austen herself.

CHAPTER 4

Sense, Insensibility, Sympathy

IN THE CASE OF JANE AUSTEN IT IS, remarkably, Austen herself who presides as the insensible of the novel.[1] Both critics and Janeites have long been preoccupied with the singularity of her unfeeling and its shaping impact on her work, making it necessary to prove either "the biographical fact that Jane Austen had loved," as Virginia Woolf put it, or, as another camp upholds, the general impression that she hated. Charlotte Brontë, annoyed at the recommendation to read more Austen, famously took issue with her forebear's dispassion: "Jane Austen was a complete and most sensible lady, but a very incomplete, and rather insensible (*not senseless*) woman; if this is heresy," Brontë concluded, "I cannot help it."[2]

Far from sacrilege, findings of Austen's insensibility are linked not only to her perceived sexlessness (in Brontë's account, Austen's neglect "of what throbs fast and full"), but also to her divinity—that is, her moral, aesthetic, and metaphysical ascendancy. "For Jane Austen has no passion, preaches no gospel, grinds no axe; standing aloof from the world, she sees it, on the whole, as silly. She has no animosity for it; but she has no affection," eulogized Reginald Farrer on the centenary of her death.[3] Fellow Austenian Lord

David Cecil boasted that the novelist was "unable to express . . . emotion directly" and that because she "surveyed her creatures with too detached an irony for her to identify herself with them," she could not "voice their unthinking gushes of feeling."[4] An icon of contempt—that cardiac "immobility" declared by Hobbes to be scandalously unaffected by either aversion or desire—Austen becomes personally subject to charges of cruelty, deviance, and *froideur*. Unthinking readers may stoop to identify with her characters' feelings, but the novelist would never.

"Distance—from her subject and from the reader—was Jane Austen's first condition for writing," begins Marvin Mudrick's classic *Jane Austen: Irony as Defense and Discovery*, which epitomizes the critical impulse to make Austen's celibacy the basis of her style.[5] For Mudrick, Austen's "single life-principle" of emotional quarantine and chilling self-exemption kept her not only from engaging in personal and, in his account, sexual relations but also from giving way to readerly pleasure. As E. N. Hayes acidly complained in a polemic against *Emma*, "Of the passion of love little is said, I think for the obvious reason that Jane Austen knew nothing of it firsthand. If her men and women feel the thrill of love, certainly the reader is never aware of the fact."[6] Too merciless or "priss[y]" or inhuman to entertain mere feelings (Mudrick 168), Austen may *appear* to concern herself with friendship, love, and, in particular, heterosexual desire, but in *fact*, this story goes, she could not care less. (Her letters and juvenilia are cited as further evidence of such deep-seated insensibility.)[7]

The reception of Austen and her novels—a history pivotal to the fortunes of the genre at large[8]—offers a potent example of how failures of feeling are entwined with narrative failure and how the charge of insensibility so often marks a disruption to protocols of fictionality. The fixation on Austen's "essentially dispassionate nature"[9] testifies to the cultural longevity of *la prude*, that warped figure of gender and narrative instability, derived from a seventeenth-century discourse of *préciosité*, which opened my genealogy of insensibles. We see in Austen's reception the same perceived overreach of female ambition once attributed to the prude's historical antecedents, *les précieuses*, the coterie of aristocratic French women writers, such as Madame de Lafayette and Madeleine de Scudéry, who crafted the *nouvelles historiques* so influential to the European novel. In retreat from failed political revolution, the *précieuses*, as I discussed earlier, remade a world of letters and were duly diminished as ridiculous, pretentious, and unnatural.

Seedbed of feminocentric literary virtuosity and catalyst of an equally eloquent libertine backlash, the maligned and exilic *précieuses* implant within the dark heart of the Richardsonian tradition an unbearably gendered claim to linguistic and political sovereignty. From *la prude et la précieuse* to Clarissa Harlowe to Jane Austen, the consistent response, not just to ridicule but to pathologize their audacity, betrays the potency of those claims. Austen's innovation in narrative technique, her syntactic precision, and stylistic *je ne sais quoi* are undoubtedly celebrated, as in D. A. Miller's paean to her "world-historical achievement . . . to have established, within the boundlessly oppressive imperiums of gender, conjugality, and the Person, something like extraterritoriality."[10] But on the flip side of tribute lies a panicked reflex to tamp down Austen's extraterritorial ambitions and rebrand them as one-dimensional *hauteur*. Early prude fictions, we recall, were constructed to puncture their subject's far-reaching aspirations by insisting on her non-transcendent, gross materiality, to remind her that she is "Unbless'd with [higher or even human] Form." As we recall of the Prude's metamorphosis, "all the Woman is become a *Bed*." So, too, Jane Austen must be held accountable to "the imprisoning psychosocial coordinates" of "the Unmarried One," of her fundamentally "injured utterance [as] a woman and spinster" that determine her possibilities of expression, even in the shape of their glittering disavowal (Miller, *Jane Austen*, 74, 73).

Revived in English protofictions, the stock figure of the prude emerged in novelized form as psychological killjoy and marital obstructionist, taking an unpopular—indeed, deadly—stance against the plaiting of narrative with conjugal felicity. We recall that in the best-selling *The Prude: A Novel*, the antiheroine, finally thwarted in her schemes of world domination, defies all the "happy Mothers and the no less happy Lovers" who dangle redemption before her as she opts easily instead for suicide. In disrupting the progress and euphonies of courtship, the prude refuses the rites of social and narrative assimilation that work to put a happy face on normative relations and structures of power. It is no stretch, I am suggesting, to understand Jane Austen as doing the same. Readers frequently construe her aborted or hyperconventionalized scenes of romantic consummation as taking place at arm's length, as if the author were holding her own nose.[11] The threat of bad faith in her representations of felicity (what Claudia Johnson captures as "Austen's distinctive dubiety")[12] corroborates the unease I discussed in Chapter 2 as immanent to Richardsonian form.[13] In Austen's unprecedented narration, what John

Bender has described as the formal realization of modernity itself,[14] and in the seemingly eternal and global reach of her compact oeuvre, Austen's powers of the novel are nonpareil. But the very impersonality of her style—Austen's free-indirect, "pure narration"[15]—conveys not only perfect linguistic pitch but, more unsettlingly, an ontologically impossible perspective that possesses both the scale and mobility of a drone camera and the interior tracking abilities of an fMRI. Austen's style thus induces, as we have seen, both religious adoration and a distinct grade of anxiety that stand alone in literary history, what Deidre Lynch has pivotally named "the history of emotional practice" that informs "an account of literature as an object soliciting its audiences' involvement and affection and fidelity"—not to mention, rancor.[16]

This chapter undertakes a reading of *Sense and Sensibility*, Austen's first published and, until a generation ago (before Ang Lee's game-changing 1995 film adaptation), her "least loved and least respected novel."[17] Soliciting the usual blowback accusations of psychological and narratological perversity, *Sense and Sensibility* does not just throw up formal impediments to courtship. It makes the long road to marriage feel like a gauntlet of unremitting torture. "This dark and disenchanted novel," writes Johnson, "exposes how those sacred and supposedly benevolizing institutions of order—property, marriage, and family—actually enforce avarice, shiftlessness, and oppressive mediocrity."[18] That the story's stalwart heroine, Elinor Dashwood, has been so closely identified with Austen herself speaks to the abiding investment in the novelist's insensibility, that affective chainmail understood as knitting together her fearsome prose.[19]

A text vitally concerned with issues of moral philosophy and, specifically, the workings of human sympathy, *Sense and Sensibility* engages key concepts of the Enlightenment.[20] Frequently paired with Austen's fiction, Hume's *Treatise of Human Nature* (1739–40) provides a central intertext for Austen studies. In her recent examination of the two writers as "mirrors to one another," E. M. Dadlez claims that Austen's "general normative stance, all told, is a great deal more like that which we can find in or infer from Hume's *Treatise* than that which we can locate in the corpus of any other philosopher" (ix). Along with Dadlez's affirmation that Hume's "sympathy mechanism is constantly at work in Austen" [77]), we might also recognize the novelist's own contribution to philosophies of the passions, part of an ongoing inquiry concerning not only the ontology of feelings but also their liability to persist, reproduce, and intensify.

Both *The Treatise of Human Nature* and *Sense and Sensibility* take a hard look at the fallout from human intimacy. Extended meditations on shared pain, they explore what John Dashwood aptly calls "complicated distress"[21]—a state inseparable from consolation, as both writers go to uncomfortable lengths to show. In its changeable field of beliefs, perceptions, and reflections, Hume's *Treatise* maps mental life according to what Adela Pinch describes as crisscrossed "epistemologies of emotion," or "transsubjective entities that pass between persons," such that "our feelings are always really someone else's."[22] If sympathy works by abrading the distinction between your pain and mine, then it inadvertently doubles suffering. But sympathy also corrects for my incapacity to ascertain my own emotions since, as I discussed in my introduction, "I am insensible of *myself*" (*T* 2.4.6.3–4: 165). In being able first to perceive and then to understand the causes of someone else's feelings (and even predict their probable effects), I gain access to my own passions—states that, otherwise, are too close for me to see. But sympathetic cognition also intensifies sensations and images, refracting and ricocheting pangs of grief and abjection across subjects so that I no longer know whose is whose. Austen begins her story with the aches of courtship (the longing, insecurity, dejection, volatility, and despair), introduces the competitive minefield of a winners-take-all market, whips up a state of migrancy and exile, and then examines the intricate microclimate of grief, worry, and confusion that takes shape in its wake. In this densely interactive arena it is all too easy to feel someone else's feelings.

Hume's answer to overpowering attunement—abetted by the qualities of resemblance, contiguity, and causation—is distance, what takes the curious form of "double contempt." In Austen's novel—barring narratorial intervention or life-saving *éclaircissement* ("Perhaps you mean—my brother—you mean Mrs.—Mrs. *Robert* Ferrars"), what cauterizes the endless and involuntary mirroring of grief is silence (407). Not a cure but a palliative to the metastases of suffering, reticence neutralizes what Hume describes as the ceaselessly "double relation" between impressions and ideas, whereby the initial impact of an object is reproduced as a mental image and then as a feeling and then again as a memory, which produces once more an image (*T* 1.1.1.2: 11). In making the concerted effort *not* to speak, one tries not to make matters worse by compounding pain—kick-starting its mental proliferation—with inquiry, concern, attention, and love: "She dared not trust herself to speak, lest she might wound" (209).

Silence stands in contrast to the weaponized speech of forced conversation, a pernicious form of intimacy tantamount to a state of war: "I certainly did not seek your confidence," Elinor tells Lucy Steele in their first confrontation over Edward Ferrars (152). The agony of speaking and of listening, the power to compel someone into speech or silence, the fast and slow violence of such communications, the claim to feel for someone you do not know or to know someone without feeling for them—these are the minute and nearly unendurable scenes of intersubjectivity dramatized in Austen's novel. *Sense and Sensibility* traffics in moments when speaking is out of the question because you have no words or there is too much to say or the sound of your own voice is excruciating: "She would have given the world to be able to speak . . . but she had no utterance. . . . Not a syllable passed aloud. They all waited in silence" (406).

From its ethic of compassionate mutism, to its heroine's unpopular "doctrine" to screen judgment with civility, to Austen's own feats of narratorial reserve, *Sense and Sensibility* reframes nonexpression as care, offering a different take on the insensible's nonresponsiveness. Because to perceive someone's situation entails reconstructing in minute detail their past, present, and future circumstances (in Hume's terms, imagining specific causes in order to grasp their effects), sympathy necessitates a certain self-erasure. But self-cancellation, as we saw in the last chapter, is bound up with sovereign power—what is eliminated by and, in the special case of Jane Austen, adapted for the impersonal, liberal state. If, as psychoanalyst David Black writes, "sympathy is [to be] with the other as a subject rather than as object,"[23] then Austen allows her reader to be with nearly every other as a subject, to inhabit each case, each situation, without exhaustion. Untethered from personhood, Austen's narrator effaces itself without cost—in fact, only enhancing its plenitude. A self-renewable source of narrative, the Austenian insensible wears the gold star for sustainability. Like Adam Smith's impartial spectator, it "does not feel [it]self worn out by the present labour of those whose conduct [it] surveys; nor does [it] feel [it]self solicited by the importunate calls of their present appetites" (*TMS* 6.1.11: 252). Only such sterling neutrality can achieve this level of productivity, make this pledge of perpetuity.

"WHAT FELT ELINOR?"

In the most satisfying scene of Ang Lee's film, Elinor, played by Emma Thompson (a self-professed Janeite who also wrote the screenplay), lashes out at Marianne, played by a still-teenage Kate Winslet. In a tranquil, celadon room, news of Edward Ferrars's engagement shocks an incredulous Marianne, who is shaken further by the discovery that her sister has long known about it. Winslet advances as in a melancholy trance toward Thompson's pillar-like figure: "Always resignation and acceptance. Always prudence and honor and duty.[24] Elinor—," cradling a face of defiance between her expressively tapered hands, "where is your heart?" Thompson, wheeling away from Winslet's touch, darts back: "What do you know of my heart? What do you know of anything but your own suffering?" (Thompson's Oscar-winning screenplay reads, "ELINOR *finally explodes.* She *turns upon MARIANNE almost savagely*").[25] At last, unleashing her pent-up emotions, Elinor indulges in the bitterness of hidden grief, a display that concludes, "Believe me, Marianne, had I not been bound to silence, I could have produced proof enough of a broken heart even for you" (167). This retort swells the drops already swimming in Winslet's doe-like eyes, as she gulps and stammers before letting them fall upon her sister's begrudging shoulder. Thompson's screenplay reads, "*Complete silence. Then* MARIANNE *speaks in a whisper.* MARIANNE: Oh Elinor. MARIANNE *bursts into sobs and flings her arms around* ELINOR *who, almost impatiently, tries to comfort her*" (167).

Poignant and revealing as this scene may be, it does not occur in Jane Austen's novel. In contrast to the film, the corresponding passage details Elinor's "painful" "office" of "undeceiving" Marianne. In this task, the narrator informs us, Elinor's "narration was clear and simple; and though it could not be given without emotion, it was not accompanied by violent agitation, nor impetuous grief" (295–96). In place of Thompson's "proof enough of a broken heart even for you" rejoinder, Austen's Elinor calmly observes, "I understand you.—You do not suppose that I have ever felt much," adding shortly, "If you can think me capable of ever feeling—surely you may suppose that I have suffered now" (298–99). In truth, Austen's text hardly makes for compelling cinema. This emotionally climactic passage is packed with action, but it is of an almost entirely mental nature. In the novel, only Elinor is present when Mrs. Jennings relays Edward's well-known engagement, and Elinor's subsequent actions consist not of vehement release but of the "constant and painful exertion" of breaking this and other bad news to her family (299).

Elinor's elaborate practices of affective management (her much discussed "exertions" of "self-command" and her constant "endeavouring" to control the passions of others) absorb most of the novel's attention, even as the text also represents her as having inscrutable or nonexistent feelings.[26] Marianne, as we know, decries her sister's "doctrine" as "reserved, spiritless, dull, and deceitful" (168, 57); their own mother exclaims, "Oh! Elinor, how incomprehensible are your feelings!" (91); and even an omniscient narrator must at times shrug, "What felt Elinor?" and "But Elinor—How are her feelings to be described?" (411). Austen thus draws attention to the very unfathomability of her heroine's emotional life and practice, repeatedly emphasizing the divide between what she is feeling and what she is doing, a separation at the center of Marianne's endless protest against "your way of thinking . . . , your resolution, your self-command" (185).[27]

In Austen studies, as well as in movie adaptations, Elinor Dashwood emerges as a figure of daunting psychic containment, on the brink, like Emma Thompson, of "savage" "explo[sion]." Mary Poovey's classic study of the bind between female propriety and female authorship showcases this reading, along with the correlation between a repressed Elinor and a repressive Austen. Noting the reader-repellent aspects of Elinor's "cautious, prim, and even repressive reserve," Poovey observes how it is only with Willoughby that "Elinor is aroused to a pitch of complex emotions" (echoing Mudrick's endearing remark that "Elinor—and presumably the author [are] almost in love, and quite amorally in love, with him").[28] Poovey casts both Elinor and Austen as moral arbiters, careful above all "to keep the reader on the outside of such 'dangerous' material" as violent erotic passions. Willoughby's attractions and the notorious "pang" (384) Elinor feels for him function as the last temptations of Sense, a structure of feeling that reflects Austen's own anxiety "to control the moral anarchy that strong appeals to feeling can unleash." A diagnosis of Elinor's repression thus extends to an aesthetic claim about Austen—that her primary goal is emotional regulation, made manifest, as Poovey writes, in a tendency to "restrict the reader's access to the romantic plot by conveying its details and its emotional affect only through indirect narration" (187).

Such narrative discretion, I am suggesting, is part of Austen's expressed concern with reticence as a mode of care or consideration. "I leave it to my reader's sagacity to determine how much of all this . . . was possible," concludes *Northanger Abbey*.[29] As Farrer observes, Austen "trust[s] the intelligence of the reader" to fill in the blanks ("Jane Austen, *ob.*," 7). In his claim that Austen's "concern is primarily with character unfolded through love, not with that love's crudities of appetite and incident," we find a restatement of Adam Smith's claim about the nontransmissibility of love itself, which is compelling only as a gateway to other, more conceivable feelings. It is only the "situation" of the lover, who hopes, fears, and suffers, that can interest anyone outside the couple: love "interests us not as a passion, but as a situation that gives occasion to other passions which interest us; to hope, to fear, and to distress of every kind" (*TMS* 1.2.2.2: 39). In general, sympathy, Smith explains, "does not arise so much from the view of the passion, as from that of the situation which excites it" (*TMS* 1.1.1.10: 15). To view erotic passion, in particular, is necessarily alienating—not only impossible to access but generally leaving one with the impression that the object does not merit the lavish attention bestowed upon it.

What Smith observes of the passion of love, Farrer applies to the love *scene*: "in the supreme moments, in point of fact, humanity becomes inarticulate, and thus no longer gives material for art. Jane Austen . . . accepts the condition, asks her reader to accept it also, and contents herself with dealing with the emotions on either side of the crucial outbreak" (9). Indeed, the only emotion that can be said to lie within the outbreak is pain, a feeling resistant to narrative representation not only because it is so definitively bound up with the body of its subject (Smith's "brother on the rack" problem) but also because it defies the kind of duration in which narrative lives. Pain, as I argued in my first chapter, colonizes mental life. Locke's *Essay* takes note of how the subject in pain can only experience the present tense of his own suffering and the consuming desire to end it: "our whole endeavours and thoughts are intent to get rid of the present evil, before all things, as the first necessary condition to our happiness; let what will follow" (*EHU* 2.21.64: 276). Pain makes us heedless of the future, of the connection between now and then. As Elaine Scarry writes, "for the person in pain, so incontestably and unnegotiably present is it that 'having pain' may come to be thought of as the most vibrant example of what it is to 'have certainty.'" In other words, there is an epistemological soundness to suffering.[30] As Locke observes, "Nothing, as we passionately think, can exceed, or almost equal, the uneasiness that sits so heavy upon us" (*EHU* 2.21.64: 277).

The same is the case with pleasure—specifically, desire. According to Locke, deprivation from the object, especially when we are close to it ("desire being inflamed by a near and tempting object"), stirs the same overwhelming uneasiness "and lessens in our thoughts what is future; and so forces us, as it were blindfold, into its embraces" (*EHU* 2.21.64: 276). Under the grip of the object, we have no choice but to attend to the uneasiness it produces. Thus, as in my earlier reading of *La Princesse de Clèves*, we let go of narrative's steering wheel, abandoning ourselves to any iteration of the future so long as the pain ceases either by possession or by elimination. Lafayette's unprecedented demonstration aside, we can appreciate how such moments, as Farrer says, would not supply "material for art." Austen's postclimactic dialogues, when the lovers review their past misprisions together, are delightful in part because they process gripping unease and time-stopping pain as coherent elements in a now resolved comedy. No longer stricken by the moment, subjects expand into retrospection, rambling over the dreamy time zones of Austenian perception: "You thought me then devoid of every proper feeling, I am sure you did. The turn of your countenance I shall never forget, as you said that I could not have addressed you in any possible way, that would induce you to accept me."[31] *Sense and Sensibility* thus stands apart in Austen's engagement of emotion *within* the outbreak, the inarticulate, narrative-resistant, blinding pain of unresolvable desire.

SCREENING

Standard hermeneutics of feeling do not adequately capture what happens in *Sense and Sensibility*. A psychically repressed Elinor, for starters, would require that she not know what she were doing—since unconscious feelings are those that consciousness cannot bear to perceive. But, of course, Elinor (like Austen) perceives all. Stoicism would appear to come closer to the mark insofar as Elinor aims to extinguish the overall quantum of passion ("I can think and speak of it with little emotion. . . . I no longer suffer materially myself"), but this categorical description is complicated by her pervasive focus on the minimization of *others'* pain: "while the comfort of others was dear to me, I was glad to spare them. . . . I would not have you suffer on my account" (297–98). Moreover, she draws on her own emotional susceptibility—"But for my mother's sake and mine" (216)—to exhort Marianne not exactly to extinguish her feelings but at least to make them less apparent.

The related charge of Elinor's hypocrisy speaks to the cover that she practices and endorses. Jenny Davidson writes, "Elinor Dashwood adopts a plan of general civility in order to advance her own interests, but the plan is continuous with her own personal practices of concealment, designed to protect herself, her mother and her sister from the painful consequences of passionate feeling. Elinor suppresses her feelings and misleads observers from a desire to protect or to limit damage."[32] Davidson's study conveys a subtle web of dependencies and codependencies that motivate practices of politeness, protection, and concealment. Female deception in her account emerges as a complex form of self-advancement and damage control, aligning with a Hobbesian model of emotion as motivated response. Yet interpretations that feature Elinor's maneuvering tend to slide into a more psychological assessment of what Davidson calls her "program of repression and self-censorship" (154), implying the internalization of any strategic masks of feeling.

In her reading of *Sense and Sensibility* in the pathbreaking "Jane Austen and the Masturbating Girl," Eve Kosofsky Sedgwick takes pointed issue with what she identifies in Austen studies as a "seemingly interminable scene of punitive/pedagogical reading, interminably structured as it is by the concept of repression."[33] Sedgwick's interpretation restores a sense of the novel's rich, conflictual, autoerotic as well as alloerotic dynamics, making the point that "the love story of *Sense and Sensibility*, no simple one, has been rendered all but invisible to most readers" (836). Taking Sedgwick's cue, I want to make visible one strand of this unorthodox love story, highlighting again *as emotion* the "complicated distress" that is "no longer available to us as passion" (834). In attending to the very deliberate and painstaking nature of Elinor's practice—the hyperconsciousness of her feelings—my reading aims to tilt the axis of interpretation away from a conceptual backformation of repressed psychic content and toward the kind of philosophical framework that has been featured throughout this book. This is not to say that mental life conceived under the discourse of psychoanalysis does not apply to Jane Austen, but that insofar as it most certainly does, its application has also obscured less accessible models.

Take, for example, Elinor's much-remarked acrobatics of physically shielding others, a form of screening that Hina Nazar has beautifully described in Austen's fiction as "an act of dissimulation as well as an act of moral respect, fairness, and even love" (*Enlightened Sentiments*, 132). In the hothouse of an evening London party, after days of watching, waiting for, and writing to her lover, Marianne finally spots Willoughby a few yards away. It is a subtle textual sequence: Elinor first perceives and catches the eye of Willoughby, inducing a quick bow but no address, "though he could not but see" her sister (200). "Involuntarily," she turns to Marianne, "to see whether it could be unobserved by her." The text catches "that moment" when Marianne "first perceived him, and her whole countenance glowing with sudden delight, she would have moved towards him instantly, had not her sister caught hold of her."

> "Good heavens!" she exclaimed, "he is there—he is there—Oh! why does he not look at me? why cannot I speak to him?"

> "Pray, pray be composed," cried Elinor, "and do not betray what you feel to every body present. Perhaps he has not observed you yet." (200)

If this scene describes a call for emotional regulation (and Marianne's failure and Elinor's screening of her failure to practice it), then it is far from elementary. The moves to be improvised in this quickfire of recognition and nonrecognition are high-risk and multiple: Elinor observes Willoughby, who perceives her and Marianne. Elinor next observes Marianne's perception of Willoughby's (deliberate) nonresponsiveness. Marianne wants to know why Willoughby does not see her and why she is not allowed to make him see her. Elinor explains it is because then others will notice her need for Willoughby's attention. The public unfolding of this dynamic makes each act of suppression (or, in Elinor's terms, nonbetrayal) oddly transparent and yet all the more necessary. One holds back feelings (anxiety, frustration, wonder, despondency, desire) easily guessed at by others. Marianne, in the depths of her disappointment, declares, "Misery such as mine has no pride. I care not who knows that I am wretched," but Elinor maintains the distinction that Anne-Lise François discerns in the "open secret" that mediates between knowledge and acknowledgment, where I am allowed "to ignore what I know."[34] At stake in this scene is the difference between others' knowledge that you are wretched and your public admission that it is so, the baleful transmutation of emotion into event. In the scene detailed above, Willoughby—newly engaged and whispering with his rich fiancée—at last comes forward. Still "determined not to observe her," he responds icily to Marianne's impassioned and bewildered plea for understanding. When Marianne, "now looking dreadfully white, and unable to stand" sinks into her chair, on the verge of blacking out, Elinor, we are told, "tried to screen her from the observation of others, while reviving her with lavendar [*sic*] water" (202).

Elinor's continual efforts "to screen Marianne from particularity" (100)—that is, from the mark of observation—plays up the decoy function of the general. As when Marianne races toward a man on horseback, thinking it is Willoughby (it is not), Elinor runs zebra-like alongside her, so they are *both* running toward the figure. Endlessly sprinting, catching, shielding, guarding, administering, and preparing, Elinor acts as self-appointed curator of her family's emotions, anticipating, arranging, and preempting the reception of their affective states. To return to the critical diagnosis of Elinor's repression, we see now that to screen emotion is not to suppress one's own feeling but to give cover to someone else's, to create an emergency shelter for the wounded subject, like a medic putting up a pop-up tent in a crisis zone. No matter that the tent is blaze orange and covered with hazmat signs reading "EMERGENCY SHELTER"—the *fact* of distress may be hypervisible, but the truth of its experience is kept private, permitted to run its course.

In Austen's novel it is not only Elinor's body but, more markedly, her civility that constructs such shelter. In one of her conversational battles with Lucy Steele, even as she is experiencing "an emotion and distress beyond any thing she had ever felt before," nominally polite conversation and "a composure of voice" mantle the total "oppression of her feelings" (154–55). Nazar, demonstrating how philosophical arguments for adopting "general rules of civility" obtain in *Sense and Sensibility*, reminds us that for Adam Smith, manners provide an autopilot function of response, allowing one to act on every occasion "with nearly equal propriety," no matter how one feels (Nazar, *Enlightened Sentiments*, 129). When the Elinor doctrine cannot be applied, when there is precisely no "time to deliberate and judge" (Austen, *Sense and Sensibility*, 108), one falls back on the muscle memory of politeness, thus maintaining the walls of composure that are so necessary to support the turmoil of the mind.

CONTIGUITY, CAUSATION

In attempting to discern "some bond of union" among simple ideas (ideas that cannot be broken down further), "by which one idea naturally introduces another," Hume lands on three "uniting principle[s]": resemblance, contiguity (in time or place), and cause and effect (*T* 1.1.4.1: 13).[35] Of these, causation forms the strongest bond. Objects can be said to exist in a causal relation when one "is the cause of any of the actions or motions of the other" or when it "is the cause of the *existence*" of the other (1.1.4.4: 13). Hume writes: "We may carry this farther, and remark, not only that two objects are connected by the relation of cause and effect, when the one produces a motion or any action in the other, but also when it has a power of producing it. And this we may observe to be the source of all the relations of interest and duty, by which men influence each other in society" (1.1.4.5: 13–14). Thus, all social ties (relations of interest and duty) derive from potentiality as much as from strict causation. Whatever has the power to move an object calls it into relation, into union with itself.

Emotion for Hume happens after the fact, in the "internal impression" that follows the perception of a sensation. (The event of sensation itself remains inexplicable, it "arises in the soul originally, from unknown causes" [*T* 1.1.2.1: 11]). Whereas Hobbes defined the passions as the "interior beginnings of voluntary motions," Hume focuses on the more attenuated, less emphatically material phenomena of "impressions of reflection." These "internal operations of the mind" mark neither the beginning nor the end of a trajectory from passion to action but are one phase in the endless looping of mental life (2.1.11.7: 208). As in earlier theories of the passions, feelings are coordinates of the pain or pleasure inspired by an object that may or may not be present. In Hume's account presence and absence are expressed not in absolute terms but along a spectrum of distance and proximity, in the fine distinctions of space, time, and probability that constitute relation. This essential but also gradational experience of relation accounts for the crucial factor of "liveliness" or "vividness" that for Hume defines the operation of fellow feeling. Sympathy begins when one person observes the "effects" or "external signs" of someone else's feelings in her "countenance and conversation." These manifestations impart an "idea" of what the person is feeling in her body (2.1.11.7: 207–8). What converts this "idea" into an "impression" reflects a process of intensification, whereby the impression "acquires such a degree of force and vivacity, as to become the very passion itself, and produce an equal emotion, as any original affection" (2.1.11.3: 206).

Relation describes the facility for conducing and, as others have discussed,[36] for cloning someone else's feelings, the process whereby "an idea of a sentiment or passion . . . be so enliven'd as to become the very sentiment or passion" itself (2.1.11.7: 207). This process is what makes Marianne, "by a resemblance in their situations [hers and Elinor's] . . . feel all her own disappointment over again" (295). Whereas for Smith, as I later discuss, there is an undeniable barrier to sympathy (the fact, as Antonio Damasio puts it, that only "your body is the reference" for affective experience),[37] the predicament of "not being united in the same persons" is for Hume remarkably not insuperable (2.1.11.16: 210). For instance, "the mere force of imagination," he posits, can make someone else's "malady real by often thinking of it" (2.1.11.7: 207–8). Physical separateness is what relation overcomes, especially between "persons, who are both related to us by blood, and contiguous in place": that is to say, between family members of a single household. David Norton and Mary Norton annotate the relevant passage of the *Treatise* accordingly: "when physically near one's family, two of the fundamental relations (contiguity, causation) will be in play and affect one's passions" (2.1.11.16n: 503). The annotation reminds us that for Hume the most powerful kind of relation (above acquaintance, education, custom) is causation and that "relations of blood [are] a species of causation" (2.1.11.6: 207).[38]

The Dashwood household fulfills the three major qualities—resemblance, contiguity, and causation—that associate ideas in Hume's theory. Their cottage forms a field of associations: resemblance (sisters and daughters), causation (either I made you, you made me, or we share the same source), and contiguity (nearly every moment of our waking and sleeping lives are spent beside each other). Once more, "Relation conveys . . . vivacity," and vivacity turns ideas into impressions (2.1.5.11: 190). To be physically near one's family does not then merely affect the passions, but it puts one in prime position for their replication: if "assisted by the relations of resemblance and contiguity," it will be possible "to feel the sympathy in its full perfection," a transfer that takes place "so perfectly as to lose nothing of it in the transition" (2.1.11.8: 208). Relations of causation ("kindred") and contiguity naturally confuse identity: "our ideas of the sentiments of others [convert] into the very sentiments, by means of the association betwixt the idea of their persons, and that of our own" (2.1.11.16: 210). Notably, the triangulation between sisters and mother in Austen's novel only contributes to the closeness: "two objects are connected together in the imagination, not only when the one is immediately resembling, contiguous to, or the cause of the other, but also when there is interpos'd betwixt them a third object, which bears to both of them any of these relations" (2.1.4.3: 13).

To return, then, to the novel's cascading patterns of sensibility, in which pain ping-pongs and proliferates among subjects, we might put it this way:

1. I, Marianne, am sad because Willoughby left.
2. You, Elinor, see that I am sad.
3. You become sad.
4. I see that you are sad for me.
5. I become sad for me (your pity allows me to take myself up as an object, i.e., to sympathize with myself).
6. I am sad that I am so sad (i.e., even sadder than in number 1).
7. I am mad that you made me this sad.

8. I am sad that I made you (and our mother) sad, which makes me even more sad as well as mad—or if not mad, then frustrated because it is almost impossible to be angry at one who has so wholly taken up my interests and well-being as her own—in fact, has done so where I have failed because of my recurrence to suicidal thinking and melancholic self-shattering.

To the extent, then, that there exist persons who can feel my feelings (the "very passion itself" and "an equal emotion") bizarrely even when I cannot, I care more about what they think and, of course, what they think of me, than I do about others. We seek the approval of those with whom we have enjoyed "a long and intimate acquaintance" while we "are, in great measure, indifferent about the opinions of the rest of mankind" (2.1.11.11: 209). Contempt, which Hume defines as a feeling of hatred (as opposed to esteem) that arises from the unpleasurable contemplation of an object, *is* bearable from strangers. What is intolerable is the contempt of our relations—a state in which we perceive ourselves as "deformed" in the eyes of those connected to us by resemblance, cause, and contiguity. This state is so unbearable that we are inclined, if not obligated, to avoid it.

Hume offers a brief sketch of this situation in one of the *Treatise*'s many embedded mininarratives.[39] Here, a gentleman bred from "birth and education" to expectations of ease must instead "seek [his] livelihood by mean and mechanical employments." In entering the laboring classes, this gentleman moves far away to live among strangers and therefore avoid the contempt of his relations. Hume curiously calls his situation a state of "double contempt," insofar as the subject endures scorn "from my relations, but they are absent" and scorn "from those about me, but they are strangers" (2.1.11.17: 210). Contempt may be doubled in this state, but its salient feature is its division along the parallel tracks of proximity ("neighbors") and familiarity ("kindred"), two lines of relation that never meet: "this difference of ideas separates the impressions arising from the contempt, and keeps them from running into each other. . . . These influences are distinct, and never unite" (2.1.11.17: 210). Severed from each other are those fundamental principles of contiguity and causation, without which perfect sympathy, or total transmission of feeling, is no longer possible. As in a Bartlebyan vision of copresence without intimacy or the urban anonymity achieved postrape in *Clarissa*, Hume sketches a sociality without the "infusion" or "diffusion" of the passions. Strangers have feelings, of course, but they do not enter, circulate, and possess the currents of my mind, as they do with my "long and intimate acquaintance," those so close to me that they feel what I feel even when I cannot stand to myself.

Like the young Sir William Thornhill of *The Vicar of Wakefield*, Hume's gentleman removes himself from the presence of his intimates and puts a stop to the transmission of shame—a piling on of one's primary (situational) response with the responses of one's family. Luckily, "the sentiments of others have little influence, when far remov'd from us, and require the relation of contiguity, to make them communicate themselves entirely" (2.1.11.6: 207). My new neighbors may detect my feelings, but these will not impress them deeply because they have such thin relations with me (and thus a low facility for conducting my emotions). Hume summarizes the parable accordingly: "the uneasiness of being contemn'd depends on sympathy, and that sympathy depends on the relation of objects to ourselves; since we are most uneasy under the contempt of persons, who are both related to us by blood, and contiguous in place. Hence we seek to diminish this sympathy and uneasiness by separating these relations, and placing ourselves in a contiguity to strangers, and at a distance from relations" (2.1.11.15: 210). A self-elected state of double contempt stanches pain ("the uneasiness of being contemn'd") by ending relation without violence—an almost geometrical solution insofar as I just have to separate contiguity from causation (or "keep them from running into each other") in order to put a merciful end to perfect sympathy.[40]

It is worth restating that Hume's solution, while technically "doubling" contempt (I now have two sets of constituents who can sympathize with me), nonetheless aspires to its termination. The parable makes clear that in sympathy's hall of mirrors, your contempt (displeasure in the contemplation of my pain) compounds my original suffering, which by itself was tolerable. The exile "himself knows his misfortunes; but as those, with whom he lives, are ignorant of them, he has the disagreeable reflection and comparison [to his former life] suggested only by his own thoughts, and never receives it by a sympathy with others; which must contribute very much to his ease and satisfaction" (2.1.11.18: 210). In exile, I aspire to treat—even preventatively—this malignant blend of hatred and humility so that, like a violent passion tempered into a calm one, it "decay[s] into so soft an emotion, as to become, in a manner, imperceptible" (2.1.1.3: 181). Such a treatment does not rely on an inside-outside framework of emotion but on the continuous calibration between individual and social states. To curtail expression does not, as in Freudian repression, intensify the feeling (increasing the pressure on the unconscious) but actually succeeds in diminishing its magnitude—a reduction that comes to generate its own pleasure. Elinor Dashwood is not just "glad to spare" her family, but her gladness, in fact, soothes the sting of her injury.

INTERLUDE: MEMORY AND IMAGINATION

A counterargument to be made in the comparison of Hume's theory of emotions to Austen's text is that there are no "simple" ideas or impressions in this novel—or in any novel—"simple" ideas being perceptions "such as admit of no distinction or separation" (1.1.1.2: 7). So when I eat an apple, I can break the experience down into its sweet taste, crunchy texture, and pale greenness, but I cannot further reduce the concepts of its sweetness, crunch, and color. An hour after I eat the apple, I have retained these ideas of it, or, in Hume's terms, I have formed copies of my original impressions of the apple. But as the day wears on (I teach a class, attend a meeting, read an unfortunate student evaluation), those ideas become fainter; they lose their force and liveliness so that my ideas of the apple lose the intensity of my impressions ("green" but not pale or speckled, "good" but not crunchy or juicy). Then, let's say, on my subway ride home at an hour when I am very hungry, I see someone directly across from me eating an apple. It is the same color and shape as mine was, and maybe the apple-eater even looks strangely like me. This encounter sparks my memory, which brings back with considerable force the idea of the apple I ate several hours ago, not just its sweetness, crunch, and greenness, but also now the feelings of pleasure and satiation that were caused by the eating of it.

The faculty of imagination works differently for Hume than does the faculty of memory, which "preserves the original form" and reproduces the "order and position" of the object (1.1.3.3: 12). The imagination is "independent of the real existence of their objects" (3.3.1.20: 373) and is "not restrain'd to the same order and form with the original impressions; while the memory is in a manner ty'd down in that respect, without any power of variation" (1.1.3.2: 12). Where I might *remember* that I ate a crunchy, green apple at lunchtime, I can *imagine* apples of every variety (macouns, ginger golds, winesaps) in the middle of a sunlit orchard that is teeming with pumpkins, kale, and kindness, its atmosphere redolent of cider and doughnuts. Enter "the liberty of the imagination to transpose and change its ideas" (1.1.3.4: 12). Hume conceives of this "liberty of the fancy" explicitly in terms of literature, of reading fiction even: "the fables we meet with in poems and romances" (1.1.3.4: 12). The literary imagination exploits complex ideas, breaking them down in order to rearrange their components: "Wherever the imagination perceives a difference among ideas, it can easily produce a separation" (1.1.3.4: 12). These separations give rise not only to chimerical figures like "winged horses, fiery dragons, and monstrous giants" but to elaborate linkages like making Edward Ferrars form an attachment to Elinor Dashwood when he was already engaged to Lucy Steele, and then to a mirroring scenario in which Willoughby attaches himself to Marianne when he knew he must marry rich, and *then* to clusters of associated ideas, including emotions that have not actually been experienced.

Not only is the imagination free to transpose and change ideas—to mix, match, and compound them—but it is so lively a faculty that it readily converts ideas into impressions. "Sympathy" is "nothing but the conversion of an idea into an impression by the force of imagination" (2.3.6.8: 273). Hume adds, "'Tis remarkable, that lively passions commonly attend a lively imagination. In this respect, as well as others, the force of the passion depends as much on the temper of the person, as the nature or situation of the object." Elinor's temperament—her "strength of understanding, and coolness of judgment, which qualified her, though only nineteen, to be the counsellor of her mother"—does not belie but affords the intensity of her feelings: "She had an excellent heart;—her disposition was affectionate, and her feelings were strong" (7). That is to say, her distinctive coolness (unlike mother and sister, "she knew how to govern them" [7]) counts as a passion, even if it is what Hume would classify as a "calm" one. Not only her temper, but her elastic imagination conduces to sympathy, a ready alchemy for converting one person's pain into another's. So rapidly does this process take place in Elinor's mind that her reflexes seem preternaturally quick, as she catches bodies just before they fall.

In Humean terms we now see how my nearness of relation to you (by resemblance, contiguity, and causation) means not just that you make an impression on me, but that I share the impressions made upon you by other objects. I can further take images of these impressions into my mind. I can then reflect on these images, as if poring over so many Polaroids with captions like Desire, Aversion, Grief, and Joy. I can commit all these feelings (attached to experiences, attached to objects) to memory, from whence my imagination can summon them in almost perfect detail. But my imagination takes them farther. I do not just reproduce these ideas, but I can separate and recombine them; I can move them around other ideas and reflections like security, family, future, Willoughby's real remorse, Colonel Brandon's sad past. Hume writes, "The passions looking farther, comprehend whatever objects are in the least ally'd or related to us. Our country, family, children, relations, riches, houses, gardens, horses, dogs, cloaths; any of these may become a cause either of pride or of humility" (2.1.2.5: 183).

"WHAT GOOD DOES TALKING EVER DO?"

Hume's remedy of double contempt is not available in Austen's novel. In a household of distressed gentlewomen already reduced to cottage life, there will be no emotional escape into the working class, the "seek[ing of] livelihood by mean and mechanical employments" (*T* 2.1.11.14: 209). As we learned from the fate of the first and fallen Eliza, to move away from your relations and dwell among strangers is to die. Moreover, the Dashwoods, cut off by patrilineal privilege, already live in exile. Elinor and Marianne may leave young Margaret and their mother for a few weeks at a time, but they are rarely out of each other's presence, confined as they are to the same small spaces. If fleeing sympathy is not an option in this crucible of resemblance, contiguity, and causation, then *Sense and Sensibility* arrives at an alternative: silence. After being wakened by Marianne's sobbing, Elinor ventures, "Marianne, may I ask?" and is flatly told "No, Elinor," as well as "not to speak to her for the world" (205). From Elinor's judicious withholding, to Colonel Brandon's endlessly "silent attention" (198), to Mrs. Dashwood's refusal to force a confidence (of whether she might simply ask Marianne if she is engaged, Mrs. Dashwood replies, "I would not ask such a question for the world" [97]), *Sense and Sensibility* stages different ways of being quiet, holding back, and not asking what it is you are dying to know.[41] "*I* long to inquire; but how will *my* interference be borne!" reflects Elinor (188). Silence, not distance, is the remedy to the uncontrollable vivacity of imagination that attends one's closest relations. Reticence may look like insensibility, but in a field charged with solicitude, it spares exchange, replication, endless transference.

We recall that in Hume's theory of causation, one body does not need to move another body; it simply needs to possess the potential to do so. Moreover, this state of potentiality defines social relations at large: "the source of all the relations of interest and duty, by which men influence each other in society" (*T* 1.1.4.5: 13–14). Expanded to a theory of the state (how men "are plac'd in the ties of government and subordination"), the principle of causation is also the essence of sovereign power: "When a person is possess'd of any power, there is no more requir'd to convert it into action, but the exertion of the will; and *that* in every case is consider'd as possible, and in many as probable; especially in the case of authority, where the obedience of the subject is a pleasure and advantage to the superior" (*T* 1.1.4.5: 14). When Mrs. Dashwood declines asking her own daughter whether she is or is not engaged to be married, she refuses to turn her causal relation into a power one. "I should never deserve her confidence again, after forcing from her a confession of what is meant at present to be unacknowledged. . . . I would not attempt to force the confidence of any one; of a child much less" (98). Marking the distance from the Harlowes' style of parenting in *Clarissa*, Mrs. Dashwood forfeits the "pleasure and advantage" of exerting her will over Marianne's. Not only would her words inflict distress, but they would also compel an answer. Mrs. Dashwood upholds Marianne's right of nonresponse—refusing even to put her in the position of having to decline and thus preserving the tender privilege of being confided in by one's child.

Speech, we know, is a special kind of action. If, "in the case of authority," the sovereign "converts [power] into action" by speaking, then reticence suggests a curious abdication (*T* 1.1.4.5: 14). Mrs. Dashwood's forfeiture opts out of a structure of domination and the claim to superiority that it implies ("the obedience of the subject is a pleasure and advantage to the superior"). We are not meant to play the cards of causation and contiguity with those we love. In matters of war confidences can be forced. When Lucy Steele divulges her engagement to Edward Ferrars, Elinor responds, "I certainly did not seek your confidence. . . . Pardon me if I express some surprise at so unnecessary a communication" (152). Against the lugubrious backdrop of Lady Middleton's drawing room, Elinor and Lucy engage in balletic passive aggression, deploying each politesse as a thrust or parry to assail or disarm her opponent. Where every word is weaponized, silence becomes a shield behind which the parties retreat when things get too hot. To Lucy's increasing menace, "Elinor thought it wisest to make no answer . . . lest they might provoke each other to an unsuitable increase of ease and unreserve" (172).

In London, observing her sister's anxious desperation, Elinor finds herself "unable to be longer silent." To her simple inquiry, "You are expecting a letter then?" Marianne quibbles, provoking Elinor's charge that "you have no confidence in me."

> "Nay, Elinor, this reproach from you—you who have confidence in no one!"
>
> "Me!" returned Elinor in some confusion; "indeed, Marianne, I have nothing to tell."
>
> "Nor I," answered Marianne with energy, "our situations then are alike. We have neither of us any thing to tell; you, because you communicate, and I, because I conceal nothing."
>
> Elinor, distressed by this charge of reserve in herself, [with] which she was not at liberty to do away, knew not how, under such circumstances, to press for greater openness in Marianne. (193)

What constitutes "openness" here is the giving of actionable information, the conveyance of my situation so that you can picture me in it, and we can share in its contemplation. Marianne's barb maintains that impossibility: You speak, but you hide. I do not hide, but I will not speak. In spite of the sentiment (said earlier of Willoughby's case) that "a plain and open avowal of [one's] difficulties" is always the better course, such candor assumes a kinder world than the one in which the Dashwoods live (94). Later, Elinor appeals to Mrs. Jennings to caution their party not to mention even Willoughby's name before Marianne: "Their own good-nature must point out to them the real cruelty of appearing to know any thing about it when she is present; and the less that may ever be said to myself on the subject, the more my feelings will be spared." Mrs. Jennings agrees: "It must be terrible for you to hear it talked of," adding, "And what good does talking ever do you know?" Elinor replies, "In this affair, it can only do harm" (222).

In *Sense and Sensibility*, not to ask is not to hurt. On the flip side of what Elinor calls "the real cruelty of appearing to know" is the charity of appearing not to know, of overlooking information, of relinquishing a claim: I will not speak of what we already know. Contrary to Smith's claim that the "bitter and painful emotions of grief and resentment . . . require the healing consolation of sympathy" (*TMS* 1.1.2.5: 19) or Patricia Meyer Spacks's observation of *Persuasion* that "healing comes from sharing,"[42] in this story, healing comes only with time—time spent *not* talking about it. This tenet applies especially where relations are strongest, when even the smallest show of "tender compassion," like a silent press of the hand, sends the loved one running, "burst[ing] into tears" (95).

When their servant Thomas informs the Dashwoods that "Mr. Ferrars is married," the narrator obligingly notes the violence of Marianne's reaction (she "fell back in her chair in hysterics" and is carted out of the room by mother and maid), but the narrator first records Marianne's primary response (as well as Mrs. Dashwood's) of catching Elinor's pale face of suffering (400). Even after "Thomas and the table-cloth" are dismissed, no one speaks. Margaret, thankful for having already eaten her dinner, vacates. The room is left to mother and daughter, who stay, absorbing "the pain of the intelligence" (402–4). "When the dessert and the wine were arranged, and Mrs. Dashwood and Elinor were left by themselves, they remained long together in a similarity of thoughtfulness and silence." In such a state, Mrs. Dashwood comes to realize her gross undervaluation of her eldest's sufferings: "She found that she had been misled by the careful, the considerate attention of her daughter," and that "every thing had been expressly softened at the time, to spare her from an increase of unhappiness, suffering as she then had suffered for Marianne." No caresses or reassurances—no speech at all—mark this scene. "Mrs. Dashwood feared to hazard any remark, and ventured not to offer consolation" (402–3).

Forbearance, not tenderness, is in order. As Adam Smith writes of the natural pleasures of sympathy, "We all desire . . . to feel how each other is affected, to penetrate into each other's bosoms, and to observe the sentiments and affections which really subsist there." Notwithstanding, "this passion to discover the real sentiments of others is naturally so strong, that it often degenerates into a troublesome and impertinent curiosity to pry into those secrets of our neighbours which they have very justifiable reasons for concealing; and, upon many occasions, it requires prudence and a strong sense of propriety to govern this" (*TMS* 7.4.28: 399). It is true that Jane Fairfax–like reserve (from one "who gives no satisfaction to our most inoffensive inquiries, who plainly wraps himself up in impenetrable obscurity") is hideously repellent (we "feel ourselves all at once pushed back with the rudest and most offensive violence") (*TMS* 7.4.28: 399–400). But the capacity to restrain one's own curiosity, to resist rubbernecking into the scene of the other's mind, is nothing short of heroic, an exercise of self-command that "is not only itself a great virtue, but [one from which] all the other virtues seem to derive their principal lustre" (*TMS* 6.3.11: 284).

Austen's prescription for the insurmountable hurdles to sharing pain is simple: you sit beside the one who suffers; you do not speak; you do not look; you remain there to contemplate her pain and its causes. Restraint—"ventur[ing] not to" speak—counts as strenuous action, the absorption of passion, what Nancy Yousef in her evocative concept of "romantic silence," describes as a "remarkably empathic calibration of silent mere presence."[43] Here, silence is an extension of shared cognition, a way of knowing and responding to the suffering of a loved one while minimizing the expression of your awareness (the cradling without comment that is so appealing in Winnicott's theory of "holding"). The mother sits with her daughter, both rapt in contemplation and wonder and misery, at a table covered with treats that neither will think to touch.

Austen makes the point two pages later that only the author can make things better—that is, can make it such that Lucy married *Robert* and not Edward Ferrars. Fiction may endow its subjects with feelings, but they are not entitled to them. And where the narrator giveth (Mrs. Dashwood's satisfying recognition of Elinor's selflessness is for the reader alone), it also taketh away ("in what manner he expressed himself, and how he was received, need not be particularly told" [409]). Here is "the case of authority," that figure of vindictive, divine withholding who began this chapter. Is the "world-historical" linguistic phenomenon of Austen's narrator the supreme case of insensibility in the novel, a sovereign who guards her rights of nonresponse and whose dispassion incites unprecedented vitriol as well as attachment, the "almost infantile desire to be close, period, as close as one can get, without literal plagiarism, to merging with the mother-text"?[44] Such a reading would overlook the narrator's own forfeiture (like Mrs. Dashwood's) of her claims to superiority and her rights of subjugation. Far from perverse, Austen's characteristic pullback from narration, usually at the peak of potential felicity ("the bells rang and every body smiled"; "What did she say?—Just what she ought, of course. A lady always does"; "exactly at the time when it was quite natural that it should be so, and not a week earlier, Edmund did cease to care about Miss Crawford"), refuses the power play of the novelist, who can always humor her readers with absurd delights (*NA* 261; *EM* 470; *MP* 544).

"WHAT HAS BEFALLEN YOU?"

It is worth remembering that Hume's totalizing account of intimacy (when proximity leaps over to identity) is no happy aspiration but an outright necessity for a condition in which the self is always uppermost and also never available to consciousness. The "impression of ourselves is always intimately present with us" since "our consciousness gives us so lively a conception of our own person" (*T* 2.1.11.4: 206), yet "I am insensible of *myself*. . . . Our eyes cannot turn in their sockets" (1.4.6.3–4: 165). The aporia of one's own subjectivity opens the door to Smith's impartial spectator, a composite mechanism of perception that allows us to gauge or, more precisely, to supply our own sentiments. For Hume, one's intimate relations obviate the need for Smith's "man within the breast" since they so effectively, "so perfectly," transfer new ideas that they alter as well as enliven "the idea of our own person" (*TMS* 3.1.2.33: 153; *T* 2.1.11.8: 208; *T* 2.1.11.5: 207). If the self is "nothing" for Hume ("Ourself, independent of the perception of every other object, is in reality nothing. For which reason we must turn our view to external objects" [2.2.2.17: 221]), then for Smith, it is simply too close to see. Just as one cannot regard one's own eye, one cannot perceive one's own capacity for perception. Without mediation we are unavailable to ourselves.

Smith's theory seizes on Hume's somewhat buried claim that sympathy works by causation: "when I perceive the *causes* of any emotion, my mind is convey'd to the effects, and is actuated with a like emotion" (*T* 3.3.1.7: 368). Smith extends the logic: in order to perceive the cause, I not only have to perceive the effects but I also have to reconstruct the situation in which they take place. I can do this by asking you for the most minute account: do not just tell me "what happened," but give me the whole story, exactly as it transpired in the order that it did. Just as Hume highlighted the interpersonal capacity to transfer feeling "in its full perfection . . . [so] as to lose nothing of it in the transition" (*T* 2.1.11.8: 208), Smith shares the fantasy of having no remainder. The perception of emotion alone is fairly leaky: "our sympathy with the grief or joy of another, before we are informed of the cause of either, is always extremely imperfect." What conduces to perfect transfer is not the passive beholding of someone's suffering (or "actual sympathy," in which "fellow-feeling is not very considerable") but rather the "curiosity to inquire into his situation." Thus, only when we ask for the story ("The first question which we ask is, What has befallen you?") are we attempting to share the feeling itself (*TMS* 1.1.1.9: 14–15). Smith elaborates: "The spectator must, first of all, endeavour, as much as he can, to put himself in the situation of the other, and to bring home to himself every little circumstance of distress which can possibly occur to the sufferer. He must adopt the whole case of his companion with all its minutest incidents; and strive to render as perfect as possible, that imaginary change of situation upon which his sympathy is founded" (*TMS* 1.1.4.6: 26).

Yousef attends to the ethical blind spot of a perception-based model of sympathy since cognition cannot prescribe action, a nonequivalence acknowledged by Smith's observation that compassion "is by no means confined to the virtuous and humane" but is shared by "the most hardened violator of the laws of society" (*TMS* 1.1.1.1: 11). But what Smith enhances in Hume's account is the sheer effort required to achieve sympathetic perception ("as much as he can," "every little circumstance," "the whole case," "all its minutest incidents," "as perfect as possible"). As Rae Greiner encapsulates, "if [Smith's book] leaves a single, unassailable impression on readers, it is that sympathy is really hard. Most of the time, it just shouldn't work, for there are too many impediments standing in its way."[45] What was involuntary cognition for Hume becomes in Smith's take extraordinary action, the most exquisite rendering of attention by which sympathy comes to overtake the ego: "Who cares about me? What *exactly* happened to *you*?" Thomas Nagel famously captures this state in his 1974 essay about the phenomenon of consciousness when he distinguishes between thinking about "what it would be like for me to behave as a bat behaves" and "what it is like for a bat to be a bat."[46] Smith makes this point in one of his test cases of grief:

> When I condole with you for the loss of your only son, in order to enter into your grief I do not consider what I, a person of such a character and profession, should suffer, if I had a son, and if that son was unfortunately to die: but I consider *what I should suffer if I was really you*, and I not only change circumstances with you, but I change persons and characters. My grief, therefore, is entirely upon your account, and not in the least upon my own. It is not, therefore, in the least selfish. (*TMS* 7.3.1.4: 374, italics mine)[47]

For Hume, the vividness of imagination can make such a strong impression that it replicates the original passion, erasing all differences between the feelings of self and other. By contrast, in Smith's insistently externalist account of emotions, to imagine someone else's feelings—to "chang[e] places in fancy with the sufferer" (*TMS* 1.1.1.3: 12)—is to *think* we can approximate the other's experience even if we know we cannot. Insensibility flags the occasions when we miss the mark: "We sometimes feel for another, a passion of which he himself seems to be altogether incapable; because, when we put ourselves in his case, that passion arises in our breast from the imagination, though it does not in his from the reality" (1.1.1.10: 15).[48] The activity of sympathy—of "enter[ing] as it were into his body, and becom[ing] in some measure the same person with him, and thence form some idea of his sensations, and even feel something which, though weaker in degree, is not altogether unlike them" (1.1.1.2: 12)—is fundamentally for Smith a fiction, a testament to the impossible desire to collapse the distance between persons, to inhabit alterity itself.[49] Jonathan Lamb, writing on *Paradise Lost,* states, "Horrid sympathy induces us to feel like a serpent or a corpse, something absolutely unlike oneself and without the least trace of social or moral value."[50]

Smith elaborates Hume's structure of sympathy as cause and consequence, emphasizing the temporal dimension of Hume's coordinating points of self and other, pleasure and pain. Smith writes: "The sentiment or affection of the heart from which any action proceeds, and upon which its whole virtue or vice must ultimately depend, may be considered under two different aspects, or in two different relations; first, in relation to the cause which excites it, or the motive which gives occasion to it; and secondly, in relation to the end which it proposes, or the effect which it tends to produce" (*TMS* 1.1.3.5: 22). An emotion, in other words, is a narrative—an explanation of temporal phenomena in which what happened before and what is presumed to happen after must be explained in order to evaluate the feeling itself (upon which "its whole virtue or vice must ultimately depend"). Narrative for Smith is the only solution to the ontological problem of difference. That problem is twofold. First, because I cannot occupy your body, I can only tell your inside (motivations and sentiments) from your outside (actions and expressions) (*TMS* 3.1.3: 129). (As *Clarissa*'s Lovelace laments, "the heart cannot be seen into but by its actions" [5:115, 789].) Second, I am held to the limits of my own person, but this is a problem (as it was for Hume) because I cannot actually feel myself. Moreover, since the basis of all knowledge is the experience of the self ("I judge of your sight by myself, of your ear by my ear, of your reason by my reason" [*TMS* 1.1.3.10: 23]), and I cannot know my own senses (because I do not have the necessary distance from them to take them up as objects of my imagination), then I have no point of relation or comparison with you—that is, no basis for moral judgment.

Critics have favored Smith's spectator as an ideological model for the novel. Emphasizing Smith's theory at work in nineteenth-century fiction, Greiner writes that "sympathy with others (including other selves) is at the very heart of the realist novel's historical enterprise."[51] But it is Hume's earlier theory that specifically posits the interpersonality of any given feeling. Fiction captures the dissonance of encounter—what allegory registers, in Gordon Teskey's account, as "a schism in consciousness."[52] Teskey writes that allegory opens the rift and repairs it at the same time. Part of allegory's legacy to the novel, then, is to provide a public language of variance, fracture—*allos egorien*: to let the other speak, that is, to permit entry into the public space of the agora, of print. But if the novel records the speech of the other, then it does so not simply as an ethical gesture. Enlightenment philosophies of emotion have allowed us to see the basic riddle that animates narrative: I cannot perceive myself (in Hume's terms), or (in Smith's) I cannot imagine my own case—that is, "bring [it] home" to myself since it is already where I live (*TMS* 2.3.5.3: 88). As Eliot writes in *Daniel Deronda*, the text treated next in my conclusion, "It must be admitted that many well-proved facts are dark to the average man, even concerning the action of his own heart and the structure of his own retina."[53] I may not be able to see my own being, but fortunately, I can see *you*. In fact, I can imagine every minute aspect of your situation, the singular circumstances in which you find yourself: capsized on an island, in involuntary flight from your home, worn out from kindness to others, too scared to speak to your own sister. To know these details is to know something, and it is as much as I can, with as much force as I can, possibly know. "My story is too long," says Clarissa Harlowe, to a room full of unbelieving strangers. But the reader, primed by Richardson, is all attention—patient, greedy, game. Psychoanalysis holds that the end of self-knowledge is impossible—that the Real, or the ceaselessly enigmatic signifier of the other's desire that alone restores the plenitude of my being—is definitively elusive. But the novel makes another promise.

HAZARDING NARRATION

The most dramatic and perhaps most discussed scene in *Sense and Sensibility*, Elinor's nighttime conversation with Willoughby, would appear to refute the novel's policy of silence. The clock strikes, a carriage clatters into the drive, Elinor rushes down the stairs into the drawing room, "and saw only Willoughby" (358). Chapter 8 of the third volume begins with Willoughby "entreat[ing]" and "insist[ing]" that Elinor hear him out and ends with assurances of her full forgiveness, topped by pity and goodwill (359, 363). Their conversation, in which Willoughby seeks "to open my whole heart to you," effects an unlikely state of truth and reconciliation (361). "If you *can* pity me, Miss Dashwood, pity my situation as it was *then*" (370). Elinor's once "incomprehensible feelings" almost magically transform from "hardening" and "angry" to "pitying" and "compassionate" (364, 362, 368, 373). Her "heart, which had undergone many changes in the course of this extraordinary conversation, was now softened" (368). After Willoughby leaves, she experiences "a tenderness, a regret," as well as an "influence over her mind" that is heightened by reflections on his beauty (377). Overwhelmed by feeling, she forgets "to think even of her sister," and in an atypically blunt sentence, the narrator informs us: "Elinor's heart was full" (377). "Willoughby, 'poor Willoughby,' as she now allowed herself to call him, was constantly in her thoughts . . . and for a moment [she] wished Willoughby a widower" (379).

Nothing short of "forc[ed]" communication has triggered Elinor's intense preoccupation, her exquisitely soft and mildly murderous sentiments (361). Exerting herself to control her feelings, she weakens in hearing and thinking about Willoughby's. When Mrs. Dashwood relates to Elinor the heart-to-heart *she* has had with Colonel Brandon, Elinor "feel[s] a pang for Willoughby" (384). But Elinor's absorption is not personal, having nothing finally to do with Marianne or herself. If narrative pleasure is aesthetic, then we might say that Willoughby's immaculate form contributes to the liveliness of Elinor's ability to reconstruct his circumstances, in response to his irresistible injunction to "pity my situation as it was *then*." Elinor's imaginative consent, her surrender to immersion, delivers nothing short of transcendence, even of her own interests. Earlier, Elinor is so absorbed in Willoughby's letter that she forgets why or even how she is reading it: "In her earnest meditations on the contents of the letter, on the depravity of that mind which could dictate it . . . Elinor forgot the immediate distress of her sister, forgot that she had three letters on her lap yet unread, and . . . entirely forgot how long she had been in the room" (210).

Home at last, Marianne regains strength of body and of mind under the "unobtrusive" and "watchful" care of sister and mother (385, 387). The sights and sounds of Barton ("every field and every tree" [387]) revive impressions of Willoughby and, with them, a stinging train of self-reproach: "not only is it horrible to suspect a person, who has been what *he* has been to *me*, of such designs,—but what must it make me appear to myself?" (390). As moral consciousness loosens Marianne's lips ("shall we ever talk on that subject, Elinor?"), Elinor fearfully remembers "her promise to Willoughby" to relay his visit, and she struggles with whether and how to keep it. "Resolved to wait till her sister's health were more secure . . . the resolution was made only to be broken." When Marianne's streak of lucid speech peters out ("If I could but know *his* heart, everything would become easy"), Elinor, "who had now been for some time reflecting on the propriety or impropriety of speedily hazarding her narration, without feeling at all nearer decision than at first, heard this; and perceiving that as reflection did nothing, resolution must do all, soon found herself leading to the fact" (393–94). Surprised into story, Elinor nonetheless "managed," "prepared," summarized, and "softened" its contents, as her sister drinks in "every syllable with panting eagerness." But the poignancy of Austen's scene is not in Elinor's titrated "recital" of Willoughby's confession but in her subsequent turning on the taps of narration, "talk[ing] of nothing but Willoughby, and their conversation together . . . carefully minute in every particular of speech and look." Moreover, Elinor—"with a mind" always "anxiously pre-arranging [the] result" of everyone's feelings—yields the details in order to spare her sister from having to express a desire to hear them ("no question was suffered to speak" her curiosity). In the dining-room scene Mrs. Dashwood steps in to spare a "disordered" Elinor from making inquiries by "immediately [taking] all that trouble" upon herself, thus giving her daughter "the benefit of intelligence without the exertion or exposure involved in seeking it": "Who told you that Mr. Ferrars was married, Thomas?" "But did she tell you she was married, Thomas?" (401). So, too, Elinor speaks so that Marianne does not have to. She hazards, she extends narrative's promise to deliver each impression, each aspect of the situation so that it becomes an object in the mind, not as the public speech of the other but as perceptions sifted into the ear, gently decanted, his words through mine, for me alone to tell and for you alone to hear. Nontoxic when folded into the soft sheets of relation, narrative approaches here the "pure contraption" and "absolute gift" of Auden's song, which "pour[s] out your forgiveness like a wine."[54]

PUBLIC SYMPATHY

In the third section of the *Treatise*, Hume counters the idea that morality is imposed by the state, that "skilful politicians endeavour'd to restrain the turbulent passions of men, and make them operate to the public good, by the notions of honour and shame." Men do not need to be shamed into virtue, Hume argues, because they hold a "natural sentiment of approbation and blame" that endows them with a basic sense of concern for "the public advantage and loss." Our innate public sympathy "takes us so far out of ourselves, as to give us the same pleasure or uneasiness in characters which are useful or pernicious to society, as if they had a tendency to our own advantage or loss."

Essential to Hume's theory of innate moral virtue is the immersive experience of fiction: the capacity to experience abstract characters with the same degree of vividness *as if* they could help or hurt our own persons. What converts the impression made by social actors into the idea of "our own advantage or loss" is the work of sympathy: "we have no such extensive concern for society but from sympathy" (*T* 3.3.1.11: 370).[55]

Blakey Vermeule's *Why Do We Care About Literary Characters?* takes up this experience of fiction and its formal vehicle of character as that which "makes us want to put ourselves in someone else's shoes or take on their psychic burdens for a time."[56] Characters that most conduce to this activity, Vermeule argues, are those "richest in mind reading," the positing of others' mental states, which is "the most important cognitive mechanism of human sociability" (52, 66). Vermeule's insights into the process of attuning to nonexistent persons help us to recognize Hume's remarkable move to base social feeling in the phenomenon of fictionality, wherein we imagine subjects (unrelated to us by resemblance, cause, or contiguity) as doing or being done to by characters useful or pernicious to us and to everyone else. As Vermeule asks and answers more broadly, "What happens when a mind, or something that looks like a mind, comes floating into our ken? It hails us" (21). For Hume, what hails subjects most profoundly is the "philosophical fiction" of Hobbes's covenant—in his account, a necessary and sufficient explanation for the existence of public feelings (*T* 3.2.2.14: 317). In extending sympathy from a tight field of individuals to the "general scheme or system of action" that comprises "law and justice" (*T* 3.3.1.12: 370), Hume entwines the capacity for narrative immersion with modernity's most consequential story. As Lamb, engaging Victoria Kahn's and Catherine Gallagher's accounts of conjectural or suppositional narrative writes, "Fiction doesn't reflect history, it makes it. Its referent is the real consequence of reading and believing it" ("Imagination," 60).[57] Hume writes, "The whole scheme . . . of law and justice is advantageous to the society and to every individual; and 'twas with a view to this advantage, that men, by their voluntary conventions, establish'd it. After it is once establish'd by these conventions, it is *naturally* attended with a strong sentiment of morals; which can proceed from nothing but our sympathy with the interests of society. We need no other explication" (*T* 3.3.1.12: 370).

Hume implicitly rewrites the parable of Hobbes's covenant such that it germinates from the perceptual apparatus of storytelling.[58] The convention of the state, he suggests, is inseparable from sympathetic perception, the process not in which I compassionately feel for your pain or pleasure but, rather, I suddenly ("naturally") and vividly imagine the existence of a common benefit or threat, hypothetical third parties (good or bad guys) that would unite our preservation and thus make me feel "the same pleasure or uneasiness" as if the threat were to me alone. This gestalt is vivid, involuntary, and, most important in Hume's account, it changes the emotional makeup of human beings, stretching their facility for converting impressions into ideas to the most abstract conception of society. Hume thus relies on the fictionalized moment of covenant to implant within the species that sixth sense for "the public advantage and loss." Once individuals consent to form a government, they possess "sympathy with the interests of society." Moreover, public sympathy overcomes the limits of relation (proximity, likeness, etc.) that conduce to affection. Born of the covenant, moral sentiments have transnational reach: "we give the same approbation to the same moral qualities in *China* as in *England*" (*T* 3.3.1.14: 371). In other words, we assume them to be the basis of any political sphere. As we recall, in Hobbes's mythologized state of nature, individuals simultaneously and unanimously agree to surrender their natural freedom to defend themselves and prosper in the world. Believing that they will be better off collectively, they consent to be governed as a commonwealth. Thus, Hume writes, "society provides a remedy" to humanity's woeful and "unnatural conjunction of infirmity, and of necessity" (3.3.2.2–3: 312). Echoing Hobbes's model of the artificial body of the commonwealth,[59] Hume observes, "the remedy, then, is not deriv'd from nature, but from *artifice*" (3.2.2.9: 314). "'Tis by this additional *force*, *ability*, and *security*, that society becomes advantageous" (3.2.2.3: 312) and, further, that its members are made aware of those advantages. Morality derives from the conscious enjoyment of those benefits, instilling "the natural sentiments of approbation and blame" within the species.

Unlike Hobbes's instantaneous account of the covenant, Hume describes "a slow progression" reinforced "by our repeated experience of the inconveniences of transgressing it" (*T* 3.2.2.10: 315). This more historical account of a social contract accommodates Hume's emphasis on the regulating powers of "custom and habit," imbuing "the tender minds of the children" with a sense of well-being rooted in collective life (3.2.2.4: 312). While the state may correct "for what is irregular and incommodious in the affections," Hume argues, this restraint does not oppose the selfish passions (including love of one's nearest relations) but "is only contrary to their heedless and impetuous movement." Worth noting is the salutary nature of long-held conventions, which even out and thus save us from ("remedy") the "partial and contradictory motions" of our tempers and tendencies (3.2.2.9: 314). Language, like the state, is another such convention.

Just as the political structure of the state solves the problem of "continual fluctuation" that defines individual subjectivity (perspective, temperament, and power), so, too, does the literary form of the novel. Despite the genre's commitment to particulars, novelistic narration—and Austen's *par excellence*—constitutes the same "general scheme or system of action" as does, in Hume's account, a legal system or code of manners or financial currency. A "whole scheme" corrects for the ethical challenges of positionality: "every particular man has a peculiar position with regard to others; and 'tis impossible we cou'd ever converse together on any reasonable terms, were each of us to consider characters and persons, only as they appear from his peculiar point of view" (*T* 3.3.1.15: 371). Austenian narration, like moral sentiments, offers the gifts of "*steady* and *general* points of view," which readers can "fix on" to acquire a "more *stable* judgment of things" even though their position relative to others is in a constant state of flux. Wayne Booth observes that Austen's readers have "the sense of standing with the author and observing with her" from her exalted position—at least "those of us readers who are wise enough, good enough, and perceptive enough to belong up there too."[60] As an expression of what Joanna Picciotto has called "plenary perspective,"[61] Austen's signature and enigmatic irony (what Hayes indicts as her cursedly unfeeling "vapid, Gioconda smile" ["*Emma*," 19]) can be seen to invite readers into a "secret communion, collusion, and collaboration" instead of repelling them from her emotional igloo.[62]

Hume observes how the steadying positions afforded by a general structure are wonderfully available whenever we need them: we can "always, in our thoughts, place ourselves in them, whatever may be our present situation" (*T* 3.3.1.15: 372). As one of Kipling's Janeites confirms in his story of soldier devotees, "You take it from me, Brethren, there's no one to touch Jane when you're in a tight place."[63] In her sweeping study of Janeite culture, Claudia Johnson clarifies that it is not only the transcendence of Austen's style but, more pointedly, her engagement with the alarming nature of the "present situation" that speaks to her acolytes: "Austen's novels are about nothing if not the perils of living in a confined, narrow, profoundly bruising place where experience unfolds under the aegis of ordeal, where vulnerable, deferent young protagonists with next to no autonomy are exposed to adversities so brutal that they cannot be essayed, much less assailed directly. In Austen's world, that narrow place is called a neighborhood; during World War I it is called a trench" (*Jane Austen's Cults*, 109). As Johnson's study so powerfully conveys, Janeism peaks at times of personal and political crises. States of precariousness and bewilderment heighten the need to read Austen, not only for the north star of her divine omniscience or the tuning fork of her flawless phrasing but, more pressingly, for her comprehension of confoundingly concrete ordeal.

STRAWBERRY AND APPLE BLOSSOM

Austenian narration abides by the Elinor doctrine, screening its subjects from the torments of self-awareness, allowing emotions quietly and sometimes deliciously to run their course. Desires, blunders, grudges, fixations—all states rise to the managed surface of narrative explication, but its subjects are, for the most part, spared from having to know about it. Readers, too, are not taken to task for their puerile feelings, however much they may complain about them later. No one is hideously shamed. If, in Austen's *ne plus ultra* scene of reputed humiliation, the picnic on Box Hill, Mr. Knightley calls out Emma Woodhouse's "unfeeling" ridicule of Miss Bates ("It was badly done, indeed!"), eliciting hot tears of mortification, it is crucial to remember that they almost instantly turn into salutary remorse and concurring gratitude. "The truth of his representation there was no denying. She felt it at her heart. . . . Emma felt the tears running down her cheeks almost all the way home, without being at any trouble to check them, extraordinary as they were" (408–9). Satire, too, works this way, calling out without shaming. As Dryden observed, its art consists in precisely not giving offense, in delivering a blow with "the fineness of a stroak [*sic*] that separates the Head from the Body, and leaves it standing in its place."[64] The life and mind of someone like Sir William Lucas may be summarily dispatched, deftly exposed in the littleness of his essence ("he had removed with his family to a house . . . where he could think with pleasure of his own importance" [*PP* 19]), but Sir William is left smilingly intact, never knowing his own victimization, never feeling the cut of narration. As Dryden writes, the "fool feels it not."

D. W. Harding famously characterized this principle of Austen's writing as a form of "regulated hatred," a coping mechanism for the "eruption of fear and hatred into the relationships of everyday social life."[65] For Harding, Austenian irony was a highly flexible and ultimately charitable mode of expression, exercising a "capacity for keeping on good terms with people without too great treachery to [one]self" (358). A social psychologist writing at the outbreak of World War II, Harding understood Austen as possessing the necessarily dual perspective of someone who can be "intensely critical of people to whom she also has strong emotional attachments" (355). Regulating ambivalence, in other words, is the most ethical as well as psychologically healthy course to take when living in a world that we at once need, and need to object to. Unlike the ironist who ridicules or the misanthrope who renounces, Harding's Austen engages in a form of opposition that preserves the dignity of her subjects without sacrificing her right of protest. Despite the role it eventually played in consolidating a pathologically repressed or sadistic Austen, Harding's figure was, as I have argued elsewhere,[66] a paragon of psychological security, a needed model in times of war.

In the archive of Harding's papers in Emmanuel College, Cambridge, there exist partial drafts of an essay entitled "Strawberries and Apple Blossom," one of the few Austen-related documents not included in the anthology of his writings on the novelist. Written late in life (the third draft is written on the back of a notice dated 1991, the same year his wife died and less than two years before his own death), Harding takes up the "slightly patronizing little joke about Jane Austen's apple orchard in flower" at Mr. Martin's farm "while Mr Knightley's guests gather ripe strawberries," a horticultural blunder committed in *Emma* and pointed out with gusto by Austen's wealthy brother, Edward Knight. According to Harding's own research, the "cultivated apple" flowers when Jane Austen says it does. She "may have been cutting it fine but she was not imagining an impossibility." He further observes that Austen would not have corrected her brother on what was ultimately his error. "Apart from the fact that [Austen, her mother, and her sister] were indebted to him for the house they lived in, she was far too secure psychologically to have any need to take him down a peg."[67] Sovereign insensibility extends to situations of misplaced ridicule, a willingness if not exactly to "stand as Butts," as in Addison's phrase, then at least to allow others to laugh at one's expense without experiencing the need to correct or expose them. Harding's fantasy here is that Austen would not have suffered, that she possessed what Hobbes describes as the insensible's singular "exemption from calamity." Apart from her firm grasp of reality (Edward was her landlord), she would have remained emotionally protected by her understanding and acceptance of human nature.

In a study of the "emotional ethics" and "affective charge" of irony, Linda Hutcheon observes its "deliberate engaging of emotion" through its powers to "mock, attack, and ridicule . . . exclude, embarrass, and humiliate." Hutcheon writes that "irony always has a 'target'" and sometimes a "victim."[68] Harding, too, refers to Austen's "admirer-victim" and coined the pithy statement that her "books are, as she meant them to be, read and enjoyed by precisely the sort of people whom she disliked" (347) (a line repurposed by Mudrick as the epigraph to his book). And yet, contrary to Mudrick's claim that in Austen, "sympathy is irrelevant to irony," we come to recognize it as irony's guiding principle, where sympathy constitutes the facility for grasping another's situation and, indeed, the *whole* situation—a panoramic vision that accommodates a vacuous Sir William Lucas, an entitled, half-witted brother, and a venomous Lucy Steele. Davidson's description of Elinor Dashwood's "tact" as resulting from "a desire not to hurt someone or to protect the other from one's own sense of superiority"[69] almost precisely recapitulates Aristotle's *eiron*,[70] a dramatic figure who, like Socrates, conceals his powers "not for the sake of one's own advantage but from a dislike for bombast and a desire to spare others the feelings of inferiority."[71] Unlike the blustering *alazon* of Greek comedy, the *eiron* is closer to the man with "no name" who "most resembles friendship." Such a person is "concerned with the pleasures and pains of social life" and manages to strike an ideal balance between obsequiousness and churlishness, conferring pleasure and even inflicting pain "in the right way" (as calibrated to the situation and the object at hand). Aristotle qualifies that this middle state "differs from friendship in that it implies no passion or affection . . . since it is not by reason of loving or hating that such a man takes everything in the right way, but by being a man of a certain kind" (*Nicomachean Ethics* 4.6: 1778).[72]

How do we describe the disposition and quality of mind conveyed in Harding's "Strawberries and Apple Blossom"? Does it register generous understatement, solipsistic contempt, or prude-like abjection? In that daisy chain of human passions discussed in the introduction from part 1 of *Leviathan*, Hobbes defines *pusillanimity* as the "Desire of things that conduce but a little to our ends; And fear of things that are but of little hindrance." Magnanimity is contempt of those "little helps, and hindrances," and "Magnanimity, in danger of Death, or Wounds" is Valour or Fortitude (*L* 1.6: 86). Valor here denotes insensibility, someone who chooses to be impervious to danger even as he or she is motivated by the safety of others. This is Elinor Dashwood's supreme feature, or what Hume conceives as an individual's "character," the "durable principles of the mind, which extend over the whole conduct" (*T* 3.1.4: 367). Annette Baier elaborates: "How a person manages her different and often conflicting passions, all keen to rule, and how she uses her intelligence to serve her prevailing passions, as well as what passions those are will be a matter of character."[73] Elinor's valor, her ability to order her passions, her style of intelligence do not consist in prioritizing the feelings of others above her own but in knowing that her feelings are not only her own—that, as she answers Marianne, who cannot fathom her sister's endurance in knowing Lucy's engagement whilst loving Edward Ferrars, "Yes. But I did not love only him" (297). Heterosexual attachment exists, but it is only one strand of love—what makes me cover, screen, and spare the other, to feel their feelings for them.

BUT BEHOLD ME IMMORTAL!

Of Austen's evanescent seascape, the unfinished *Sanditon*, D. A. Miller notes the mercilessness required for a dying writer to satirize illness: "In Austen, so completely does her subject remain the negation of her subjectivity that, even when she is most seriously ill, she elects to write about hypochondria" (*Jane Austen*, 56). As we know by now, the maddening thing about the insensible is that she does not respond to her *own* case. Sympathy compensates for unfeeling, as Smith explained, supplying the "emotion which the person principally concerned is incapable of feeling, and which yet we feel by an illusive sympathy with him." As elaborated in the last chapter, so powerful are the fictionalizing properties of sympathy that we can project "the foresight of our own dissolution," putting us in the situation of our own newly dead self, "and thence conceiving what would be our emotions in this case" (*TMS* 1.1.1.13: 16). Austen's final composition, known as "When Winchester Races," the curiously high-spirited poem penned in a still elegant though decidedly looser hand (seen by biographers as "badly written," potentially "dictated," and decidedly "misspelled")[74] imagines the situation of a being long dead and then pictures it bouncing back to life in the form of a spry deity, who disrupts the revels of his "subjects rebellious" only to rebuke them.[75]

The poem—written on 15 July 1817, three days before Austen succumbed to some variety of illness that ravaged her joints, face, and eyesight—commemorates St. Swithin's Day, when locals watch the skies to see if their patron saint, the Anglo-Saxon Bishop of Winchester, will curse them with forty days of rain in retribution for once removing his remains. Like the unkillable prude or the author function of Clarissa Harlowe, St. Swithin stands "aloof" in supernal judgment to make "The Lords and the Ladies" pay for their depravity:

"*But behold me immortal!* By vice you're enslaved / You have sinned & must suffer. Then farther he said" (lines 12, 7, 15–16). But unlike the prude, St. Swithin is no obstructionist. He urges on the company's "dissolute" races:

> Let them stand—You shall meet with your curse in your pleasures
> Set off for your course, I'll pursue with *my* rain.
> Ye cannot but know my command o'er July
> Henceforward I'll triumph in shewing my powers
> Shift your race as you will it shall never be dry
> The curse upon Venta is July in showers—. (19–24)

The speaker announces his triumph in the form of imminent weather, which will chase his listeners (in appropriate anapestic tetrameter) and soak their joys with yearly rains that will fall like beads from an immortal language. The insensible, grand spoiler of narrative felicity, refuses its offers of assimilation, opting instead to die in its own way. In her last piece of writing Austen giddily frees herself from fiction's long march forward, laying down instead the circular tracks of the divine. (As the impish Lumpkin riddles, "What's that goes round the house, and round the house, and never touches the house?") Explaining the phenomena of "Duration and Expansion, considered together," Locke gleaned something like narrative's curse of linearity. Whereas expansion involves lengthening in so many directions as to "make Figure, and Breadth, and Thickness," he writes, "*Duration is but as it were the length of one streight Line*" (*EHU* 2.15.11: 203). Expansion allows embodiment, "Multiplicity, Variation, or Figure" pulled through space. Even with its points reordered, duration still moves along the same, one-dimensional plank of time. Distinguishing between mortal temporality and "infinite Duration," Locke writes that whereas for man, "What is once passed, he can never recal, and what is yet to come, he cannot make present," for God, "there is nothing, which he cannot make exist each moment he pleases" (*EHU* 2.15.12: 204). In his exhilarating powers to make weather, chase races, pounce from heaven to earth ("He made but one Spring from his Shrine to the Roof"), St. Swithin stands as a waggish tribute to Austen's own knack for pulling "Figure, and Breadth, and Thickness" out of narrative language, spinning objects of "Multiplicity" and "Variation" from skeins of prose, crafting novels somehow bestowed with infinite duration.

CONCLUSION

Death Wish for the Novel

GEORGE ELIOT'S LAST NOVEL FEATURES the relentless punishment of Gwendolen Harleth, a deliciously insensible heroine whose surname tags her Richardsonian descent.[1] "I believe all men are bad, and I hate them," declares this "Spoiled Child," another pale "immovable" beauty, who refuses to crawl out of bed for her mother's pills, throttles her sister's bird for out-singing her, fantasizes about stabbing her husband with a desk ornament, and laughs when her cousin breaks his bones falling off a horse.[2] The charge of insensibility in this case is an understatement ("You have no feeling, child!" [24]). Like Defoe's impervious heroines before her, Gwendolen's unfeeling is born of detailed socioeconomic calamity: what happens when a woman of extraordinary charm (what Joseph Roach, in his study of *It*, calls the quality of being "abnormally interesting")[3] and therefore a lifelong sense of entitlement, faces toppling collapse—an unthinkably wholesale ruin that threatens to destroy not only the subject herself but also the only person she has ever loved (Mom). Too cool to fail, the subject goes to compromising lengths to preempt devastation. So well do things work out that she looks like a clean success: "The sylph was a winner" (10). Only Gwendolen knows the hidden costs and, in fact, she would give it all up to escape her unremitting states of "mortal humiliation," "torture," "hatred and rage," "fits of spiritual dread," "terror," "indignation and loathing," "weariness and disgust," and "world-nausea" (424, 668, 693, 63, 311, 298, 429, 272).

Appropriately married to a washed-out, sociopathic libertine,[4] Gwendolen Harleth-now-Grandcourt lives a half-life, brittle with suppressed abhorrence and self-reproach—until she meets Deronda, whose mere presence compels her to stop performing and speak only raw truths: "I will tell you everything as God knows it. I will tell you no falsehood; I will tell you the exact truth" (692). Early in their acquaintance, during what began as a casual conversation about music, she probes, "Do *you* never find fault with the world or with others? . . . And hate people? Confess you hate them." Disarmed by the new bride, who speaks "with a hard intensity unaccountable in incidental talk," Deronda deflects with a commonplace: "We are often standing in each other's way when we can't help it" (412). But his attempt to steer Gwendolen back to polite speech—to a nonrevelatory, nonintimate type of exchange—goes unheeded. Gwendolen presses on, so thinly disguising her own circumstances ("But if they injure you and could have helped it?" [412]) that she commits something akin to emotional flashing in her sudden, "unaccountable," and intense acts of self-exposure. Successful in leaving a "painful impression," Gwendolen forces relation, knowledge—eagerly taking up what Deronda started when he interfered with her roulette streak at the novel's start, "entangling her in helpless humiliation" (20). *Nobody knows me; no one sees who I really am. You did, and so now you must.*

Shamed into encounter, Gwendolen phases into a "beseeching persistent need" for Daniel Deronda (587). In this almost unbearably tilted dynamic ("The feeling Deronda endured in these moments he afterwards called horrible" [610]), Eliot stages a fantasy to bypass the process of getting to know someone—the prosaic staple, in other words, of romantic courtship. A twenty-year-old woman who still sleeps in a "little white bed" next to her mother's, experiences "physical repulsion" when men make love to her, and erupts in "hysterical violence" on her wedding night (311, 70, 359), Gwendolen Harleth has understandably been read as an example of Victorian hysteria, as mad as the queen in "Snow White" and as repressed as Freud's Dora.[5] But in this aborted bildungsroman, which outstrips any hermeneutic of repression, desire and even love (that "word of all work") do not suffice to explain Gwendolen's "hunger to speak to" Deronda, a sensation so pressing that it blunts "her sensibility to everything else" ("the wish to speak to him and have him speaking to her was becoming imperious") (415, 592, 336). Already coerced and stunned into conjugality, she is not after admiration ("There was not the faintest touch of coquetry in the attitude of her mind towards him" [415]). Empathy—what critics discern in Gwendolen's stark appeal to "tell me again. What should you do—what should you feel, if you were in my place?"—comes closer, except that Deronda would much prefer not to ("I should rather be inclined to run away from her" [449, 163]). Intoxicated by a stranger's freakish attunement—what makes Deronda's secret-sharing feel more like autonomic mirroring than shaky attraction[6] ("that he should misunderstand her had never entered into her mind" [448])—Gwendolen stands as Eliot's neuroticized version of an insensible, that is to say, someone who is not actually insensible.

Truer impassivity, we remember from Goldsmith, does not proceed from the frigid woman but from the male practitioner of "profound sensibility," whose "rare and massive power" to sympathize with any and every emotion ("there was hardly a delicacy of feeling this lad was not capable of") must be shut off or rechanneled in order to preserve himself (168). Deronda's eighteenth-century roots lay not only in the sentimental novel's tapped-out man of feeling but also in amatory fiction's irresistible man, whose tender attentiveness and enchanting beauty make anyone who enters his orbit feel instantly, albeit mistakenly, loved. Part 3 of *The Prude* presents the Chevalier D'Avimont, whose killer feature is not his "agreeable, easy Air" or "just-proportion'd Limbs" but "a peculiar Softness in his Eyes, *as if* the lovely Object, on which he gaz'd, had inspir'd him."[7] The rake's trick is not to feign love but, more insidiously, to feign its particularity, as if only "their very Foibles, as well as their Perfections" could have sparked "his Tongue," "his Looks," his "amorous, tender Desires" (3.5). The truth—unsurprising in this study—is that "tho' he knew how to create the greatest Passion in the Breast of the Fair, yet he was insensible of it himself" (3.5). D'elmont, the "insensible" who is "not an object to be gazed at safely" in Eliza Haywood's baroque novel of unreciprocated desire, *Love in Excess* (1719), drives women to madness "with that softness in his eyes, and that engaging tenderness in his voice, as would half persuade [one] that god had touched his heart."[8] "Think but what you are," sighs one of his victims, resigned to submit to "a form like yours" (208). Daniel Deronda inherits D'elmont's fated form. His eyes, Eliot writes, "had a peculiarity which has drawn many men into trouble; they were of a dark yet mild intensity which seemed to express a special interest in every one on whom he fixed them" (332).

What is horrible about befriending a man of feeling is that eventually you come to see that the "pleasure[s] inconceivable" of being addressed by this godlike creature are "but the effects of his natural complaisance, and that to whom soever he addressed, he carried an equality in his behaviour" (Haywood, *Love in Excess*, 38). The flaw of Deronda/D'elmont/D'Avimont is that they "creat[e] in the minds" of their objects a sense of individualized attention, *as if* the other were "special." "That sort of effect was penetrating Gwendolen" (*Daniel Deronda*, 332). The Deronda Effect flags a proverbial distinction between sympathy and empathy. In psychoanalyst David Black's example we might consider the professional torturer a gifted sympathizer insofar as he can vividly imagine what his victim will experience in any given position.[9] What is different about the empathic person is not his facility to feel what the other feels but that doing so costs him something, alters his understanding of himself. Empathy, Black proposes, "entails not only a knowing of the other person's feeling, but also an identification with the other as the one having that feeling" (585). Deronda is always affected in the moment (his "anguish was intolerable. . . . His eyes too were large with tears"), but the fact is, his plans never change: "She was the victim of his happiness. 'I am cruel'," he thinks (805). Cruel, compassionate, cruelly compassionate—in any case, he is off the hook: "How could Deronda help this?" "He could not help himself" (587, 805). "The grave beauty of his face" and "that exquisite voice of soothing which expresses oneness with the sufferer" just invite telepathic communion (589, 638). Gwendolen muses, "I wish he could know everything about me without my telling him" (630). So desirable is faultless, noninvasive, almost nonverbal intimacy that it does not even register as desire. Like a phototropic creature ("You will find yourself growing like a plant" [769]), one simply turns toward "receptiveness," or that "keenly perceptive sympathetic emotiveness" that inspires "unreflecting openness" in all of its objects (771, 496). No matter that (apart from his pull to Jewish objects) Deronda's empathy is neither voluntary nor personal but "so infused with kindliness that it easily passed for comradeship" (179). In other words, he doesn't mean it.

In fact, Deronda "dreaded hearing [Gwendolen's] confession . . . shrank from the task that was laid on him [and] he wished . . . that she could bury her secrets in her own bosom. He was not a priest" (694, 695).[10] If, as critics are fond of observing, Deronda is not Gwendolen's priest but rather her therapist ("Tell me all you feel it a relief to tell" [694]), then, as Jerome Thale remarks, he is "a poor one."[11] Yet psychoanalysis depends on impersonality—on the analyst's special technique, as Freud advises, of "not directing one's notice to anything in particular and in maintaining the same 'evenly-suspended attention'" to everything offered.[12] For Freud, this principle of nonselectivity is imperative for both the analyst's self-preservation and the patient's treatment, even if it comes off as impassivity: "The justification for requiring this emotional coldness in the analyst is that it creates the most advantageous conditions for both parties." Freud famously urges analysts to imitate "the surgeon, who puts aside all his feelings, even his human sympathy, and concentrates his mental forces on the single aim of performing the operation as skillfully as possible."[13] Unlike the "particular movement" of Descartes's pineal gland, which is activated by the presence of a certain form (*you and only you*), clinical feeling is not object-specific. Sympathy—like narrative, like psychoanalysis—I am suggesting, has no a priori commitments. It shines its light on whoever walks into the room, whatever sentient being can make the claim, *I'm here*.

Psychoanalytic transference nonetheless depends on emotional projection—a miscalculation that in the space of the novel proves far from curative.[14] Gwendolen "had never before had from any man a sign of tenderness which her own being had needed, and she interpreted its powerful effect on her into a promise of inexhaustible patience and constancy" (691). Her interpretation is wrong, of course, and although Gwendolen may not run into Deronda's sword as she flies down a corridor in the dead of night (as happens in *Love in Excess*), she is equally gutted. The novel leaves her where it found her, unwilling to import her "small life" into its hero's epic ambitions (804). Confined to the kids' table of narrative possibility, the character who used to "play at reigning" is now made continuously aware of her "thraldom"—not to mention the constraints of her own mind: "Can I understand the ideas, or am I too ignorant?" (316, 601, 803). In this "history of a young lady hitherto well provided for," Eliot draws out the dysphoric essence of Richardsonian fiction to make the point that history has never provided for young ladies (253). "Girls' lives are so stupid: they never do what they like" (69). Freed from girlhood but now chained to a reptile, Gwendolen is the subject of a history of forms and forces that have conspired to put her in this no-exit situation, in which her shining amour-propre (the rights of which have been conferred on her by nature and by culture) is shocked into "something spiritual and vaguely tremendous that thrust her away, and yet quelled all her anger into self-humiliation" (804). "The Nereid in sea-green robes" who sails through any room is "brought to kneel down like a horse under training for the arena" (12, 320).

BAD DREAM

If that arena is marriage, then Henleigh Mallinger Grandcourt is unquestionably the master. Without needing to represent marital rape exactly (almost a redundancy here), Eliot makes Gwendolen's bind of nonconsent explicit enough: "Of what use was the rebellion within her? She could say nothing that would not hurt her worse than submission" (427). As in most scripts of abuse, countermotion seems to initiate greater motion, such that to pull away only provokes the other to tug harder: "his eyes showed a delight in torturing her. How could she be defiant? She had nothing to say that would touch him—nothing but what would give him a more painful grasp on her consciousness" (427). As *Clarissa* teaches, sensibility baits the sadist, for whom "protest [only] . . . add[s] to the piquancy of despotism" (672). But as *Clarissa* also teaches, insensibility baits the sadist even more: Grandcourt "had a peculiar triumph in conquering her dumb repugnance" (602). Whereas stillness can at least camouflage a hunted animal, immobility just gives Gwendolen away, reinforcing a vise-grip that strangles its object while stifling its cries of pain: "what he required was that she should be as fully aware as she would have been of a locked hand-cuff, that her inclination was helpless to decide anything in contradiction with his resolve" (584). Lovelace resorted to drugging his victim, but Grandcourt wants his kept awake, "eyes open," paralyzed but "aware" (602).

Grandcourt gets the drowning he deserves, and it is a scene to which his wife will be fully present ("a wild amazed consciousness in her eyes . . . 'I saw his dead face'" [686, 691]). With his waterlogged head now bobbing up and down the Mediterranean ("he was gone down again, and I had the rope in my hand—no, there he was again—his face above the water—and he cried again—and I held my hand, and my heart said, 'Die!'—and he sank" [696]), Grandcourt comes off worse than Lovelace, who at least dies in a duel. But neither does Gwendolen win this story. What the novel announces, from its first chapter to its seventieth, is that women are born losers, that even their most triumphant victory (securing a single man in possession of a good fortune) will turn out to be their most wrenching, consciousness-crushing, self-estranging loss. A textbook prude whose placidity belies her cruelty ("too markedly cold and neutral not to have in it a little of that nature which we call art concealing an inward exultation"), Gwendolen must own up to the truth of her soul (homicidal ideation)—but that, for Eliot, is less a manifestation of individual psychology than an outcome of historical and narrative logic (10). Contemplating female wreckage in the form of Grandcourt's used-up mistress, Gwendolen has one of her regular "ghastly vision[s]," which speaks prophetically this time: "I am a woman's life" (762, 152).[15] In the rigged game of female *Bildung* ("a lure through a long Satanic masquerade" [762]), women are made to know their own powerlessness, turned into ghosts or, as in prude fictions, cats, beds.

Denied by Deronda and the Richardsonian novel, "this delicate-limbed sylph of twenty [who had] meant to lead" ends her history back inside of her family's recessed home, surrounded again by the "worn beauty" of her mother and the "shabby" dresses of her sisters, with only a faraway pen-pal to remind her of her single attempt at cathexis (39, 25). What F. R. Leavis famously called the "good" half of *Daniel Deronda* thus signals Eliot's best effort to entomb, or at least quarantine, the novel's blighted formula of gendered insensibility, sending it back to its crib with the half-hearted hope that it might try again ("I will try—try to live" [806]).[16] "Turned away" by Deronda, Gwendolen shrieks and sobs throughout the night before looking up to see her mother's face: "I shall live. I shall be better" (807). If Gwendolen finally awakens from the bad dream of Richardsonian form, then her desperate appeal to know "what to think and what to do" cannot be answered (445). Failures of feeling, this book has argued, go hand in hand with narrative failure. Not surprisingly, much of *Deronda*'s reception history (like nearly every text treated in this study) has been marked by disappointment. As one reader staged by Henry James complains, "A silly young girl and a heavy, overwise young man who *don't* fall in love with her! That is the *donnée* of eight monthly volumes" (*CH* 432). Daniel Deronda, a disgusted Saintsbury declares, is "so intolerably dreadful that we not only dislike, but refuse to admit him as possible" (*CH* 373). In this novel, Adela Pinch writes, George Eliot "in a totally unprecedented fashion, places at its center a heterosexual relation between a man and a woman that cannot possibly be subsumed under any of the varieties of amatory plotting—courtship, seduction—known to English fiction."[17]

Is *Deronda* a mercy killing, what allows Eliot to euthanize Richardsonian fiction before pursuing her subsequent and final work, the experimental and sketch-like *Impressions of Theophrastus Such*?[18] What does it mean for Eliot to give up on the novel and its theory of mind, to shrug it off like an exoskeleton or, better yet, a sea-green feather boa? By the end of the novel, Deronda's irresistible tenderness has finally misfired, and he trades in his second sight: for once and forever, "he could not quite divine what was going on within her" (802). The burnt-out man of feeling / exhausted psychoanalyst / disillusioned novelist ("my brains are melting" [791]) quits his practice, opting for something less claustrophobic, less one-on-one, less *known*. Deronda announces a new "object"—"purposes" that will "force me to leave England," as well as everyone unlucky enough to be stuck there. Left to fend for herself on the crumbling estate of realist fiction, Gwendolen tries to construe Deronda's banal advice to "be among the best of women" (769). "I do not yet see how that can be," she writes, correct for once in her self-assessment (810). What's more, a throwaway suggestion that Gwendolen could still marry her cousin Rex is the plot's insulting offer of an afterlife. No believer in the redemptive possibilities of domestic fiction, Eliot stretches the form to its usual crisis and leaves it excitedly behind for "the East" and whatever counterforms of narrative life it might offer. And yet, isn't self-exposing failure exactly what the novel does best?

In *Deronda*, David Kurnick writes, "Eliot gives voice to a desire to exceed the constraints of her form."[19] Proposing that we read the novel as a play (as Eliot had considered), Kurnick revisits the text not as a work of competing plotlines (in which Deronda wins) but as "a world where such plots coexist in the same fictive space"—that is, the unifying space of a "universal theater" (103, 94). Individual *Bildung*, successful or failed, would in Kurnick's interpretation, give way to a "sense of collective plenitude [that] is always ready to reassert itself as the phenomenological ground" of fiction (94).[20] In Lisa Freeman's account, what novelistic character must keep repressing *is* theatricality, "a contrivance that must be internalized and concealed in order to maintain the fiction of the subject's stability."[21] In other words, Freeman writes, the formal realism of the novel "depended upon, and could be maintained only to, the extent that the fictionality or artifice of its own enterprise could be concealed, with the subject situated behind a stabilizing fourth wall" (14). The failed fictions that have been featured in this book are poor concealers; their fourth walls are deliberately flimsy or, worse, decorated to look weird. Swayed by Kurnick's and Freeman's readings, we might wish to conceive of this failure as an attempt to leave the novel itself behind, to plant one foot boldly back onto the boards of the theater. As tempting and even true as that explanation would be (and what I argued in Goldsmith's case), what interferes with that move is the stickiness of the novel itself—its freakish tendency to cannibalize all forms, even its own. The novel, this story goes, is the ultimate insensible. As Bakhtin summarized, "it gets on poorly with other genres."[22] Like its political correlative, the modern nation-state, the novel proposes to take everybody in, to absorb or at least contain every difference within its policed but hungry borders. The Bartlebyan subject marks the internal limit of the novel's engulfing tendencies, igniting and defying its unprecedented powers of assimilation. In fiction's history *Daniel Deronda* delivers perhaps the most electrifying such figure: not a hysterical woman or a man of feeling but yet another insensible long rooted in the history of the English novel, the unmaternal mother.

ANOTHER LIFE

"I am your mother. . . . I did not want a child"; "I am not a loving woman That is the truth," speaks Leonora Alcharisi, a.k.a. the Princess Halm-Eberstein, Deronda's mother and the final insensible in this study (623).[23] Gwendolen Harleth, with her serpent costume and neck-winding airs, proves to have been only the opening act for this "Melusina," whose defections from nearly every regime (emotional, religious, sexual, familial) speak to her choice of "another life" (666). Outing herself as the Jewish mother she never wanted to be ("I did not wish you to be born" [223]),[24] the Alcharisi encounters Deronda in two rarefied sessions that take place in a hushed suite of rooms at a Genovese resort. These interviews form the emotional climax of what David Marshall calls *Deronda*'s "private theater" of sympathy.[25] Except in this dramatic, certifiable family romance (*my real mother is a princess*), Eliot stages a dazzling repudiation of fellow-feeling. "I did not send for you to comfort me," says the dying actress to her beautifully grown and pantingly solicitous son. "Is it not possible that I could be near you often and comfort you?" Deronda persists. "No, not possible," she answers (638).[26]

The actor, like the psychoanalyst, obeys a professional imperative to be insensible ("*Nulle sensibilité!*") so that, as Diderot writes, he can deliver the same affecting performance each time he hits the stage: "At the very moment when he touches your heart he is listening to his own voice; his talent depends not, as you think, upon feeling, but upon rendering so exactly the outward signs of feeling, that you fall into the trap. He has rehearsed to himself every note of his passion. He has learnt before a mirror every particle of his despair."[27] The actor harnesses its entire expressive mechanism (every note, every particle) for the sake of performance. So, the Alcharisi, "the greatest lyric actress of Europe" (who practices "sincere acting," dramatizing "her own emotions"), instantly transmutes passion into action: "this woman's nature was one in which all feeling—and all the more when it was tragic as well as real—immediately became matter of conscious representation" (629). Like a centrifuge or a cistern, the actor has almost no time or even physiological tolerance for interiority. The vessel takes in all that it can but only to convert and expel its contents. It would be even more difficult to classify this process as sympathy since the actor's "genius" to live "myriad lives in one" is premised on *not* "be[ing] hampered with other [actual] lives" (629, 639). Leonora's capacity to inhabit any role (ostensibly similar to her son's "plenteous, flexible sympathy") necessitates a refusal of the single one for which she was born: to serve the needs of others, "to adore" a patriarchal Judaism (630).[28] "I did not care at all. I cared for the wide world, and all that I could represent in it" (630). This is not involuntary self-loss or erasure but willed and inexhaustible transmigration.

If—like Gwendolen, Gwendolen's mother, Lydia Glasher, and any other female besides Catherine Arrowpoint—the princess loses out ("I have after all been the instrument my father wanted"; "I am the loser"; "I miscalculated" [662, 663, 666]), then her failure nonetheless indicts men's own frustrated sovereignty: "They would rule the world if they could; but not ruling the world, they throw all the weight of their will on the necks and souls of women" (631). The Alcharisi channels here the manifesto of another unfeeling mother and retired performer, Defoe's Roxana (1724), who spells out her misprision: "I thought a Woman was a free Agent, as well as a Man, and was born free, and cou'd she manage herself suitably, might enjoy that Liberty to as much Purpose as the Men do." Instead, she discovers that law and society "acted quite upon other Principles; and those such, that a Woman gave herself entirely away from herself . . . that the very Nature of the Marriage Contract was, in short, nothing but giving up Liberty, Estate, Authority, and every-thing, to the Man, and the Woman was indeed, a meer Woman ever after, that is to say, a Slave."[29] In a restatement of Mary Astell's infamous question posed a generation earlier ("If all Men are born free, how is it that all Women are born slaves?"), Roxana asserts a transgendered freedom: "I would be a Man-Woman; for as I was born free, I wou'd die so" [171]). As Elizabeth Wahl observes of the *précieuses*, female liberation involves a "rejection of heterosexual as well as maternal norms."[30] For the Alcharisi, acting is a strategic part of that rejection: "Others have loved me—and I have acted their love. I know very well what love makes of men and women—it is subjection. It takes another for a larger self, enclosing this one. . . . I was never willingly subject to any man. Men have been subject to me" (666).

The plot of maternal failure, Toni Bowers argues, was an obsession during the long eighteenth century. In a culture still processing the forced flight of a sovereign, "representations of failed authority and abdicated responsibility" saturated narrative forms (musical, visual, dramatic, political, religious, and literary).[31] Bad mothers, in particular, as Bowers illuminates, captured an anxiety-producing porousness between aggression and resistance, acquiescence and agency, which preoccupied social consciousness. The Alcharisi, like her predecessors, is "both innocent and guilty, victimized and victimizing" (22)—a testament to sociocultural failings but still held personally accountable. "Maternal guilt," Bowers explains, "is always overdetermined, maternal innocence always interested and compromised" (22). "Well," as the Alcharisi says of her motives, "there are reasons. I feel many things that I can't understand" (628). Yet, Bowers argues, stories of maternal failure also capitalized on this murkiness to reconceptualize female subjectivity, launching "the revolutionary notion that maternal virtue and authority take a multitude of forms, and can even inhabit absence, abdication, and transgression" (33). New figurations thus introduced "forms of complicity that constitute forms of resistance, places supposedly outside that redefine what an inside might mean" (25). Deronda's mother, a fabulous diva who (in Kurnick's excellent gloss) challenges the interpretive "regime of novelistic depth," "its mutually reinforcing logics of narrative supervision, ethnic truth, and psychological legibility," is part of a long legacy of feminist experimentation within fiction to define and redefine interior life (*Empty Houses*, 96–97).

With her magisterial scene-stealing, Deronda's mother nonetheless seems to draw from a different source of energy than the psychological narrative otherwise epitomized by Eliot's text. Burdened but unrepentant, admiring but withholding, dying but larger than life, the princess performs a set of contradictions too grand for ego psychology. Kurnick argues that it is theater itself that comes back in the Alcharisi's second scene, reasserting its phenomenological difference from the novel: "The Princess's ability to survive her submission to the novel—even to comment skeptically on its progress—makes her an unprecedented instance in Eliot's work of the theater being permitted to look back dubiously at the novel that would contain it" (100).[32] But the fact is that the novel does contain it. The Alcharisi may be terminally ill, but she dies offstage in her own way, and what resonates is her assertion, "I am not a monster" (626). Central to *Deronda*—and, as I have been claiming, to the Richardsonian text at large—is the staging of what certain theorists have located as fiction's singular instance of ethical knowledge: "the confrontation with alterity, an experience of the other that surprises us in its intractability, its refusal to conform to what we imagine we know," as Dorothy Hale writes.[33] For Judith Butler, only this encounter of failed recognition can reveal the social and historical norms that "delineat[e] who will qualify as a subject" and who will not.[34] Butler draws on the ethical relation formulated by Adriana Cavarero as one that "does not support empathy, identification, or confusions," that says, "Your story is never my story."[35] Or, as the princess tells her son, "You may try—but you can never imagine" (629). To refuse sympathy ("I *am suffering*. But with a suffering that you can't comfort" [625]) is to refuse story. "I beseech you to tell me what moved you," Deronda demands. "Oh—the reasons for our actions!" brushes off the princess, "with a ring of something like sarcastic scorn" (629). (The analogy in *Middlemarch* would be if in response to Dorothea Brooke's "I beseech you to tell me how everything was," Lydgate, instead of melting into confidence, gave a hard laugh and strode off to his ruin.) To take Kurnick's cue of adaptation:

> DANIEL. Mother! take us all into your heart—the living, and the dead. Forgive everything that hurts you in the past. Take my affection.
>
> LEONORA. (*kisses Daniel on the head and replies sadly*) I reject nothing, but I have nothing to give. (634)

The Alcharisi's neutrality, here so full of pathos ("I cannot make you a joy" [663]), returns us to Hobbes's definition of insensibility as immobility—neither aversion nor desire, neither no nor yes—and to its undeniable incitement of the passions. Deronda leaves the room, blinded by grief, his feelings "wrought to a pitch of acuteness in which he was no longer quite master of himself" (666). "Good-bye, my son, good-bye. We shall hear no more of each other. Kiss me" (666). *Curtain closes.*

The prude fictions with which this book began established a narrative agenda to punish women's expectations to "be better," as if to say, this world is not for you, and you will be punished for daring to make (or even *thinking* you could make) another one. As literary historians tell us, the defeated women of the civil uprisings of *la Fronde* rechanneled their political aspirations into a linguistic revolution that made the European novel, reclaiming indifference and recultivating *repos* as their affective estate. Such presumptions of *le triomphe de l'indifférence* lit a flight of misogynistic eloquence, with its devastating rewriting of women's political failure as sexual shame. But what this strange archive also records is an enduring belief in female sovereignty—a counterfactual commitment to a feminocentrism that is unachieved but somehow continuously imaginable. What I'm saying is that if the novel is a form that records and restages real failure, its gifts come in what Frances Ferguson, writing on Philomela, describes as literature's shining "overcompensation."[36]

Novels, John Bender writes, "make visible the means of production of the social text," in other words, "the symbolic practices [institutions, structures of domination, emergent imagery and discourse] through which we manifest our social presence."[37] Moreover, novels "not only reveal ideology" by making such practices and voices visible; "they *must* do so in order to maintain their generic identity" (134). *Failures of Feeling* has endorsed that immanently "dual structure" of the novel to "spea[k] out and ac[t] out," its mandate to symptomatize and to go on strike (134). What distinguishes the Richardsonian project is not only its representation of clashing voices but also a self-appalled staging of protest, or what Ferguson calls a "self-negation," embedded like a cry for help within its own form ("Rape," 109). Psychological fiction is profoundly nontranscendent. It is, as Ferguson writes (and as discussed in Chapter 2), a "form that insists that forms can never be outrun" (109). Unlike the bildungsroman, the psychological text "can never get ahead [because] its way of manifesting itself in the world is to make apparent its own subjection" (107). In a lighter key, we might say that Richardsonian form is campy. It calls out its own flimsy construction while taking itself dead-seriously at the same time. As Joseph Roach writes, "Camp reveals no hidden depths because what is hiding in plain sight needs all the therapeutic recuperation it can get."[38] What is then so bizarre and so fundamental to the Richardsonian text—its "catch me if you can," self-stigmatizing style of play—is the distinctive, compulsive, Lovelacean desire to be found guilty: "no one shall say worse of me than I will of myself. . . . And if you can say worse, speak it" (7:263 [1280]). If all of the police procedurals and psychological thrillers that we now binge-watch, and that testify to Samuel Richardson's long reach over narrative entertainment, have forgotten that legacy of doubleness (what Bakhtin calls the novel's "ambivalent laughter, at the same time cheerful and annihilating" [*The Dialogic Imagination*, 21]), then at least they possess a genetic disposition toward self-rebuke, as well as a tendency to outrage. Hanging over these stories—all set in motion by the appearance of a dead woman's body and the need to know how it came to be and who she thought she was—is the unfinished insensible (raped and unrapeable, scandalized and unshameable, blindsided and omnipotent), speaking through a dismal plot: *still here* and *not yet*.

Acknowledgments

I would like first to thank my colleagues in the Princeton and Yale English Departments, whose early insights and support were so invaluable to this project. Special acknowledgment goes to April Alliston, Anne Cheng, Maria DiBattista, Reneé Fox, Diana Fuss, Simon Gikandi, Bill Gleason, Patricia Gugliemi, Jeff Nunokawa, Starry Schor, Alyson Shaw, and Susan Wolfson at Princeton; and Jill Campbell, Jacqueline Goldsby, David Kastan, Stefanie Markovits, Claude Rawson, Joseph Roach, Katie Trumpener, Michael Warner, and Ruth Yeazell at Yale. I am eternally indebted to Claudia Johnson and Deborah Nord, the models of so many virtues. The friendship and wisdom of Adrienne Brown, Sophie Gee, Meredith Martin, and Jacqueline Shin have sustained me throughout this process. The gracious company of GerShun Avilez, Shital Pravinchandra, and Brian Walsh provided crucial support and solidarity. This book could not have been completed without my favorite New Yorkers: the staff, students, and faculty of the NYU English Department, whose originality, humanity, and endless funds of gallows humor have kept me and my work afloat. Particular mention is owed to Thomas Augst, Christopher Cannon, Juliet Fleming, Elaine Freedgood, Maureen McLane, Mary Mezzano, Patricia Okoh-Esene, Catherine Robson, Lytle Shaw, and Jini Kim Watson for targeted support and advice. Paula McDowell and Gabrielle Starr provided immaculate feedback and the warmest encouragement. Without Julia Jarcho and Sonya Posmentier all would be lost. Very special thanks to Tanya Schmidt, whose research, editorial, and translation skills were a salvation.

Several institutions and groups have enabled the evolution of this project. For their enormously helpful feedback and enlivening conversation, I want to thank my interlocutors at Columbia, Harvard, the University of Chicago, the University of Maryland, Lehigh University, the University of Pennsylvania, Princeton, Yale, Rutgers, and NYU. The organizers and members of the American and Canadian Societies for Eighteenth-Century Studies, Columbia Faculty Seminar in Eighteenth-Century Culture, and the Jane Austen Society of North America have been crucial sounding boards and sources of inspiration. I also want to thank the editors and readers at *ELH*, *Eighteenth-Century Fiction*, and *PMLA* for their exceptional guidance and critique. Portions of this book have appeared in *Eighteenth-Century Fiction* and *PMLA*, and I am grateful to the editors for their permission to use that material here. Special mention is owed to the generosity and encouragement of the following individuals: Scott Black, Jenny Davidson, Helen Deutsch, Joseph Drury, Frances Ferguson, Lynn Festa, Jonathan Flatley, Stephanie Hershinow, Lauren Kopajtic, Jonathan Kramnick, Kathleen Lubey, Sandra Macpherson, and Samuel Otter. The time and resources to write this book were made possible by the generosity of New York University, the NYU Center for the Humanities, Yale University, the Woodrow Wilson National Fellowship Foundation, and the New York Public Library. The entire team at Stanford University Press has been nothing short of remarkable. I owe a world of thanks to Emily-Jane Cohen for her galvanizing confidence in the project, to Faith Wilson Stein for her meticulous shepherding of it until the end, and to Jessica Ling and Joe Abbott for their patient exertions on my behalf. I cannot express gratitude enough to my impeccable readers, Sarah Tindal Kareem and Deidre Lynch, who took such care in helping me to make this book better.

Finally, I want to thank my family: Mandy, Scott, Justin, Jeremy, and Buddy Tachiki; Emelia Miguel, Trevor and Talulah Bridge; my mother, Jong Sook Noh, and the other Korean line-dancing ladies of Newport News; and my late mother-in-law, the peerless and terribly missed Janice M. Bridge. To Colin and Delia: it takes big hearts to live with someone immersed in unfeeling. I love you so much, and the next book is going to be about goodness!

Note on Citations

References to several primary works are made parenthetically, using the abbreviated titles below. For philosophical texts the abbreviated title is followed by numerals indicating internal divisions such as book, part, chapter, section, and so forth, with page numbers preceded by a colon. For examples, a reference to book 2, chapter 21, section 64, page 277 of Locke's *Essay Concerning Human Understanding* will appear as *EHU* 2.21.64: 277; and to part 4, axiom 1, proposition 50, page 574 of Spinoza's *Ethics* as *E* 4.A1.P50: 574.

All references to Jane Austen texts are to *The Cambridge Edition of the Works of Jane Austen* (Cambridge: Cambridge University Press, 2005–8) and are abbreviated by title.

References to Descartes's writings are to *Descartes: Selected Philosophical Writings*, trans. John Cottingham, Robert Stoothoff, and Dugald Murdoch (Cambridge: Cambridge University Press, 1988).

CW Collected Works of Oliver Goldsmith*. Edited by Arthur Friedman. 5 vols. Oxford: Oxford University Press, 1966.

E Baruch Spinoza, *Ethics*. In *The Collected Works of Spinoza*. Vol. 1. Edited and translated by Edwin Curley. Princeton, NJ: Princeton University Press, 1985.

EHU John Locke, *An Essay Concerning Human Understanding*. Edited by Peter H. Nidditch. Oxford: Clarendon, 1975.

EL Thomas Hobbes, *The Elements of Law, Natural and Politic*. Edited by Ferdinand Tönnies. London: Simpkin, Marshall, 1889.

EM Jane Austen, *Emma*. Edited by Richard Cronin and Dorothy McMillan. Cambridge: Cambridge University Press, 2005.

EP Thomas Hobbes, *Elements of Philosophy*. Edited by William Molesworth. Vol. 1 of *The English Works of Thomas Hobbes of Malmesbury*. London: John Bohn, 1839.

EPM David Hume, *An Enquiry Concerning the Principles of Morals*. Edited by Tom L. Beauchamp. Oxford: Clarendon Press, 1998.

L Thomas Hobbes, *Leviathan: The English and Latin Texts*. Edited by Noel Malcolm. Oxford: Oxford University Press, 2012. Vols. 3–5 of the Clarendon Edition of the Works of Thomas Hobbes.

M Descartes, *Meditations on First Philosophy*. In *Descartes: Selected Philosophical Writings*. Translated by John Cottingham, Robert Stoothoff, and Dugald Murdoch, 73–122. Cambridge: Cambridge University Press, 1988.

MP Jane Austen, *Mansfield Park*. Edited by John Wiltshire. Cambridge: Cambridge University Press, 2005.

NA Jane Austen, *Northanger Abbey*. Edited by Barbara M. Benedict and Deirdre Le Faye. Cambridge: Cambridge University Press, 2006.

P Jane Austen, *Persuasion*. Edited by Janet Todd and Antje Blank. Cambridge: Cambridge University Press, 2006.

PP Jane Austen, *Pride and Prejudice*. Edited by Pat Rogers. Cambridge: Cambridge University Press, 2006.

PS Descartes, *The Passions of the Soul*. In *Descartes: Selected Philosophical Writings*. Translated by John Cottingham, Robert Stoothoff, and Dugald Murdoch, 218–38. Cambridge: Cambridge University Press, 1988.

SS Jane Austen, *Sense and Sensibility*. Edited by Edward Copeland. Cambridge: Cambridge University Press, 2006.

T David Hume, *A Treatise of Human Nature*. Edited by David Fate Norton and Mary J. Norton. Oxford: Oxford University Press, 2000.

TMS Adam Smith, *The Theory of Moral Sentiments*. Edited by Knud Haakonssen. Cambridge: Cambridge University Press, 2002.

Notes

Introduction: The Bartleby Problem

1. See especially Sianne Ngai's formulation of "the Bartlebyan question of suspended agency" in *Ugly Feelings* (Cambridge, MA: Harvard University Press, 2005), 33.

2. See James Fowler on the " 'flickering' effect" between *prude* and *vertueuse* in *romans libertins*, where "*prude* can function as an antonym of *vertueuse*, or as a virtual synonym." James Fowler, *The Libertine's Nemesis: The Prude in "Clarissa" and the Roman Libertin* (London: Maney, 2011), 4.

3. *Selected Letters of Samuel Richardson*, ed. John Carroll (Oxford: Clarendon, 1964), Letter 60.1, 253.

4. Histories of the English novel constitute an archive nearly as rich and heterogeneous as fiction itself. The post-Watt era alone (crucially announced by Michael McKeon's *The Origins of the English Novel* and Nancy Armstrong's *Desire and Domestic Fiction*, and elaborated in their subsequent studies) has given rise to numerous methodologies and principles of literary studies. A sampling of such diversity can be found in Margaret Doody's *The True Story of the Novel*; Lennard Davis's *Factual Fictions*; Deidre Shauna Lynch's *Economy of Character*; Srinivas Aravamudan's *Enlightenment Orientalism*; and Franco Moretti's *Maps, Graphs, Trees*. For a range of approaches to eighteenth-century fiction see John Bender's *Imagining the Penitentiary*; Barbara Benedict's *Framing Feeling*; Rosalind Ballaster's *Seductive Forms*; Ruth Perry's *Novel Relations*; John Richetti's *Popular Fiction Before Richardson*; Patricia Meyer Spacks's *Novel Beginnings*; and William Warner's *Licensing Entertainment*. For background see W. B. Carnochan's " 'A Matter Discutable': The Rise of the Novel," *Eighteenth-Century Fiction* 12, no. 2–3 (2000): 167–84.

5. Nicholas Paige, *Before Fiction: The Ancien Régime of the Novel* (Philadelphia: University of Pennsylvania Press, 2011), xii–xiii.

6. See especially Macalester Bell's *Hard Feelings: The Moral Psychology of Contempt* (Oxford: Oxford University Press, 2013); William Ian Miller's *Anatomy of Disgust* (Cambridge, MA: Harvard University Press, 1997); and Ngai's *Ugly Feelings*.

7. See C. B. Macpherson's pivotal argument that possessive individualism is modernity's reconceptualization of persons from contributors to a moral and social whole to independent proprietors of their own capacities. Macpherson presents Hobbes's

philosophy as premised on the establishment of a possessive market society, in which individuals are forced into a ceaseless grab for power. While this totalizing structure of competition, in which all land and labor are subject to market forces, was still in the making in seventeenth-century England, Macpherson argues that its fundamental transformation of social life had become clear enough to Hobbes and to others. In particular, wage-earning had already substantially replaced more paternal forms of relation between workers and owners. C. B. Macpherson, *The Political Theory of Possessive Individualism: Hobbes to Locke* (Oxford: Clarendon, 1962), 61–68.

8. Victoria Kahn calls the publication of *Leviathan* "a watershed in the construction of the new political subject," that is, one who believes in the possibility of rewriting their political obligations. "*Leviathan* was the turning point because it emphasized the fictional dimension of contract to a greater degree than before, because it offended contemporary beliefs on both sides of the political divide, and because it was more powerfully argued than any other account of contractual obligation." Victoria Kahn, *Wayward Contracts: The Crisis of Political Obligation in England, 1640–1674* (Princeton, NJ: Princeton University Press, 2004), 6.

9. Giorgio Agamben, "Bartleby, or On Contingency," in *Potentialities: Collected Essays in Philosophy*, ed. and trans. Daniel Heller-Roazen (Stanford: Stanford University Press, 2000): 243–71, 253–54.

10. René Descartes, *Meditations on First Philosophy*, in *Descartes: Selected Philosophical Writings*, trans. John Cottingham, Robert Stoothoff, and Dugald Murdoch (Cambridge: Cambridge University Press, 1988), 73–112, 100 (hereafter cited as *M*).

11. George Eliot, *Daniel Deronda*, ed. Terence Cave (London: Penguin, 1995), 253.

12. See, e.g., Lauren Berlant's account of "the theatrical or scenic structure of fantasy" and the recognition of "its fundamentally social character." Lauren Berlant, *Desire/Love* (Brooklyn: Punctum, 2012), 8. Berlant's elegant study attends specifically to the encounter staged by desire and its "drive to be embodied and reiterated," or what she calls "desire's formalism" (20).

13. Michael Frazer, *Enlightenment of Sympathy: Justice and Moral Sentiments in the Eighteenth Century and Today* (Oxford: Oxford University Press, 2010), 4.

14. See Ngai's broader argument that modernity calls for a new repertoire of emotions: "in the transnational stage of capitalism that defines our contemporary moment, our emotions no longer link up as securely as they once did with the models of social action and transformation theorized by Aristotle, Thomas Hobbes, and others under the signs of relatively unambiguous emotions like anger or fear" (*Ugly Feelings*, 5). As tantalizing as such a call for a modernist theory of emotions may be, earlier philosophies of the passions still contribute to a contemporary understanding of affects. For starters, the elaborate taxonomies of feeling that so occupy Western philosophers after Aristotle grapple precisely with the instability of phenomena such as anger and fear and their relation to each other and to other emotions. For studies of earlier theories of the passions that emphasize their ongoing significance, see especially the interdisciplinary contributions of Miranda Burgess, Antonio Damasio, Daniel Gross, Jonathan Israel, Victoria Kahn, Catherine Malabou, Martha Nussbaum, Adela Pinch, Adam Potkay, Jesse Prinz, and Barbara Rosenwein. See also Amanda Bailey

and Mario DiGangi, eds., *Affect Theory and Early Modern Texts: Politics, Ecologies, and Form* (New York: Palgrave, 2017).

15. A short list of influential scholars of eighteenth-century sensibility includes G. J. Barker-Benfield, Michael Bell, Markman Ellis, David Fairer, Paul Goring, John Mullan, Christopher Nagle, Thomas Pfau, Mark Phillips, William Reddy, G. S. Rousseau, Geoffrey Sill, Gillian Skinner, Janet Todd, and Ann Jessie Van Sant. Specific studies are treated throughout this book, especially in Chapter 3.

16. Catherine Gallagher, *Nobody's Story: The Vanishing Acts of Women Writers in the Marketplace, 1670–1920* (Berkeley: University of California Press, 1994), 168.

17. Catherine Gallagher, "The Rise of Fictionality," in *The Novel*, vol. 1, *History, Geography, and Culture*, ed. Franco Moretti (Princeton, NJ: Princeton University Press, 2006), 336–63, 351, 349, 346.

18. See Adela Pinch's thought experiment in her reading of "really" and "actually" in *Daniel Deronda*: "To focus on the way characters in novels—in which there are no actual people—may become 'real' to each other, without being shockingly 'actual,' may serve as a model for how fictional characters may become real (but not 'actual') to readers (as in this thought-experiment: 'Adela was reading *Daniel Deronda*. In an hour or so she actually met Deronda')." Adela Pinch, *Thinking About Other People in Nineteenth-Century British Writing* (Cambridge: Cambridge University Press, 2010), 149.

19. Rae Greiner, *Sympathetic Realism in Nineteenth-Century British Fiction* (Baltimore: Johns Hopkins University Press, 2012), 2–3.

20. Henri Bergson, *Laughter: An Essay on the Meaning of the Comic* (Mansfield Center, CT: Martino, 2014), 5.

21. Oliver Goldsmith, *She Stoops to Conquer: or, The Mistakes of a Night. A Comedy*, in *Collected Works of Oliver Goldsmith*, ed. Arthur Friedman, 5 vols. (Oxford: Oxford University Press, 1966), 5:85–217, 154, 108.

22. See Helen Thompson's influential critique of conjugal authority in her *Ingenuous Subjection: Compliance and Power in the Eighteenth-Century Domestic Novel* (Philadelphia: University of Pennsylvania Press, 2005).

23. See Ann Thomson's detailed account of the contemporary shock at Hobbes's "denial of incorporeal substance, as it entailed great problems for the nature of the deity and the explanation of thought in humans." Ann Thomson, *Bodies of Thought: Science, Religion, and the Soul in the Early Enlightenment* (Cambridge: Cambridge University Press, 2008), 47.

24. Thomas A. Spragens Jr., *The Politics of Motion: The World of Thomas Hobbes* (Lexington: University Press of Kentucky, 1973), 71. See Daniela Coli's summary: "All is motion in Hobbes's philosophy, and at the root of his anthropology lies movement, from which arises all our passions, the aim of which is our personal pleasure, every individual being dominated by his own self-interest." Daniela Coli, "Hobbes's Revolution," in *Politics and the Passions, 1500–1850*, ed. Victoria Kahn, Neil Saccamano, and Daniela Coli (Princeton, NJ: Princeton University Press, 2006), 75–92, 81. See also Sara Landreth's fascinating "Breaking the Laws of Motion: Pneumatology and *Belles Lettres* in Eighteenth-Century Britain," *New Literary History* 43 (2012): 281–308.

25. See Jesse Prinz's definition of emotions as "perceptions (conscious or uncon-

scious) of patterned changes in the body." He writes, "At their core, emotions are more like judgments or thoughts than perceptions." Jesse Prinz, "Embodied Emotions," in *Thinking About Feeling: Contemporary Philosophers on Emotions*, ed. Robert C. Solomon (Oxford: Oxford University Press, 2004), 44–58, 45, 44. Solomon's volume makes clear the persistence of debate in contemporary philosophy about, in Prinz's words, what qualifies or "deserves to be called emotions" (50). See also Solomon's earlier *What Is an Emotion? Classic and Contemporary Readings* (Oxford: Oxford University Press, 2003).

26. Susan James, *Passion and Action: The Emotions in Seventeenth-Century Philosophy* (Oxford: Clarendon, 1997), 131. My study, like so many others, is indebted to James's illuminating exposition of Hobbes's theories of emotions and to her discussion of the discourse of passion and action more generally in early philosophy.

27. Hume, while noting that Hobbes and Locke "maintained the selfish system of morals [but] lived irreproachable lives" (*EPM* App. 2.3: 91), nonetheless casts Hobbes as either an insensible or a lax theorist: "What heart one must be possessed of who professes such principles, and who feels no internal sentiment that belies so pernicious a theory . . . what degree of affection and benevolence he can bear to a species, whom he represents under such odious colours, and supposes so little susceptible of gratitude or any return of affection. Or if we should not ascribe these principles wholly to a corrupted heart, we must, at least, account for them from the most careless and precipitate examination" (*EPM* App. 2.1: 90).

28. See Frazer's argument that Smith's theory "fully appreciates the distinctions among individuals in a way that Hume's public-interest-based theory fails to do" (*Enlightenment of Sympathy*, 90).

29. On Melville's engagement with Descartes see Branka Arsić's chapter "Bartleby or the Cloud," in *Passive Constitutions; or, 7½ Times Bartleby* (Stanford: Stanford University Press, 2007), 155–66.

30. Hume at first draws on the metaphor of the eye that cannot see itself, but because that analogy still assumes the existence of an eyeball, he moves on to the less durable metaphor of the mind as a theater, still qualifying that "the comparison of the theatre must not mislead us. They are the successive perceptions only, that constitute the mind; nor have we the most distant notion of the place, where these scenes are represented, or of the materials, of which it is compos'd" (*T* 2.4.6.3–4: 165).

31. Isabel Rivers observes of the ambivalence toward Hobbes maintained by eighteenth-century philosophical culture: "It seems fair to say that the freethinkers drew on aspects of Hobbes's treatment of religion and natural philosophy while discounting the uncongenial aspects of his moral and political thought." Isabel Rivers, *Reason, Grace, and Sentiment: A Study of the Language of Religion and Ethics in England, 1660–1780*, vol. 1, *Whichcote to Wesley* (Cambridge: Cambridge University Press, 2005), 21.

32. See Ruth Leys, "The Turn to Affect: A Critique," *Critical Inquiry* 37, no. 3 (2011): 434–72; Ruth Leys, "Critical Response II: Affect and Intention: A Reply to William E. Connolly," *Critical Inquiry* 37, no. 4 (2011): 799–805; and Ruth Leys,

"Critical Response III: Facts and Moods: Reply to My Critics," *Critical Inquiry* 38, no. 4 (2012): 882–91.

33. Charles Altieri, "Critical Response II: Affect, Intentionality, and Cognition: A Response to Ruth Leys," *Critical Inquiry* 38, no. 4 (2012): 878–81, 880.

34. Leys's intentionalist account of emotions calls explicitly for a narrative model: "the moment one abandons the Tomkins-Ekman [nonintentionalist] paradigm in favor of some kind of intentionalist interpretation of the affects, one finds oneself forced to provide thick descriptions of life experiences of the kind that are familiar to anthropologists and novelists but are widely held to be inimical to science." Leys, "The Turn," 471. See also Leys, "Critical Response II"; and Leys, "Critical Response III."

35. Miranda Burgess, "On Being Moved: Sympathy, Mobility, and Narrative Form," *Poetics Today* 32, no. 2 (2011): 289–321, 294.

36. See Gilbert Ryle on why affective "tendencies or propensities," such as vanity and indolence, "cannot be construed as expressing categorical narratives of episodes" (85). In Ryle's analysis, dispositions are not occurrences in the way that "feelings" (pangs, twinges, aches) are. Thus, dispositions cannot serve as causes even though they present a causal explanation in which behavioral signs (attention-seeking and boasting) signify "momentary actualisations" (87). For example, a certain remark (x) causes a man to boast (y) because of his preexisting vanity (z). Gilbert Ryle, *The Concept of Mind* (1949; Chicago: University of Chicago Press, 2000), 83–93.

37. See Jonathan Kramnick's *Actions and Objects from Hobbes to Richardson* (Stanford: Stanford University Press, 2010), which emphasizes the externalism of Hobbes's theory of causation. Kramnick argues that Hobbes's grounding of human action in interior states like appetite and fear has obscured the diffusiveness of his theory, in which those very mental states originate in numberless external events and objects.

38. Daniel M. Gross, *The Secret History of Emotion from Aristotle's "Rhetoric" to Modern Brain Science* (Chicago: University of Chicago Press, 2006), 80.

39. Jonathan Lamb, *The Evolution of Sympathy in the Long Eighteenth Century* (London: Pickering and Chatto, 2009), 2. To my regret, I only learned of Lamb's remarkable study in the final stages of preparing this book.

40. See Michael Betancourt, *Glitch Art in Theory and Practice* (New York: Routledge, 2016).

41. Cees Leijenhorst, "Sense and Nonsense About Sense: Hobbes and the Aristotelians on Sense Perception and Imagination," *The Cambridge Companion to Hobbes's Leviathan*, ed. Patricia Springborg (Cambridge: Cambridge University Press, 2007), 89.

42. Distinctions among feelings, emotions, affects, and so on—untenable as they are—have become part of the debate about affect studies. As Julie Ellison writes, "One of the reasons why it is difficult to stabilize the meanings of terms like 'sensibility,' 'sympathy,' and 'sentiment' is that they not only vary according to their usage in distinct historical contexts but they also change as scholars seek an integrated understanding of emotions." Julie Ellison, *Cato's Tears and the Making of Anglo-American Emotion* (Chicago: University of Chicago Press, 1999), 5. Even within a very localized

context, terminology is difficult, if not impossible, to pin down. See Thomas Dixon's observation that "affective discourses and terminologies in the eighteenth century were too complex for it to be possible to discern in them any single attitude to human passions (or to 'emotions' or 'feeling' or 'sentiment')." Thomas Dixon, *From Passions to Emotion: The Creation of a Secular Psychological Category* (Cambridge: Cambridge University Press, 2003), 66. For those who work on the history and philosophy of emotions, such slipperiness of terms is both an unavoidable frustration and a rich subject of study in itself. On the changing discourses see Amélie Oksenberg Rorty, "From Passions to Emotions and Sentiments," *Philosophy* 57, no. 220 (1982): 159–72. See also Burgess's engagement with the critique of emotions in affect studies ("a skeptical post-psychoanalytic rethinking of the subject of emotion itself") and "the heterogeneity inscribed *within* the category of affect," especially as articulated by Eve Kosofsky Sedgwick (Burgess, "On Being Moved," 293, 291).

43. Adrian Johnson and Catherine Malabou, *Self and Emotional Life: Philosophy, Psychoanalysis, and Neuroscience* (New York: Columbia University Press, 2013), 36.

44. Where Miller reads Hobbes as "clear that . . . contempt is a passion, not simply the absence of affect" (214), I am treating the "absence of affect" as what is neither clear nor simple.

45. Herman Melville, "Bartleby, the Scrivener: A Story of Wall-Street," in *The Piazza Tales and Other Prose Pieces, 1839–1860*, ed. Harrison Hayford, Alma A. MacDougall, and G. Thomas Tanselle (Evanston, IL: Northwestern University Press; Chicago: Newberry Library, 1987), 13–45, 19.

46. Compare Bartleby's nonpreference to Nippers, who "knew not what he wanted. Or, if he wanted any thing, it was to be rid of a scrivener's table altogether" (17). Incidentally, Ngai focuses on Bartleby, but the "negative," "nasty," and "ignoble" feelings under examination apply easily to the "restive" and "insolent" Nippers, whose "nervousness," "diseased ambition," and "irritable, brandy-like disposition" readily line up with "ugly feelings" (Ngai, *Ugly Feelings*, 3, 7; Melville, "Bartleby," 17, 18).

47. See Ralph James Savarese's reading of Bartleby's "hopeless metabolism" in the "catastrophe of capitalist labor practices [that] has made him sick." Ralph James Savarese, "Nervous Wrecks and Ginger-Nuts: Bartleby at a Standstill," *Leviathan* 5, no. 2 (2003): 19–49, 37.

48. In the same paragraph in which he accuses Bartleby of an aggravating "passive resistance," the lawyer rationalizes that "his eccentricities are involuntary" (23). See also the "little, dried-up man" in chapter 10 of *The Confidence-Man*, "who looked as if he never dined" and is "naturally numb in his sensibilities." Herman Melville, *The Confidence-Man: His Masquerade*, ed. Harrison Hayford, Hershel Parker, and G. Thomas Tanselle (Evanston, IL: Northwestern University Press, 2002), 53.

49. Daniel Heller-Roazen, *The Inner Touch: Archaeology of a Sensation* (Brooklyn: Zone, 2007), 133.

50. The image of the millstone is another link to Hobbesian insensibility. It features in Job 41, in the description of the Leviathan: "His heart is as firm as a stone; yea, as hard as a piece of the nether millstone." The lower millstone is the fixed and

hard stone on which the upper stone revolves on a shaft. See also Deleuze on Melville's characters who are "presque stupides, créatures d'innocence et de pureté, frappes d'une faiblesse constitutive, mais aussi d'une étrange beauté, pétrifiés par nature, et qui préfèrent . . . pas de volonté de néant (le 'négativisme' hypocondriaque). Ils ne peuvent survivre qu'en devenant Pierre, en niant le volonté, et se sanctifient dans cette suspension." Gilles Deleuze, "Bartleby, ou la Formule," in *Critique et clinique* (Paris: Minuit, 1993), 89–114, 102.

51. See Bell, *Hard Feelings*, on Aristotle's *megalopsychos*, or great-souled man: "Non-*megalopsychoi* are not worthy of his attention—they cannot harm him, and he is emotionally unaffected by harms that befall them. The attitude the *megalopsychos* evinces is one of haughty indifference, and it is reasonable to interpret this indifference as a kind of passive contempt" (141).

52. As Ruttenburg observes, "theoretical readings have cut closer to the bone in disclosing the metaphysical import of Bartleby's aberrance, while Americanist scholarship has targeted those cultural-historical specificities of context which identify the aberration as such, often through a defamiliarizing exploration of normative social practices in relation to which the scrivener is seen as both marginal and representative." Nancy Ruttenburg, " 'The Silhouette of a Content': 'Bartleby' and American Literary Specificity," in *Melville and Aesthetics*, ed. Samuel Otter and Geoffrey Sanborn (New York: Palgrave, 2011), 137–55, 139.

53. See also Derrida's sense of touching as "limitrophe": "Le toucher en tout cas reste ainsi limitrophe, il touche ce qu'il ne touche pas, il ne touche pas, il s'abstient de toucher à ce qu'il touche et, dans une abstinence qui le retient au cœur de son désire et de son besoin, dans une inhibition qui constitue en vérité son appétit, il mange sans manger ce dont il se nourrit, touchant, sans y toucher." Jacques Derrida, *Le toucher, Jean-Luc Nancy* (Paris: Galilée, 2000), 82.

54. Arsić, *Passive Constitutions*, 55.

55. The lawyer recounts earlier repulses; for example, he asks Bartleby "to put his finger" on the knot tied around some of his papers, presumably in hopes of bringing their fingers to touch through the "bit of red tape" (26).

56. Aristotle, *Metaphysics*, trans. W. D. Ross, in *The Complete Works of Aristotle*, ed. Jonathan Barnes, vol. 2 (Princeton, NJ: Princeton University Press, 1985), 12.6.1071b13–15.

57. Sean Gaston, "The Impossibility of Sympathy," *The Eighteenth Century* 51, no. 1/2 (2010): 129–52, 139. According to Gaston, philosophy's search for the untouchable as a concept that unifies individual moral judgment and the organization of a moral society "can be traced at least back to Hobbes" and specifically to *Leviathan* as "at once a very serious response to the philosophical, political, and religious events of the 1640s and a utopian tract" that idealizes the social benefits of sovereignty (141).

58. Herman Melville, *The Confidence-Man: His Masquerade*, ed. Harrison Hayford, Hershel Parker, and G. Thomas Tanselle (Evanston, IL: Northwestern University Press, 2002).

59. Kareem theorizes wonder as "a durational affect," constituting a double experience *at* and *about* a "verisimilar marvelous" object, such that one experiences recognition and estrangement, enchantment and disenchantment, suspense and admiration. See Sarah Tindal Kareem, *Eighteenth-Century Fiction and the Reinvention of Wonder* (Oxford: Oxford University Press, 2014), 8–10, 42.

60. Phineas Taylor Barnum, *The Life of P. T. Barnum: Written by Himself, Including His Golden Rules for Money-Making* (Buffalo: Courier, 1888), 61.

61. Lisa Zunshine, *Why We Read Fiction: Theory of Mind and the Novel* (Columbus: Ohio State University Press, 2006), 6.

62. Michael Orsini and Joyce Davidson, "Introduction: Critical Autism Studies: Notes on an Emerging Field," in *Worlds of Autism: Across the Spectrum of Neurological Difference*, ed. Joyce Davidson and Michael Orsini (Minneapolis: University of Minnesota Press, 2013), 1–28, 10.

63. See Amit Pinchevski, "Bartleby's Autism: Wandering Along Incommunicability," *Cultural Critique* 78 (2011): 27–59, 39. In one of many insightful lines of analysis, Pinchevski discusses the gendered history of writing machines: "The manual scrivener almost preempts the technology of writing with his repetitive, mechanical toil, to the point where it is no longer clear whether he is a copyist or a typewriter" (42).

64. A recent move in medical ethics to understand autism as "affective difference" rather than "affective deficit" asks us to regard the insensible in yet another light. Instead of "an absence of emotionality," autism might be recognized as "an alternative sensitivity or sensual perceptionality" to neurotypical functioning. See Jenny Bergenmar, Hanna Bertilsdotter Rosqvist, and Ann-Sofie Lönnggren, "Autism and the Question of the Human," *Literature and Medicine* 33, no. 1 (2015): 202–21, 206.

65. See Anne-Lise François, *Open Secrets: The Literature of Uncounted Experience* (Stanford: Stanford University Press, 2008).

66. Jean-Jacques Rousseau, *Émile, or On Education*, trans. Allan Bloom (New York: Basic Books, 1979), 61.

67. Nancy Yousef, *Romantic Intimacy* (Stanford: Stanford University Press, 2013), 8.

Chapter 1. A Brief History of the Prude

1. "The Triumph of Beauty: or, The Prude Metamorphos'd" (London: C. Corbett, 1740).

2. See Festa on how the anthropomorphic object "is both a symptom of humanity's overweening drive to refashion the world in its own likeness and a sign of its blind dispossession before things and forces that exceed its comprehension: a testament both to enduring bafflement before the enigmatic face of the world, and to the unending endeavor to recast it into intelligible form." Lynn Festa, *Fiction Without Humanity: Person, Animal, Thing in Early Enlightenment Literature and Culture* (Philadelphia: University of Pennsylvania Press, forthcoming).

3. Anonymous, *The Prude: A Novel by a Young Lady*, pts. 1–3 (London: J. Roberts, 1724–25), 3.80. See my entry in *The Cambridge Guide to the Eighteenth-Century*

Novel, 1660–1820, ed. April London (Cambridge: Cambridge University Press, forthcoming).

4. J. Paul Hunter, *Before Novels: The Cultural Contexts of Eighteenth-Century English Fiction* (New York: Norton, 1990), 26.

5. See especially Paula Backscheider, *Elizabeth Singer Rowe and the Development of the English Novel* (Baltimore: Johns Hopkins University Press, 2013); Paula Backscheider and John Richetti, *Popular Fiction by Women, 1660–1730* (Oxford: Clarendon, 1996); and Susan Staves, *A Literary History of Women's Writing in Britain, 1660–1789* (Cambridge: Cambridge University Press, 2006).

6. See chapter 2, "Seventeenth-Century Foundations," in Cheryl Turner's *Living by the Pen: Women Writers in the Eighteenth Century* (London: Routledge, 1992), 18–30.

7. The prude testifies to the porousness between English and French writing. For example, Voltaire's *La Prude* (1747) is an adaptation of Wycherley's *Plain Dealer* (1676), which was influenced by Molière. See Marvin A. Carlson, *Voltaire and the Theatre of the Eighteenth Century* (Westport, CT: Greenwood Press, 1998), 52. See also Richard Flecknoe's rewrite of Molière in *The Damoiselles a la Mode* (1667).

8. Elizabeth Susan Wahl, *Invisible Relations: Representations of Female Intimacy in the Age of Enlightenment* (Stanford: Stanford University Press, 1999), 181.

9. Eugenia Zuroski Jenkins and Patrick Coleman, "Introduction: The Sense of Humour," *Eighteenth-Century Fiction* 26, no. 4 (2014): 505–14, 509. See also Simon Dickie's *Cruelty and Laughter: Forgotten Comic Literature and the Unsentimental Eighteenth Century* (Chicago: University of Chicago Press, 2011).

10. Samuel Boyse, *Miscellaneous Works, Serious and Humorous: In Verse and Prose. Design'd For the Amusement of the Fair Sex* (London: 1740). See April Alliston's reading of Germaine de Staël's *Corinne* (1807), emphasizing the heroine's performative and linguistic dexterity as an "improvisatrice," in April Alliston, *Virtue's Faults: Correspondences in Eighteenth-Century British and French Women's Fiction* (Stanford: Stanford University Press, 1996).

11. Rebecca Armstrong, *Ovid and His Love Poetry* (London: Duckworth, 2005), 56. For the Latin text (*illa uerecundis lux est praebenda puellis, / qua timidus latebras speret habere pudor* [1.5.7–8]), see J. C. McKeown, *Ovid: Amores*, vol. 1, *Text and Prolegomena* (Liverpool: Francis Cairns, 1987); and *Ovid: Amores*, vol. 2, *A Commentary on Book One* (Leeds: Francis Cairns, 1989). Armstrong's translation can be compared to John Barsby's standard English translation ("That is the light to offer to shy girls, / in which their timid modesty may hope to find a hiding-place"), in *Ovid's Amores: Book One* (London: Oxford University Press, 1973); and to the Loeb edition ("It was such a light as shrinking maids should have / whose timid modesty hopes to hide away"), in *Ovid I, Heroides and Amores*, Loeb Classical Library, trans. Grant Showerman (Cambridge, MA: Harvard University Press, 1914); see also ibid., 2nd ed., revised by G. P. Goold, 1977.

12. Armstrong, *Ovid and His Love Poetry*, 57. See McKeown, *Ovid: Amores* (*cumque ita pugnaret tamquam quae uincere nollet, / uicta est non aegre proditione sua*

[1.5.15–16]); Barsby, *Ovid's Amores* ("But, since she was struggling like one who had no will to conquer, / she was conquered without difficulty by self-betrayal"); and the Loeb edition ("Even while thus she struggled, as one who would not overcome, / was she overcome—and 'twas not hard—by her own betrayal").

13. For more on the coquette see Shelley King and Yaël Schlick, eds., *Refiguring the Coquette: Essays on Culture and Coquetry* (Lewisburg, PA: Bucknell University Press, 2008).

14. Felicity Nussbaum, *The Brink of All We Hate: English Satires on Women, 1660–1750* (Lexington: University Press of Kentucky, 1984), 139. Nussbaum's study examines, in particular, the myths of "the permissive female or whore, the powerful Amazon, the learned lady, the ideal woman, the angel" (4).

15. Jenny Davidson, *Hypocrisy and the Politics of Politeness: Manners and Morals from Locke to Austen* (Cambridge: Cambridge University Press, 2004), 11.

16. *Clélie, histoire romaine, seconde partie* (Paris: Augustin Courbé, 1655), livre premier, 233–34. See its famous inset map of emotions, *La carte du tendre.*

17. Ruth Yeazell, *Fictions of Modesty: Women and Courtship in the English Novel* (Chicago: University of Chicago Press, 1991). Yeazell highlights the "confusions and contradictions" that inhere in modesty as a cultural practice in the eighteenth and nineteenth centuries. Examining modesty "not as a set of rules but as a series of changing responses" to women's roles, especially as wives, she argues that novels, especially, "could accommodate" what "her modesty might superficially appear to deny" (ix).

18. Jean-Claude Bologne, *Histoire de la pudeur* (Paris: O. Organ, 1986), 10.

19. "C'est que je treuve le mariage une chose tout à fait choquante. Comment est-ce qu'on peut souffrir la pensée de coucher contre un homme vraiment nu?" Molière, *Les précieuses ridicules. Comédie, œuvres complètes.* 2 vols. (Paris: Gallimard, 1971), 2:247–87 (scène 4, p. 270; my translation).

20. *An Epistle to the most Learned Doctor W—d—d; From a Prude, that was unfortunately Metamorphos'd on Saturday, December 29, 1722* (London: J. Roberts, 1723).

21. Henry Fielding, *Tom Jones* (1749; Oxford: Oxford University Press, 1996), 58.

22. See Ian Watt's discussion of "Fielding's avoidance of the subjective dimension" and his refusal "to go too deep into the minds of his characters" in Ian Watt, *The Rise of the Novel* (Berkeley: University of California Press, 1957), 273.

23. See Jesse Molesworth's reading of *Amelia* as "a radical rethinking of the epistemological terrain of the novel." Molesworth characterizes *Amelia* and *Tristram Shandy* as "Humean fictions," or "anti-fictional fictions, works that, paradoxically, reject the assumptions necessarily underpinning them." Jesse Molesworth, *Chance and the Eighteenth-Century Novel: Realism, Probability, Magic* (Cambridge: Cambridge University Press, 2010), 170, 175.

24. *Œuvres complètes de J. de La Bruyère: Les caractères: I–XII* (Paris: Garnier frères, 1876). See also Christian Biet, "Du critère de la misogynie appliqué au XVIIe siècle: Le cas de La Bruyère," *Les cahiers du GRIF* 47, no. 1 (1993): 25–36.

25. See La Bruyère on la femme's control over manner and speech (*de maintien et de parole*) (78). See James Fowler, *The Libertine's Nemesis: The Prude in "Clarissa" and*

the Roman Libertin (London: Maney, 2011) on how the libertine's spectrum always collapses into a single position: "*(for all her Prudery) a mere Helen.*" "The Metamorphosis of a Prude: A Poem" (London: M. Cooper, 1756), 4. See also Michel Baron, *Coquette et la fausse prude: Comédie* (Paris: Thomas Guillain, 1687).

26. Fowler, *The Libertine's Nemesis*, 9.

27. Eliza Haywood, *Female Spectator* 1, no. 1 (April 1744): 32.

28. See Erica Harth's *Cartesian Women: Versions and Subversions of Rational Discourse in the Old Regime* (Ithaca, NY: Cornell University Press, 1992). See also Wahl, *Invisible Relations*, on the poem "Aux précieuses," which sends the offenders to a brothel, where they use their books as dildos (202–3).

29. Molière, *Les femmes savantes. Comédie, œuvres complètes*, 2 vols. (Paris: Gallimard, 1971), 1:973–1072, 3.2.1023 (my translation). References are to act, scene, and page.

30. Molière formulates the spousal conflict over their daughter in terms of maternal dualism versus paternal monism:

> Je lui montrerai bien aux lois de qui des deux
> Les droits de la raison soumettent tous ses vœux;
> Et qui doit gouverner, ou sa mère, ou son père,
> Ou l'esprit, ou le corps; la forme, ou la matière.
>
> I will show her whose laws (yours or mine)
> Possess the rights of reason to subject her wishes
> And who should govern: her mother or her father,
> Spirit or body, form or matter.
>
> Molière, *Les femmes savantes*, 1:973–1072,
> 4.1.1043 (my translation)

31. As in Judith Butler's endlessly fertile theory of "the iconographic figure of the melancholic drag queen" (where "drag imitates the imitative structure of gender, revealing gender itself to be an imitation"), the prude does not authenticate female goodness but makes the performance of it bathetically visible. If, as Butler writes, "gender is produced as a ritualized repetition of conventions," then the rigidity of the prude's performances of modesty and virtue only highlight their utter conventionality. Judith Butler, *The Psychic Life of Power: Theories in Subjection* (Stanford: Stanford University Press, 1997), 144–45.

32. Susan Sontag, "Notes on Camp," *Partisan Review* 31, no. 4 (1964): 515–30, 522.

33. Judith Halberstam, *The Queer Art of Failure* (Durham, NC: Duke University Press, 2011), 88, 109.

34. J. Hillis Miller, "Narrative and History," *ELH* 41, no. 3 (1974): 455–73, 456. See also Rebecca Tierney-Hynes, *Novel Minds: Philosophers and Romance Readers, 1680–1740* (London: Palgrave, 2012).

35. Victoria Kahn, *Wayward Contracts: The Crisis of Political Obligation in England, 1640–1674* (Princeton, NJ: Princeton University Press, 2004), 135.

36. Aphra Behn, *Oroonoko: or, The Royal Slave. A True History. By Mrs. A. Behn* (London: William Canning, 1688), 2.

37. Françoise Jaouën, "Civility and the Novel: De Pure's *La prétieuse ou le mystère des ruelles*," *Yale French Studies* 92 (1997): 105–25, 106.

38. Wahl's translation (Wahl, *Invisible Relations*, 206).

39. Saint-Evremond, "La Prude et la précieuse, A Madame ***," *œuvres de Monsieur de Saint-Evremond*, 12 vols. (Paris: Barbin, 1753), 4:304–6, 305).

40. Nussbaum, *The Brink*, 4.

41. Abbé Michel de Pure, *La prétieuse ou le mystère des ruelles*, 2 vols., ed. Antoine Adam (1656–58; Paris: Droz, 1938–39), 61.

42. *An Epistle to the most Learned Doctor W—d—d*, 5.

43. *The Female Politician: Or the Statesman Unmask'd. A Novel* (London: J. Wilford, 1733), 28.

44. Joan DeJean, *Tender Geographies: Women and the Origins of the Novel in France* (New York: Columbia University Press, 1991). As Susan S. Lanser argues of the seventeenth and eighteenth centuries, "the Sapphic served the social imaginary as one way to confront challenges to the predictable workings of the universe." Representations of female intimacy thus "became a flash-point for epistemic upheavals that threatened to dismantle the order of things." Susan S. Lanser, *The Sexuality of History: Modernity and the Sapphic, 1565–1830* (Chicago: University of Chicago Press, 2014), 2.

45. "Metamorphosis of a Prude," 4. Carole Levin writes of Elizabeth I's forty-five-year reign as the "Virgin Queen": "her success as monarch was inextricably woven into her refusal to wed." The proof of female rule, Elizabeth also represented a "third sex": "both woman and man in one, both king and queen together, a male body politic in concept while a female body natural in practice." Carole Levin, *The Heart and Stomach of a King: Elizabeth I and the Politics of Sex and Power* (Philadelphia: University of Pennsylvania Press, 2013), 121. The queen was also known for her flounces: "Elizabeth's delight in gorgeous apparel . . . was notorious during her own [reign] and vital to her self-representation as monarch" (12).

46. See Wahl, *Invisible Relations*, 221.

47. Kathryn King writes that the authorship of *The Prude* "remains a tantalizing literary puzzle," particularly in connection with Eliza Haywood's *Rash Resolve*, a text singled out in the dedication to *The Prude*. See Kathryn R. King, "New Contexts for Early Novels by Women: The Case of Eliza Haywood, Aaron Hill, and the Hillarians, 1719–1725," in *Companion to the Eighteenth-Century English Novel and Culture*, ed. Paula Backscheider and Catherine Ingrassia (London: Wiley, 2009), 261–75, 271.

48. Jane Austen, *Emma*, ed. Richard Cronin and Dorothy McMillan (Cambridge: Cambridge University Press, 2005), 90. See Claudia Johnson's reading in *Jane Austen: Women, Politics, and the Novel* (Chicago: University of Chicago Press, 1988).

49. Jane Austen, *Persuasion*, ed. Janet Todd and Antje Blank (Cambridge: Cambridge University Press, 2006). The meddling, learned widow Lady Russell is a figure of financial independence ("extremely well provided for"), singledom (with

"no thought of a second marriage"), and social power ("rank is rank," agrees William Elliot) (5, 163). Attached to both Anne and her mother before her (so much so, we are told, that she follows Lady Elliot to Kellynch), Lady Russell reprises the prude's classic role of obstructionist, balefully interfering in the amours of her innocent, young charge and thus tasked with putting up the novel's necessary impediments to felicity: "internally her heart revelled in angry pleasure, in pleased contempt, that the man who at twenty-three had seemed to understand somewhat of the value of an Anne Elliot, should, eight years afterwards, be charmed by a Louisa Musgrove" (135). But, in Austen's more naturalized contours of fiction, the prude becomes forgivably flawed, a poor judge of character but no malignant iconoclast. Confirmed as having been "pretty completely wrong," Lady Russell remains a "truly sympathising friend" and surrogate mother to Anne Elliot and eventually to Captain Wentworth (271, 46).

50. Elizabeth Povinelli, *The Empire of Love: Toward a Theory of Intimacy, Genealogy, and Carnality* (Durham, NC: Duke University Press, 2006), 17.

51. Lee Edelman, *No Future: Queer Theory and the Death Drive* (Durham, NC: Duke University Press, 2004), 4.

52. Madame de Lafayette, *The Princesse de Clèves*, trans. Terence Cave (Oxford: Oxford University Press, 1992), 95, 99.

53. Anne-Lise François, *Open Secrets: The Literature of Uncounted Experience* (Stanford: Stanford University Press, 2008), 75.

54. See François's reading, flagged in the introduction, of the "strangely passive, all but agentless and guiltless, exchange" in Lafayette's novel. For François, the "unavailable, untouchable, nonpossessable" of the "open secret" implies "a relation to the beloved that neither appropriates nor denies" (81). François writes that "the essential paucity or minimalism defining subjective acts" registers the fact that they are "easily discharged, not hard to complete, not a matter of violent interpretive work on the self" (86).

55. See Jess Keiser's fascinating "Nervous Figures: Enlightenment Neurology and the Personified Mind," *ELH* 82, no. 4 (2015): 1073–1108.

56. Jonathan Lamb, "Imagination, Conjecture, and Disorder," *Eighteenth-Century Studies* 45, no. 1 (2011): 53–69, 66–67.

57. See Alliston's ingenious reading of the paintings in the novel, especially those representing the siege of Metz (*Virtue's Faults*, 66–74).

58. See François's reading of the scene's "simultaneous sense of hours flying and time not mattering" as "conjoin[ing] history as waste and love as vanity." François argues here again for the bare temporality of Lafayette's narrative: "the minimal, all but imperceptible passage from one kind of blank to another" (90–93).

59. On the physical changes that experience makes on the brain's structure in Descartes, see Susan James, *Passion and Action: The Emotions in Seventeenth-Century Philosophy* (Oxford: Clarendon, 1997), 98–99.

60. *The Vicar of Wakefield* [1766], in *Collected Works of Oliver Goldsmith*, ed. Arthur Friedman, 5 vols. (Oxford: Oxford University Press, 1966), 4:3–184, 161.

61. *Rambler* 32, "The Vanity of Stoicism. The Necessity of Patience," in *The Yale Edition of the Works of Samuel Johnson*, ed. W. J. Bate and Albrecht B. Strauss (New Haven, CT: Yale University Press, 1969), 3:174–79, 176.

62. Madame de Lafayette, *La Princesse de Clèves* (Geneva: Librarie Droz, 1950), 198, 200.

Chapter 2. Clarissa's Marble Heart

1. Samuel Richardson, *Clarissa; or, The History of a Young Lady*, 3rd ed., intro. Florian Stuber, 8 vols. (1751; New York: AMS, 1990), 8:41. References are to this edition. To accommodate most readers, I have also placed in brackets the equivalent pages from the more readily available *Clarissa, or, The History of a Young Lady*, ed. Angus Ross (Harmondsworth: Penguin, 1985), 1382. Because the Penguin edition is based on the first edition of the novel, there may be some discrepancies in the text.

2. Sarah Fielding, *Remarks on Clarissa* (1749; Los Angeles: William Andrews Clark Memorial Library, UCLA, 1985), 13.

3. See, e.g., Lovelace to Belford: "Don't tell me, that Virtue and Principle are her guides on this occasion!—'Tis *Pride*, a greater Pride than my own, that governs her. Love, she has none, thou seest; nor ever had; at least not in a superior degree. Love that deserves the name, never was under the dominion of *Prudence*, or of any *reasoning* power. She cannot bear to be thought a *woman*, I warrant!" (5:263 [868]).

4. See, e.g., Joan DeJean's claim for the definitive place of seventeenth-century French women's writing in the history of the novel, as well as the immanence of feminist ideals to the genre: "if the relation between prose fiction and an ideology that can be qualified as feminist is linked to the history of women writers' involvement with the creation of what came to be known as the modern novel, it becomes possible to claim a more central role for feminism in the shaping of that genre." Joan DeJean, *Tender Geographies: Women and the Origins of the Novel in France* (New York: Columbia University Press, 1991), 5.

5. Richardson omits the parenthetical about Cromwell in the third edition; see 3:31–32 [401–2].

6. See Frances Ferguson, "Rape and the Rise of the Novel," *Representations* 20 (Autumn 1987): 88–112.

7. Samuel Richardson to Astraea and Minerva Hill, 14 Dec. 1748, in *Selected Letters of Samuel Richardson*, ed. John Carroll (Oxford: Clarendon, 1964), 102–3.

8. Samuel Richardson to Lady Bradshaigh, 26 Oct. 1748, in *Selected Letters*, 97.

9. See, e.g., Lady Elizabeth Echlin, *An Alternative Ending to Richardson's "Clarissa,"* ed. Dimiter Daphinoff (1755; Berne: Francke, 1982), which removes the rape even though both Clarissa and Lovelace die.

10. S. Fielding, *Remarks on Clarissa*, 13.

11. Jean Hagstrum, *Sex and Sensibility: Ideal and Erotic Love from Milton to Mozart* (Chicago: University of Chicago Press, 1980), 200, 202.

12. Lovelace draws out this narrative in greater detail: "Oh but truly, she hoped

to have the merit of reclaiming him. She had formed pretty notions how charmingly it would look to have a penitent of her own making dangling at her side to church, through an applauding neighborhood: and, as their family increased, marching with her thither at the head of their boys and girls, processionally, as it were, boasting of the fruits of their *honest desires*" (6:100 [970]).

13. Several studies explore the reception history of *Clarissa*. See especially Carol Houlihan Flynn and Edward Copeland, eds., *Clarissa and Her Readers: New Essays for the Clarissa Project* (New York: AMS, 1999); and Lois E. Bueler, ed., *"Clarissa": The Eighteenth-Century Response, 1747–1804*, 2 vols. (New York: AMS, 2010). For an introduction to the Clarissa Project see Florian Stuber and Margaret Anne Doody, "The Clarissa Project and *Clarissa*'s Reception," *Text* 12 (1999): 123–41.

14. Tom Keymer, *Richardson's "Clarissa" and the Eighteenth-Century Reader* (Cambridge: Cambridge University Press, 1992), 76–77.

15. See also Anna Howe after the rape: "I charge you, if you *can*, to get over your aversion to this vile man" (6:370 [1113]); and Mrs. Norton's call to the Harlowes to join the campaign along with "Lord M., from the two Ladies his Sisters, and from both his Nieces, and from the wicked man himself, to forgive and marry him" (7:31 [1155]). Mrs. Harlowe agrees with Clarissa in replying that she would be better off dead than married.

16. Anna Laetitia Barbauld, "Life of Samuel Richardson, with Remarks on His Writings," *The Correspondence of Samuel Richardson*, vol. 1, ed. Anna Laetitia Barbauld (London: Lewis and Roden, 1804), v. References are to this edition.

17. See Stephanie Insley Hershinow's reading of Clarissa as a figure of stasis in "Clarissa's Conjectural History: The Novel and the Novice," *Eighteenth Century* 56, no. 3 (2015): 297–319.

18. Samuel Richardson to Aaron Hill, sometime between Hill's letter of 15 Jan. 1741 and Hill's response of 9 Feb. 1741, and to George Cheyne, 31 August 1741, in *Selected Letters*, 41, 46–47.

19. Samuel Richardson to Aaron Hill, 26 Jan. 1747, in *Selected Letters*, 81.

20. Scott Paul Gordon, "Disinterested Selves: *Clarissa* and the Tactics of Sentiment," *ELH* 64, no. 2 (1997): 473–502, 482. Gordon depicts a "contagion model" of sympathy at work in Richardson's novel, or one which "denies that individuals author their own sympathetic distress; sympathy is inscribed on one body by another. The reader's tears echo another's passions, reproducing experiences already suffered by another reader or by Clarissa herself" (491).

21. Terry Castle, *Clarissa's Ciphers: Meaning and Disruption in Richardson's "Clarissa"* (Ithaca, NY: Cornell University Press, 1982), 16.

22. Ian Watt, *The Rise of the Novel* (Berkeley: University of California Press, 1957), 237.

23. Ferguson, "Rape and the Rise of the Novel," 106.

24. See Ferguson on the rape of Philomela: "It is not so much that the art of poetry operates as a compensation for the reality of suffering; it is that the very process of searching for equivalences becomes an account of overcompensation, of Philomela's

being able to tell her story by weaving when she had no voice and then of gaining a new voice with which to sing, if only in a speech that must be translated" (109).

25. See especially Katherine Binhammer, "Knowing Love: The Epistemology of *Clarissa*," *ELH* 7, no. 4 (2007): 859–79; Kathleen Lubey, "Sexual Remembrance in *Clarissa*," *Eighteenth-Century Fiction* 29, no. 2 (2016–17): 151–78; and Julie Park, *The Self and It: Novel Objects in Eighteenth-Century England* (Stanford: Stanford University Press, 2010).

26. See Sandra Macpherson, *Harm's Way: Tragic Responsibility and the Novel Form* (Baltimore: Johns Hopkins University Press, 2010), 66.

27. See Jonathan Kramnick, *Actions and Objects from Hobbes to Richardson* (Stanford: Stanford University Press, 2010), 204. Kramnick explores the status of human action in the seventeenth and eighteenth centuries and argues that the model of intentionality to which Clarissa Harlowe adheres, in which motives justify actions, conflicts with the model ascribed to by everyone else in the novel, in which intentions are imputed from events. Quoting Watt's *Rise of the Novel*, Kramnick writes, "Whether or not Clarissa 'withhold[s] her sexual feelings from Anna Howe, and even from her own consciousness,' is for our current purposes immaterial" (203).

28. Peter DeGabriele, *Sovereign Power and the Enlightenment: Eighteenth-Century Literature and the Problem of the Political* (Lewisburg, PA: Bucknell University Press, 2015), 27. See also Ferguson on how rape "dramatizes a problematic about the relationship between the body and the mind; although a rake like Lovelace may imagine that carnal 'knowing' includes knowing someone else's mind, a character like Clarissa—virtuous even in her violation—suggests that one knows about mental experience as much in despite of the body as through it" ("Rape and the Rise of the Novel," 99).

29. DeGabriele argues that Lovelace eschews consent because of the impossibility of intimacy it implies by constructing "an intact subjectivity" or "self-propriety, which remains immune to the very touch to which it consents" (41). Lovelace, according to DeGabriele, tries to solve the problem of touch that obtains in Enlightenment empiricism: in Locke's principle of the solidity of bodies that does not permit two bodies to occupy the same space and in Hume's understanding of penetration as annihilation (33–38).

30. Defined as "a type of body that is not entirely sensible of itself," the insensible becomes "a radical remainder that cannot be accommodated into the violent patriarchal order of the rapist, or into the new bourgeois order of sensibility in which the novel seems to be invested" (27). Ingeniously, DeGabriele connects Hobbes's dream of a unified body politic with the libertine's fantasy of an eminently graspable female body: "Lovelace imagines women's bodies as absolutely open to and constructed by the pertinent (even sovereign) touch of the rake, and it is on this basis that he fantasizes about a form of consent that would hold nothing back from his touch" (31). The insensible thwarts both dreams of a unified object and a unified state, "interrupt[ing] liberal relations of consent and locat[ing] the site of the political at the zone of contact, or non-contact, between, and at the limit of, two bodies" (xxxiii).

31. In her reassessment of the genre (see especially the chapter titled "How the Misfit Became a Moral Protagonist") Nancy Armstrong departs rather profoundly from the outlook of *Desire and Domestic Fiction*, in which she argued that the rise of the novel tracks the domestication of the female subject and that the increasingly self-disciplining heroine of the novel organizes a middle class around the home instead of the state. Her *How Novels Think: The Limits of Individualism from 1719–1900* (New York: Columbia University Press, 2006) does not exactly refute her earlier trajectory of self-regulation, but it does turn to a residual "bad subject" of the novel, as one who cannot be trained by the genre's ideological program to create compliant bourgeois subjects. Armstrong thus casts the novel not as a medium of domestication but as an expression of resistance, a tension between "free subjectivity" and "social subjection" (29). Armstrong observes that "the raw energy of individualism is dangerously antisocial" (58). The ethical shift in rise-of-the-novel narratives from ideological submission to antisocial resistance is also evident in Michael McKeon's dialectic between "public subjection" and "private ethical subjectivity" in his sweeping account of early fictions (649). In his *The Secret History of Domesticity* (Baltimore: Johns Hopkins University Press, 2005), McKeon takes up how domestic novels negotiate the process of privatization, or the internalization of public, political structures into private, affective life. Just as Armstrong conceives of the novel as the realm of the misfit, McKeon writes that the novel (here *Pride and Prejudice*) describes an "actively contradictory process of ideological inquiry" (714). For example, Pamela Andrews's closet becomes an "ambivalent" and "multipurpose" site of both privacy and publicity, subjection and subjectivity, where she is locked up by her persecutors and also escapes them to record her experiences.

32. On Lovelace's "continued struggle with the meaning of the body and the meaning of gender" see Tassie Gwilliam's *Samuel Richardson's Fictions of Gender* (Stanford: Stanford University Press, 1993): "Through intense observation or sexual intercourse Lovelace imagines that he can strip off the disguise he associates with women; by flattening femaleness to a single meaning, he will be able to subjugate women, reduce them to mere bodies, or make them echo his desires. He will force women to acknowledge their bodies, to acknowledge desires that the developing ideology of femininity tries to deny, repress, or erase—and those desires will turn out to be identical with his" (71, 68).

33. On "auto-affection" see Derrida's *Le toucher, Jean-Luc Nancy* (Paris: Galilée, 2000); and Catherine Malabou's opening discussion of auto-affection in Adrian Johnson and Catherine Malabou, *Self and Emotional Life: Philosophy, Psychoanalysis, and Neuroscience* (New York: Columbia University Press, 2013).

34. Toni Bowers, *Force or Fraud: British Seduction Stories and the Problem of Resistance, 1660–1760* (Oxford: Oxford University Press, 2011), 266. "Even though Lovelace short-circuited her choice, manipulated her apprehensions, and physically 'lifted' her into the coach while she was screaming 'no, no, no,' Clarissa remains accountable" (273–74). More broadly, Bowers argues that marriage must be understood on a spectrum of violent usurpation, which resonated in the Glorious

Revolution of 1660. Just as James II's exit was not a strict case of "abdication" or "usurpation" but some disconcerting form of both, Clarissa's flight from Harlowe Place is neither and both "elopement" nor/and "abduction"—that is to say, some overdetermined instance in which neither and both of these phenomena seem to take place (270). For Britons still loyal to James, the moral and political quandary in which they found themselves gave rise to this preoccupation. By Richardson's time, Tory Britons "had spent a generation dreading the worst while remaining unsure about precisely where the worst might hide, and occupying an uneasy place not unlike Richardson's heroine and countless other fallen maidens, simultaneously guilty and unfortunate" (276).

35. See Lovelace's description of the irretrievability of an affair in which "a Clarissa could not move me" (5:295 [885]); Belford's appeal: "It is my design to make thee *feel*" (8:33 [1378]); or Clarissa's accusation of his "hardened insensibility" (8:123 [1426]).

36. *Rambler* 97, "Advice to Unmarried Ladies," in *The Yale Edition of the Works of Samuel Johnson*, ed. W. J. Bate and Albrecht B. Strauss (New Haven, CT: Yale University Press, 1969), 4:153–59, 158. Working-class women in the eighteenth century could come out as rape victims. For a discussion of a hard-hearted eighteenth-century British culture in which rape was a disturbingly popular topic of humor, see Dickie's chapter, "Rape Jokes and the Law," in *Cruelty and Laughter*. Dickie observes that although rape cases in the midcentury rarely advanced to capital trial, cases were regularly brought to and resolved at the level of the local magistrates, who usually administered monetary compensation to the plaintiff. "Repugnant as this transactional logic may be, it does at least suggest that ordinary women were not completely helpless" (228).

37. Insensibility as incapacitated consent is, of course, a staple of courtship because of the prohibition against women knowing, much less announcing, their desires (as memorialized in *Rambler* 97). Adela Pinch captures this illogic in her description of the eighteenth-century heroine as "looking for signs of love and also . . . blind to them. Blinded by her education, the constraints of courtship, and the constraints of form, she must wish to know feelings without knowing that she knows them." Adela Pinch, *Strange* Fits *of Passion: Epistemologies of Emotion, Hume to Austen* (Stanford: Stanford University Press, 1997), 144.

38. To paraphrase the logic of this bind: If I let you see that I mistrusted you, the appearance of my mistrust would confirm your suspicions and grounds for mistrusting me; that is, your treatment of me makes me fear for my life, which makes me want to run away. But if I prepare now to run away and you catch me in those preparations, then you will think I intended to run away all along, which will seem to justify your mistreatment of me, even though it was your mistreatment and nothing else that motivated me to run away in the first place.

39. Regarding what she describes as her sister's "*consenting negatives*," Clarissa glosses the loopy predicament in which women must refuse the marriage proposals

of men they are eager to accept in order to maintain the very respectability of character necessary to any renewal of the offer (fully vindicating Mr. Collins's style of courtship in *Pride and Prejudice*). Clarissa ponders, "What can any young creature in the like circumstances say?" before she places the blame (by way of a remembered poem) on men's "false hearts" that "*Compel* our Sex to act dissembling parts" (1:11 [44]).

40. Helen Deutsch, *Loving Dr. Johnson* (Chicago: University of Chicago Press, 2005), 155.

41. Ibid., 156–57. These passages are taken from Deutsch's analysis of the Ephesian matron, in brief: "the widow who would have died of grief making love with another man on her husband's coffin" (158). Engaging Elisabeth Bronfen's study of the aesthetic of the dead woman, Deutsch observes that in Lovelace's fantasy, "the visual scenario of sexual difference replaces specific narrative complicities of desire and death that compromise all distinctions, including those between the sexes, as well as the clear division between anatomist and corpse" (48).

42. "This romance is queer," she writes, "precisely because the desires and identifications it sets in motion cannot be reduced to or exposed as a particular kind of sexuality" (45).

43. Catherine Gallagher, *Nobody's Story: The Vanishing Acts of Women Writers in the Marketplace, 1670–1920* (Berkeley: University of California Press, 1994), 171.

44. Gilles Deleuze, *Masochism: Coldness and Cruelty* (New York: Zone, 1989), 86. In Deleuze's account the sadistic superego advances toward totalization in its progress from "the negative as a partial process of destruction" to "negation as an absolute idea of reason" (127). Deleuze writes that "insofar as the sadistic superego expels the ego and projects it into its victims, it is always faced with the task of destroying something outside itself again and again" (126). Total negation ("the cold purity of thought in the superego" that "bypass[es] the law") can only be achieved when the sadist "add[s] up and totalize[s] all the partial processes" (86). My thanks to Julia Jarcho for her insights into this text.

45. Lovelace, after the rape, hits on the immanent contradiction of secrecy as both impenetrable and what precisely exists to be opened up. He announces to Belford, "And now the whole secret is out" while only a few lines later enjoining him to "inviolable secrecy" (5:299–300 [888]).

46. Lovelace faults Clarissa for *her* contempt: "and she, to appearance, a Runaway, an Eloper, from a tender, a most indulgent Husband!—To neglect to cultivate the opinion of individuals, when the whole world is governed by appearance!" (5:114–15 [789]).

47. Macpherson, *Harm's Way*, 63.

48. Sigmund Freud, "Creative Writers and Day-Dreaming," *The Standard Edition of the Complete Psychological Works of Sigmund Freud*, ed. James Strachey, 24 vols. (London: Hogarth, 1959), 9:146–53.

49. Cynthia Wall, *The Prose of Things: Transformations of Description in the Eighteenth Century* (Chicago: University of Chicago Press, 2006), 106.

50. Regarding Locke's influence on eighteenth-century literature, see Richard A. Barney, *Plots of Enlightenment: Education and the Novel in Eighteenth-Century England* (Stanford: Stanford University Press, 1999); and Christopher Fox, *Locke and the Scribblerians: Identity and Consciousness in Early Eighteenth-Century Britain* (Berkeley: University of California Press, 1988). For a discussion of Richardson's and Richardsonians' particular engagement with Locke, see Derek E. Taylor, *Reason and Religion in Clarissa* (Abingdon, UK: Ashgate, 2009). Taylor observes that while "the evidence would seem to suggest that Samuel Richardson was moderately interested in—if somewhat unsure of—John Locke," the fact that "Richardson lived in the age of Locke" has suggested the philosopher's saturation into the novelist's thinking and writing, especially in *Clarissa* (34). In the chapter titled "Un-Locke-ing Samuel Richardson," Taylor argues that while Richardson scholars, including Jocelyn Harris, Florian Stuber, John Dussinger, and Terry Castle, emphasize the novelist's fundamentally Lockean worldview (a sense of empiricism, religion, and hermeneutics all filtered through the philosopher), they ultimately interpret Locke's influence as "shortsighted, misplaced, or self-defeating" (37).

51. According to his letters, Locke originally intended *Of the Conduct of the Understanding* as a new and significant chapter for the fourth 1700 edition of *An Essay Concerning Human Understanding*. Instead, it was published unfinished in 1706 in *Posthumous Works of Mr. John Locke*, edited by Peter King. Different published editions are available of the *Conduct*. It is included in the ten-volume Scientia reprint of *The Works of John Locke* (1823; repr., Aalen, Germany: Scientia, 1963), 3:203–89. Two modern versions have also been published: a reprint of the 1706 *Posthumous Works* edition by Thoemmes Press and a volume by Hackett that combines the *Conduct* with Locke's 1693 treatise *Some Thoughts Concerning Education*. The *Conduct* will also be included in vol. 3 of *Drafts for the Essay Concerning Human Understanding, and Other Philosophical Writings*, ed. Paul Schuurman and Jonathan Walmsley (Oxford: Oxford University Press, forthcoming). The Hackett edition draws on both the 1706 version and the 1901 Oxford version edited by Thomas Fowler. See John Locke, *Of the Conduct of the Understanding*, intro. John Yolton (Bristol, UK: Thoemmes Press, 1996), §12, at 47; and *Some Thoughts Concerning Education and Of the Conduct of the Understanding*, ed. Ruth W. Grant and Nathan Tarcov (Indianapolis, IN: Hackett, 1996), 187. References here and in the text proper are to section and page numbers in the Thoemmes edition. To accommodate readers, I have also placed in brackets the equivalent pages from the Hackett edition. Misnumbered sections from the 1706 edition, reproduced in the facsimile by Thoemmes, have been silently corrected.

52. "Indifferency" is the only heading that appears in the *Conduct* as three distinct sections (§§11, 34, and 35). Its repetition and its appearance within several other sections in Locke's treatise speak to both its slipperiness and its importance.

The *Oxford English Dictionary* attests to the complex usage of the term, especially in the early modern period. The sense of an impartial or neutral stance in *indifferency*, used by Thomas More and John Donne and adopted in the *Conduct*, has since given way to the more negative shades of apathy and unimportance conveyed by "indifference." *OED*, 2nd ed. (online version June 2011), s.v. "indifferency," "indifference."

53. See Descartes's *Meditations*, in which indifference reflects "a defect in knowledge or a kind of negation" (*M* 102). Mary Astell writes that "when [men] Marry with an indifferency, to please their Friends or encrease their Fortune, the indifferency proceeds to an aversion, and perhaps even the kindness and complaisance of the poor abus'd Wife shall only serve to encrease it." Mary Astell, "Some Reflections Upon Marriage," in *Astell: Political Writings*, ed. Patricia Springborg (Cambridge: Cambridge University Press, 1996), 32–80, 38–39. See another take in Jane Barker's "To my *Indifferent Lover*, who complain'd of my *Indifferency*" or a state of both contemptible lack of feeling and laudable disinterestedness in *A Patch-Work Screen for the Ladies*, in *The Galesia Trilogy and Selected Manuscript Poems of Jane Barker*, ed. Carol Shiner Wilson (New York: Oxford University Press, 1997), 105–6.

54. To practice indifferency, Locke assumes two things in the *Conduct*: that the truth is self-evident and that one has unmediated access to it. Assent, he writes, "should be regulated by the evidence which things carry with them" (§33, at 99 [210]). He adds later, "I never saw any reason yet why truth might not be trusted to its own evidence" (§34, at 104 [212]).

55. *Indifferent* is an important word in a much earlier context, in Locke's contribution to the early modern debate, heightened by Restoration politics, over "matters indifferent," or adiaphora, described by historian Jacqueline Rose as "circumstantial details of worship (time, place, and ceremonies) unspecified in the Bible, imposed by temporal authority." See Rose's study of Locke's *Two Tracts on Government* (1660–1662): "John Locke, 'Matters Indifferent,' and the Restoration of the Church of England," *Historical Journal* 48, no. 3 (2005): 601–21, 603.

56. The appearance of indifferency in the second book of Locke's *Essay Concerning Human Understanding* (1690) in chapter 21, "Of Power," clarifies how the concept is bound up with the question of liberty or the "power to act or not to act according as the Mind directs." See *Essay Concerning Human Understanding*, ed. Peter H. Nidditch (Oxford: Clarendon, 1975), 2.21.71: 282, line 33. Whereas the *Conduct* is concerned with indifferency of opinion, the *Essay* is concerned with indifferency of action. For example, Locke describes the power to move one's hand or to let it rest as demonstration of the freedom of indifferency. He writes, "If during the rest of my Hand, it be seized by a sudden Palsy, the *indifferency* of that operative Power is gone, and with it my Liberty: I have no longer Freedom in that respect, but am under a Necessity of letting my Hand rest." Furthermore, it is important that "the Power of moving my Hand, is not at all impair'd by the determination of my Will" (*EHU* 2.21.71: 284, lines 8–15). Even if one decides to move, one must still be physically free to forbear moving. This very nonabstract example of constraint or

freedom demonstrates for Locke "what sort of *indifferency* Liberty seems to me to consist, and not in any other, real or imaginary" (*EHU* 2.21.71: 284, lines 19–21), or what Raymond Polin calls "the power of organizing one's thoughts and movements according to one's own preferences." See Raymond Polin, "John Locke's Conception of Freedom," in *John Locke: Problems and Perspectives, a Collection of New Essays*, ed. John W. Yolton (Cambridge: Cambridge University Press, 1969), 1–18, 2. The *Oxford English Dictionary* includes Locke's usage in the *Essay* under the definition of "indifferency" as "indetermination of the will; freedom of choice; an equal power to take either of two courses." For a full study of Locke's difficult and much reworked chapter "Of Power," see Gideon Yaffe, *Liberty Worth the Name: Locke on Free Agency* (Princeton, NJ: Princeton University Press, 2000). See also Gross's treatment of apathy as "the rhetorically constituted shadow economy against which a positive economy of emotion is fashioned," in Daniel M. Gross, *The Secret History of Emotion from Aristotle's "Rhetoric" to Modern Brain Science* (Chicago: University of Chicago Press, 2006), 51–84, 55; and Kramnick's discussion of Locke's "Of Power" chapter in *Actions and Objects*, 155–62.

57. See Jonathan Lamb's reading of Catherine Morland's "indifferen[ce] to conjecture." Austen's heroine, he writes, is committed to "a formidable simplicity of vision, a persistently literal use of language, and a fierce loyalty to her own sensations." Jonathan Lamb, "Imagination, Conjecture, and Disorder," *Eighteenth-Century Studies* 45, no. 1 (2011): 53–69, 63. See also Erik Gray, *The Poetry of Indifference: From the Romantics to the Rubáiyát* (Amherst: University of Massachusetts Press, 2005). Gray defines "poetic indifference" as the representation of indifference, as well as a carelessness for the form of poetry itself. An indifferent poem disregards its readers' expectations: "it manifests indifference not only in what it says but in what it does, or rather in what it fails to do" (5). Under the romantic prescription to express strong feeling in order to elicit strong feeling, Gray argues, "a detectable strain of indifference began to appear in English poetry" (3). For example, of Keats's personal letters and epistolary poem "The Eve of St. Agnes," Gray writes, "the epistolary mode offers special ways not only of addressing but also of *avoiding* issues of deep human concern" (29).

58. Sharon Cameron, *Impersonality: Seven Essays* (Chicago: University of Chicago Press, 2007), x.

59. On impersonality and the eighteenth-century novel see especially Deidre Shauna Lynch, *The Economy of Character: Novels, Market Culture, and the Business of Inner Meaning* (Chicago: University of Chicago Press, 1998), which relates the impersonality of eighteenth-century fictional character to the impersonality of commodity exchange; and Pinch, *Strange Fits of Passion*, which argues that impersonal feelings are actually "transpersonal" in that they move from person to person and can be experienced as actually belonging to someone else (15).

60. Kathryn L. Steele examines *Clarissa* through the Christian reading practice of "diffidence, or the practice of avoiding direct interpretive struggle." See Kathryn L. Steele, "*Clarissa*'s Silence," *Eighteenth-Century Fiction* 23, no. 1 (2010): 1–34,

4. For other compelling religious interpretations of the novel see Lois Chaber, "Christian Form and Anti-Feminism in Clarissa," *Eighteenth-Century Fiction* 14, nos. 3–4 (2003): 507–37; Elizabeth Heckendorn Cook, *Epistolary Bodies: Gender and Genre in the Eighteenth-Century Republic of Letters* (Stanford: Stanford University Press, 1996); and John A. Dussinger, " 'Stealing in the Great Doctrines of Christianity': Samuel Richardson as Journalist," *Eighteenth-Century Fiction* 15, nos. 3–4 (2003): 451–506.

61. Leslie Richardson, "Leaving Her Father's House: Astell, Locke, and Clarissa's Body Politic," *Studies in Eighteenth Century Culture* 34, no. 1 (2005): 151–71, 153. Richardson reads Clarissa's loss of self through Locke's theory of possessive individualism, such that rape is "a crime against property," as well as against identity (162).

62. Impersonated by Lovelace and his accomplices before the rape and unconscious during it, Clarissa issues this frank disclaimer to Anna Howe: "But how to defend myself in every-thing that has happened, I cannot tell: Since in some part of the time, in which my conduct appears to have been censurable, I was not myself" (6:146 [996]).

63. G. Gabrielle Starr, *Lyric Generations: Poetry and the Novel in the Long Eighteenth Century* (Baltimore: Johns Hopkins University Press, 2004), 28. Starr's book emphasizes the signifying limits and community-building challenges of epistolarity in Richardson's novel. Letters, in Starr's analysis, aim for a transparency of feeling but ultimately demonstrate the "asymptotic" nature of intimacy and the permanence of solitude—existential conditions only reinforced by the inadequacies and abuses of language. In *Clarissa*, she writes, "we are alone and fallen, and writing seems only to confirm that isolation" (29). Starr's intervention consists in a turning to lyric as the more effective means within the novel for participating in the pain of another. In her intertextual reading of Clarissa's postrape fragments with the book of Job and the poems of George Herbert, Starr invests the texts commonly referred to as Clarissa's "mad papers" with lyric's power "to create emotional consensus" (15, 21). Starr emphasizes the equivocal nature of what she describes as the novel's overall aesthetic of self-alienation, which draws out "the social contours of intimacy" (23). Although Starr privileges Richardson's formal fragmentation and condensation of poems (as well as the elaborate emblems on Clarissa's coffin), her insights extend to the broader postrape narrative that those embedded texts initiate.

64. *Le triomphe de l'indifférence*, ed. André Beaunier (Paris: Librairie José Corti, 1937), 155–206.

65. DeJean quotes Virginia Woolf, "Anon had great privileges. He was not responsible. He was not self conscious. He is not self conscious" (*Tender Geographies*, 242).

66. Starr, *Lyric Generations*, 38.

67. Gilbert Ryle, *Concept of Mind* (1949; Chicago: University of Chicago Press, 2000), 73.

68. In Clarissa's mad Paper VIII, which begins with her well-known acknowledgments of Lovelace's early appeal ("At first I saw something in your air and person that displeased me not"), she draws on allegory to cut through any ambiguity: "Yet,

God knows my heart, I had no culpable inclinations!—I honoured Virtue!—I hated Vice!—But I knew not, that you were Vice itself!" (5.307 [892]).

69. Claudia Brodsky, "Narrative Representation and Criticism: 'Crossing the Rubicon' in *Clarissa*," in *Reading Narrative: Form, Ethics, Ideology*, ed. James Phelan (Columbus: Ohio State University Press, 1989), 207–19, 216.

70. Cook, *Epistolary Bodies*, 104–11. See also Pinch, *Strange Fits of Passion*, on "the impersonality of eighteenth-century personification" of feelings (44–50); and Paula Backscheider and John Richetti, *Popular Fiction by Women, 1660–1730* (Oxford: Clarendon, 1996), on characters' "semi-allegorical effects" (264).

71. John Richetti, *The English Novel in History* (London: Routledge, 1999), 105–6. Richetti aims to unseat the reading of *Clarissa* as a "struggle for psychosexual domination" and instead to open up the novel's engagement with concepts about personality and sociability. Richetti's analysis makes us aware of the correlation between depth-readings of Clarissa (deciphering her interiority) and interpretations locked into plots of violence and loss.

72. Hilary Schor, "Notes of a Libertine Daughter: Clarissa, Feminism, and the Rise of the Novel," *Stanford Humanities Review* 8, no. 1 (2000): 94–117, 98–99.

73. Edward Copeland, "Remapping London: *Clarissa* and the Woman in the Window," in *Samuel Richardson: Tercentenary Essays*, ed. Margaret Anne Doody and Peter Sabor (Cambridge: Cambridge University Press, 1989), 51–69, 55.

74. Amanda Anderson, *The Powers of Distance: Cosmopolitanism and the Cultivation of Detachment* (Princeton, NJ: Princeton University Press, 2001), 63.

75. See Anne-Lise François, *Open Secrets: The Literature of Uncounted Experience* (Stanford: Stanford University Press, 2008), which examines "nonemphatic revelation," challenging critical models that value exposure and are not "prepared to accept something that does not require either the work of disclosure or the effort of recovery" (xvi).

76. Perhaps an instance of giving too much information, Clarissa also informs Mrs. Smith, "I have not had my clothes off since Thursday night" (6:288 [1072]). Four days without laundry (she returns to the glove shop on a Monday) do not appear to affect her stain-proof white damask nightgown, described by Belford as "beyond imagination white" (6:274 [1065]). My emphasis on Clarissa's chattiness about her rape differs significantly from Kathryn Steele's focus on her silence. Steele observes, "After Lovelace rapes her, Clarissa retreats into an increasingly silent world" ("*Clarissa*'s Silence," 12).

77. Patricia Meyer Spacks reads Clarissa's openness as a critique of "the self-elected doom of privacy" suffered by women as submissive as her mother. Spacks glosses that such a gesture "also declares Clarissa's posthumous transcendence of convention and of concealment." Here I address the transcendence she achieves whilst still living. See Patricia Ann Meyer Spacks, *Privacy: Concealing the Eighteenth-Century Self* (Chicago: University of Chicago Press, 2003), 16.

78. For an alternative interpretation see Leslie Richardson, who argues that "the arrest and imprisonment powerfully demonstrate that Clarissa does not have power

over her own movements, that she is without claim to the liberty, the freedom, granted to those who own themselves" ("Leaving Her Father's House," 166).

79. William Ray, *Story and History: Narrative Authority and Social Identity in the Eighteenth-Century French and English Novel* (Cambridge: Blackwell, 1990), 178.

80. Rachel K. Carnell, "Clarissa's Treasonable Correspondence: Gender, Epistolary Politics, and the Public Sphere," *Eighteenth-Century Fiction* 10, no. 3 (1998): 269–86, 282.

81. S. Fielding, *Remarks on Clarissa*, 46.

82. Paula McDowell, *The Women of Grub Street: Press, Politics, and Gender in the London Literary Marketplace, 1678–1730* (Oxford: Clarendon, 1998), 213.

83. Roland Barthes, *Image Music Text*, trans. Stephen Heath (New York: Hill and Wang, 1977), 172–74.

84. Felicity Nussbaum, *Rival Queens: Actresses, Performance, and the Eighteenth-Century British Theater* (Philadelphia: University of Pennsylvania Press, 2010), 19.

Chapter 3. The Man of No Feeling

1. See Mary Nyquist's expansive take in *Arbitrary Rule: Slavery, Tyranny, and the Power of Life and Death* (Chicago: University of Chicago Press, 2013).

2. William Harris, *An Historical and Critical Account of the Life and Writings of Charles I. King of Great Britain. After the Manner of Mr. Bayle. Drawn from Original Writers and State-Papers* (London: R. Griffiths, 1758), 66–67.

3. See parliamentarian lawyer Bulstrode Whitlocke's *Memorials of the English Affairs; or, An Historical Account of What Passed from the Beginning of the Reign of King Charles the First to King Charles the Second His Happy Restauration* (London: Nathaniel Ponder, 1682). Whitlocke had expressed reservations about trying the king and absented himself during the trial.

4. See vol. 4 of *Cobbett's Complete Collection of State Trials, and Proceedings for High Treason and Other Crimes and Misdemeanors* (London: R. Bagshaw, 1809–29), 1072. All citations of *Cobbett's Complete Collection* refer to this volume.

5. See Ernst Kantorowicz's classic exposition of the medieval political theology of "the king's two bodies" (one natural and mortal, the other political and perpetual): "the Pythagoreans claimed that the metamorphosis" of the king's body from personal to divine "was the result of the king's *mimesis*, his imitation of the godhead. Grace and *mimesis*, however, are not mutually exclusive, since Grace (at least in this connection) is the power enabling man to be, or act as, the 'image of God.'" Ernst Kantorowicz, *The King's Two Bodies: A Study in Mediaeval Political Theology* (Princeton, NJ: Princeton University Press, 1958), 500. See also Michael McKeon, "Parsing Habermas's 'Bourgeois Public Sphere,'" *Criticism* 46, no. 2 (2004): 273–77. McKeon writes that "the killing of the king in 1649 also killed the doctrine of the king's two bodies by showing that the death of the natural or private body of monarchy—its separation out from the political or public body of monarchy—did not result in the death of the state, or even of monarchy" (276–77).

6. James I, *The True Lawe of Free Monarchies* (London: Thomas Creede, 1603), 8.

7. Michael Frazer's description of Humean detachment flags the necessity of

something like sovereign neutrality to a conception of perfect sympathy: "Normally, the results of this sympathy are not very strong, overwhelmed as they are by other sentiments, but we can imagine their dominance growing as our impartiality increase[s]. If we can successfully imagine an omniscient, entirely rational and perfectly impartial being (emphasis on the 'if'), then we can also imagine that this being is endowed with sympathy so great as if to feel the sentiments of all individuals with all of their original vehemence." Michael Frazer, *Enlightenment of Sympathy: Justice and Moral Sentiments in the Eighteenth Century and Today* (Oxford: Oxford University Press, 2010), 92.

8. *Eikon Basilike: The Pourtracture of His Sacred Majestie and His Solitudes and Sufferings. With a perfect Copy of Prayers used by his Majesty in the time of his sufferings* (London, 1649). *Eikon Basilike* may have been largely the work of cleric John Gauden. See Hugh Trevor-Roper, "'*Eikon Basilike*': The Problem of the King's Book," *Historical Essays* (London: Macmillan, 1957). For further context see also *Eikon Basilike: The Portraiture of His Sacred Majesty in His Solitudes and Sufferings, with Selections from Eikonoklastes*, ed. Jim Daems and Holly Faith Nelson (Toronto: Broadview, 2006).

9. "He was no more affected with a List that was brought into Oxford of five or six thousand slain at Edgehill, than to read one of Ben Jonson's Tragedies. . . . If ye had lost your lives for his sake, you see he would have no more pitied you, by his own confession, than you do a poor worm: and yet what heart but would cleave, if it were a rock; melt, if it were ice; break, if it were a flint; or dissolve, if it were a diamond" (*Cobbett's*, 4:1018).

10. George Bate, *Elenchus motuum nuperorum in Anglia: or, a short historical account of the rise and progress of the late troubles in England* (London: Abel Swalle, 1685), 144.

11. Geoffrey Robertson, *The Tyrannicide Brief* (London: Vintage, 2006), 189.

12. See especially Lauren Berlant and Sianne Ngai, "Comedy Has Issues," *Critical Inquiry* 43, no. 2 (2017): 233–49; and Simon Critchley, *On Humour* (New York: Routledge, 2002).

13. My reading cuts against the well-documented claim that indifference fell out of favor in the eighteenth century. See R. S. Crane's key 1934 essay, "Suggestions Towards a Genealogy of the 'Man of Feeling,'" *ELH* 1, no. 3 (1934): 205–30. Citing an anonymous 1755 text, Crane depicts the culture's indictment of a "stoical insensibility." See also Margaret Anderson's engagement of Crane in her "Stoic Constructions of Virtue in *The Vicar of Wakefield*," *Journal of the History of Ideas* 69, no. 3 (2008): 419–39.

14. Jacques Derrida, *The Beast and the Sovereign*, vol. 1, trans. Geoffrey Bennington (Chicago: University of Chicago Press, 2009), 57.

15. Robertson, *The Tyrannicide Brief*, 362–63.

16. *The Spectator* 47 (April 24, 1711).

17. Francis Hutcheson, *Reflections upon Laughter, and Remarks upon the Fable of the Bees. Carefully Corrected* (Glasgow: R Urie, 1750), 13.

18. Daniel M. Gross, *The Secret History of Emotion from Aristotle's "Rhetoric" to*

Modern Brain Science (Chicago: University of Chicago Press, 2006), 2, 46. Gross elaborates that "passions in the Hobbesian world are thus anterior to and constitutive of political agency, though they are by no means biological givens. An emotion such as jealousy originates not from within—not in the biological organism jealous of scarce resources, for instance—but rather is constituted without, in the contested space *between* politically and historically situated agents" (45).

19. *England's Black Tribunall, Set Forth in the Triall of King Charles I* (London, 1660), 13; *Cobbett's*, 4:1074. See also William L. Sachse, "England's 'Black Tribunal': An Analysis of the Regicide Court," *Journal of British Studies* 12, no. 2 (1973): 69–85.

20. See Norbert Elias, "Essay on Laughter," ed. Anca Parvulescu, *Critical Inquiry* 43, no. 2 (2017): 281–304.

21. Harris also records that just "when the president *Bradshaw* gave judgment against him, 'the king was observed to smile'" (*Cobbett's*, 4:413).

22. Edward Hyde, Earl of Clarendon, *History of the Rebellion and Civil Wars in England begun in the year 1641*, vol. 4, *1702–1704*, ed. W. Dunn Macray (Oxford: Clarendon, 1888), 488.

23. *Elenchus motuum* records the commissioners' concern that "the *King* would not submit his Neck to the Ax of his *Subjects*," leading them to "order iron Rings and Staples to be made upon the Scaffold, that if he resisted, he might be drawn down to the Block by the head and hands" (151).

24. On hearing that his confidant, George Villiers, the Duke of Buckingham, had been executed, Harris records from one source that "His majesty continued unmoved, and without the least change in his countenance, till prayers were ended; when he suddenly departed to his chamber, and threw himself upon his bed, lamenting, with much passion, and with abundance of tears, the loss he had" (Harris, *An Historical and Critical Account*, 66).

25. Richard Halpern, *Eclipse of Action: Tragedy and Political Economy* (Chicago: University of Chicago Press, 2017), 40, 46.

26. David Marshall, "Adam Smith and the Theatricality of Moral Sentiments," *Critical Inquiry* 10, no. 4 (1984): 592–613, 599.

27. Harris, *An Historical and Critical Account*, 412.

28. *Elenchus motuum*, 197.

29. "The Pleasures of the Imagination," *The Spectator* 411 (June 21, 1712).

30. See Laura Brown's "The Romance of Empire: *Oroonoko* and the Trade in Slaves," in *The New Eighteenth Century: Theory, Politics, English Literature*, ed. Felicity Nussbaum and Laura Brown (New York: Methuen, 1987), 41–61.

31. See Cynthia Wall: "Aphra Behn shaped her narrative space, not surprisingly, like a dramatist, with a particular eye toward the piece of furniture, the position of a room, the dramatic possibilities of small, enclosed spaces. In fact, all the stage directions that are implicit in her plays tend to emerge almost explicitly in her fiction, to a greater degree than in other novelist-playwrights." Cynthia Wall, *The Prose of Things: Transformations of Description in the Eighteenth Century* (Chicago: University of Chicago Press, 2006), 125.

32. Ramesh Mallipeddi, *Spectacular Suffering: Witnessing Slavery in the Eighteenth-Century British Atlantic* (Charlottesville: University of Virginia Press, 2016), 25. Mallipeddi's analysis details how "Behn first elevates the black body to an admirable spectacle via the conventions of Restoration drama, then shows how it is reduced to an exchangeable commodity, and finally documents its violent dismemberment at the scaffold" (26).

33. See Mallipeddi: "The affinity between the novella's complex system of representation and theater is further underscored by the fact that it was successfully adapted, most famously by Southerne and Hawkesworth, for the stage in the next century—adaptations that were more popular than their novelistic counterpart" (28–29).

34. *Rambler* 4, "Saturday, 31 March 1750," in *The Yale Edition of the Works of Samuel Johnson*, ed. W. J. Bate and Albrecht B. Strauss (New Haven, CT: Yale University Press, 1969), 3:19–24, 22.

35. Jonathan Lamb, *The Evolution of Sympathy in the Long Eighteenth Century* (London: Pickering and Chatto, 2009), 130.

36. Rebecca Tierney-Hynes, *Novel Minds: Philosophers and Romance Readers, 1680–1740* (London: Palgrave, 2012) 90–91.

37. David Hume, *The History of England from the Invasion of Julius Caesar to the Revolution of 1688*, vol. 5 (1754; Indianapolis: Liberty Fund, 1983), 535.

38. Ibid., 537–38, 541. "Women are said to have cast forth the untimely fruit of their womb: Others fell into convulsions, or sunk into such a melancholy as attended them to their grave: Nay some, unmindful of themselves, as though they could not, or would not survive their beloved prince, it is reported, suddenly fell down dead" (541).

39. See also Smith: "All the innocent blood that was shed in the civil wars, provoked less indignation than the death of Charles I" (*TMS* 1.3.2.2: 63).

40. Mary Fairclough, *The Romantic Crowd: Sympathy, Controversy and Print Culture* (Cambridge: Cambridge University Press, 2013), 3.

41. Henry Mackenzie, *Man of Feeling*, ed. Maureen Harkin (Peterborough, Ontario: Broadview, 2005), 138.

42. See Claudia Johnson, "A 'Sweet Face as White as Death': Jane Austen and the Politics of Female Sensibility," *Novel* 22, no. 2 (1989): 159–74. Johnson argues that the involuntary, corporeal, and totalizing forces of sensibility amount to the tidy self-destruction of women, such that men of feeling can enjoy the spectacle of their violent sufferings and then be released from it, guilt-free, when the show is over. Johnson argues that Austen—through overt parodies of such conventions, an emphasis on the robust physical health and appetites of her female characters, and also in their stubborn tendency to survive their wrongs—exposes and defies an economy of male sensibility that is yoked to female pain and morbidity.

43. Herman Melville, "Bartleby, the Scrivener: A Story of Wall-Street," in *The Piazza Tales and Other Prose Pieces, 1839–1860*, ed. Harrison Hayford, Alma A. MacDougall, and G. Thomas Tanselle (Evanston, IL: Northwestern University Press; Chicago: Newberry Library, 1987), 45.

44. Rae Greiner, *Sympathetic Realism in Nineteenth-Century British Fiction* (Baltimore: Johns Hopkins University Press, 2012), 17.

45. See Michael Frazer on the "two separate but interrelated ways in which sympathy may be said to threaten the separateness of individuals: first by eliminating the distinction between a sympathizer and the individual object of her feeling and second by eliminating the distinction between the multiple objects of a single person's sympathy" (*Enlightenment of Sympathy*, 93).

46. John Mullan, *Sentiment and Sociability: The Language of Feeling in the Eighteenth Century* (Oxford: Oxford University Press, 1990), 3.

47. Edmund Burke, *Reflections on the Revolution in France*, ed. L. G. Mitchell (Oxford: Oxford University Press, 1993), 86; Tobias Smollett, *The Letters of Tobias Smollett*, ed. Lewis M. Knapp (Oxford: Clarendon, 1970), 33.

48. Oliver Goldsmith, *The Good Natur'd Man*, in *Collected Works of Oliver Goldsmith*, ed. Arthur Friedman, 5 vols. (Oxford: Oxford University Press, 1966), 5:11–83, 63 (hereafter *CW*).

49. Robert Burton, *The Anatomy of Melancholy*, vol. 1, ed. Thomas C. Faulkner et al. (1620; Oxford: Clarendon, 1989), 136, 257.

50. Sean Gaston, "The Impossibility of Sympathy," *Eighteenth Century* 51, no. 1/2 (2010): 129–52 (emphasis in original). Understood through an early Puritan model, sympathy is less about "enter[ing] imaginatively into the feelings of another" than about advancing "intolerance, warfare, and persecution" (130, 137). Over the course of the eighteenth century, a broader, more secular notion of sympathy, Gaston argues, "hollow[ed] out" the earlier version, such that it came to be defined by the very "*absence* of its militant theological and political heritage" (138). And yet, he observes, Hutcheson's belief in innate benevolence, Shaftesbury's promulgation of political sympathy, and sentimental fiction's copious scenes of distressed, lachrymose virtue continue to record the difficulties hashed out in the earlier "wars over fellow feeling"(141, 145–46).

51. Mullan, *Sentiment and Sociability*, 146.

52. See Fred Kaplan, *Sacred Tears: Sentimentality in Victorian Literature* (Princeton, NJ: Princeton University Press, 1987), 34. Kaplan describes at length how much the "Victorians loved *The Vicar of Wakefield*" (35). Where texts like Mackenzie's *Man of Feeling* had lost much of their currency, Goldsmith's "Dr. Primrose seemed a paragon of virtue whose adventures exemplify the good heart and the moral sentiments, and to see virtue was not only to admire but to love it" (34).

53. Goldsmith is not included in recent studies of sentimental fiction such as Michael Bell's *Sentimentalism, Ethics and the Culture of Feeling* (London: Palgrave, 2000); Ildiko Csengei's *Sympathy, Sensibility and the Literature of Feeling in the Eighteenth Century* (New York: Palgrave, 2011); and Alex Wetmore, *Men of Feeling in Eighteenth-Century Literature: Touching Fiction* (New York: Palgrave, 2013).

54. See, e.g., in "An Essay on the Theatre": "A friend of mine, who was sitting unmoved at one of these sentimental pieces, was asked how he could be so indifferent?" (*CW* 3:209–13, 212–13).

55. Nigel Wood, "Goldsmith's English Malady," *Studies in the Literary Imagination* 44, no. 1 (2011): 63–83, 64.

56. See especially Robert Hopkins, *The True Genius of Oliver Goldsmith* (Baltimore: Johns Hopkins University Press, 1969).

57. Oliver Goldsmith, "Advertisement" for *The Vicar of Wakefield* [1766], in *Collected Works*, 4:14.

58. R. F. Brissenden, *Virtue in Distress: Studies in the Novel of Sentiment from Richardson to Sade* (New York: Macmillan, 1974), 248–49.

59. See my "The Vicar and the Sovereign: Monarchism as Narrative Theory in Oliver Goldsmith's *The Vicar of Wakefield*." *Eighteenth Century: Theory and Interpretation* (forthcoming).

60. Goldsmith, *The Good Natur'd Man*, 73.

61. See Daniel M. Gross's discussion of Hobbes's vainglory as "the fundamental distortion in social relations" that is nonetheless "built into the very fabric of society." Gross, *The Secret History of Emotion*, 45–46.

62. Richard Tuck points us to the comparison in Bacon's essay *Of Vaine-Glory*, which begins, "It was prettily Devised of *Aesope; The Fly sate upon the Axletree of the Chariot wheele, and said, What a Dust doe I raise!* So are there some *Vaine Persons*, that whatsoever goeth alone, or moveth upon greater Means, if they have never so little Hand in it, they thinke it is they that carry it." Richard Tuck, "Hobbes's Moral Philosophy," in *The Cambridge Companion to Hobbes*, ed. Tom Sorell (Cambridge: Cambridge University Press, 1996), 175–207, 201.

63. Victoria Kahn claims that "Hobbes saw in conscience and vainglory the Calvinist officeholder and the knight errant, two sides of the same coin, two manifestations of the same politically troublesome link between the passions, the imagination, metaphorical thinking, and rebellion." Ironically, Kahn claims, *Leviathan*, "the canonical text of rational theories of contractual obligation," can be read as a romance narrative about the reunited bond between subject and sovereign. Victoria Kahn, *Wayward Contracts: The Crisis of Political Obligation in England, 1640–1674* (Princeton, NJ: Princeton University Press, 2004), 136, 170.

64. Vivasvan Soni, *Mourning Happiness: Narrative and the Politics of Modernity* (Ithaca, NY: Cornell University Press, 2010), 278–79.

65. John Bender, *Ends of Enlightenment* (Stanford: Stanford University Press, 2012), 146, 141, quoting E. P. Thompson, "Eighteenth-Century English Society: Class Struggle Without Class?" *Social History* 3, no. 2 (1978): 133–65, 140.

66. Norma Clarke, *Brothers of the Quill: Oliver Goldsmith in Grub Street* (Cambridge, MA: Harvard University Press, 2016), 323. Goldsmith "was immersed in a male world of philosophy and raking," and "we know almost nothing about [his] sexual and emotional life" (244).

67. Lisa A. Freeman, *Character's Theater: Genre and Identity on the Eighteenth-Century English Stage* (Philadelphia: University of Pennsylvania Press, 2002), 10.

68. Berlant and Ngai, "Comedy Has Issues," 233.

69. Henri Bergson, *Laughter: An Essay on the Meaning of the Comic* (Mansfield Center, CT: Martino, 2014), 4–5.

70. E. H. Mikhail, *Goldsmith: Interviews and Recollections* (Houndmills: Macmillan, 1993), 85.

71. See ibid., 85–86. See also Goldsmith's preface to *The Good Natur'd Man*, in which he argues that gentrification of the stage has killed not only humor but also character. Thus, "to delineate character has been [my] principal aim" (*CW* 5:14).

72. "Will with a Whisp to Robbin Goodfellow" (London: T. Davies, 1680), 4.

73. "The Character of a Coffee-House, with the Symptomes of a Town-Wit" (London: Jonathan Edwin, 1673), 4–5.

74. Michael Griffin, *Enlightenment in Ruins: The Geographies of Oliver Goldsmith* (Lewisburg, PA: Bucknell University Press, 2013), 84; Berlant and Ngai, "Comedy Has Issues," 234; Critchley, *On Humour*, 5.

75. Louise Geddes, "Playing No Part but Pyramus: Bottom, Celebrity and the Early Modern Clown," *Medieval and Renaissance Drama in England: An Annual Gathering of Research, Criticism and Reviews* 28 (2015): 70–85, 71. Geddes depicts Puck's affiliation with the early modern celebrity clown, itself a "continuation of the Lord of Misrule" from the Tudor period. Engaging Bente Videbaek, *The Stage Clown in Shakespeare's Theatre* (Westport, CT: Greenwood Press, 1996), Geddes argues that Puck's autonomy is partly a function of Shakespeare's splitting of the clown into Puck and Bottom, who absorbs the ridicule attached to that figure (70).

76. Tim Reid, "Clown and the Death Drive: What Could Go Wrong?" paper presented at the Annual Meeting of the American Comparative Literature Association, Los Angeles, CA, March 2018.

77. Winifried Schleiner, "Imaginative Sources for Shakespeare's Puck," *Shakespeare Quarterly* 36, no. 1 (1985): 65–68, 67, 68. Schleiner conveys Puck's multicultural claim to witchcraft and magic (English *pouke*, Welsh *pwka*, Icelandic *puki*), folk figurations that also appear across literary texts (Langland, Drayton, Spenser, Jonson). See also William Bell's multivolume, illustrated *Shakespeare's Puck and His Folkslore* (London: Richards, 1852), which Schleiner calls "nineteenth-century antiquarianism gone rampant" (65).

78. Haldeen Braddy, "Shakespeare's Puck and Froissart's Orthon," *Shakespeare Quarterly* 7, no. 2 (1956): 276–80, 278. Braddy's quotation is from Lord Berners's 1524–25 version of the *Chronicles*, "one of the more famous English translations known in Elizabethan times" (277).

79. Richard Tarlton, *Tarltons newes out of purgatorie Onely such a iest as his iigge, fit for gentlemen to laugh at an houre, &c. Published by an old companion of his, Robin Goodfellow* (London: R. Robinson, 1590), 2.

80. The *OED* lists this text as its first entry for the second definition of *quaint* as "to act in a prim, affected, or pretentious manner."

81. Anonymous, *A pleasant comedie, called Wily beguiled* (London: Humphrey Lownes for Clement Knight, 1606).

82. Sonnet 94 explores the potentiality of the insensible:

> They that have power to hurt and will do none,
> That do not do the thing they most do show,
> Who, moving others, are themselves as stone,
> Unmoved, cold, and to temptation slow. (1–4).

83. "The Bare-Faced Tories" (London: H. Jones, 1682).
84. "Will with a Whisp," 1.
85. Marjorie Garber, *Shakespeare After All* (New York: Pantheon, 2004), 224.
86. Emily Hodgson Anderson, *Eighteenth-Century Authorship and the Play of Fiction: Novels and the Theater, Haywood to Austen* (New York: Routledge, 2009), 9.
87. "Speech at the anniversary of the *People's Paper*, Delivered in London, April 14, 1856," in *The Collected Works of Marx and Engels*, vol. 14 (Charlottesville, VA: International Publishers, 1975), 656. First published in the *People's Paper*, April 19, 1856.

Chapter 4. Sense, Insensibility, Sympathy

1. In Ian Watt's classic metafiction, the novel rises to Austen, who solved the narrative dualism between Samuel Richardson's subjective, individual-centered approach and Henry Fielding's objective, society-centered one (a binary that encapsulates the problem of realism if not, Watt suggests, the problem of Cartesian dualism itself). See Ian Watt, *The Rise of the Novel* (Berkeley: University of California Press, 1957).
2. "To W. S. Williams, 12 April 1850," in *Selected Letters of Charlotte Brontë*, ed. Margaret Smith (Oxford: Oxford University Press, 2007), 161–62.
3. Reginald Farrer, "Jane Austen, *ob.* July 18, 1817," *Quarterly Review* 228, no. 452 (1917): 1–30, 11. Included in *Jane Austen: The Critical Heritage*, vol. 2, *1870–1940*, ed. B. C. Southam (London: Routledge, 1987), 245–72. For more on Farrer and other wartime Janeites see Claudia Johnson's landmark study *Jane Austen's Cults and Cultures* (Chicago: University of Chicago Press, 2012). Johnson writes, "Victorian Janeites turned to Austen for reenchantment; Farrer and other writers of his generation celebrate their 'radiant and remorseless Jane' as the supreme figure of disenchantment, a strong-minded artist whose allegiance is solely to the truth of her art" (103).
4. David Cecil, *Jane Austen* (Cambridge: Cambridge University Press, 1935), 12.
5. Marvin Mudrick, *Jane Austen: Irony as Defense and Discovery* (Princeton, NJ: Princeton University Press, 1952), explicates Austenian irony as a fundamentally self-protective style that expresses the author's phobia of personal intimacy. Modern biopics, adaptations, and erotic fictions also address the pressing matter of Austen's celibacy. See Deidre Lynch, "See Jane Elope: Why Are We So Obsessed with Jane Austen's Love Life?" in *Slate*, August 2007, www.slate.com/articles/arts/culturebox/2007/08/see_jane_elope.html. Eric C. Walker describes Austen as a writer who "ducks marriage in her own life and appears to write about nothing else"; see Eric

C. Walker, *Marriage, Writing, and Romanticism: Wordsworth and Austen After War* (Stanford: Stanford University Press, 2009), 3.

6. E. N. Hayes, "*Emma*: A Dissenting Opinion," *Nineteenth Century Fiction* 4, no. 1 (1949): 1–20, 6.

7. See Mudrick's correlation between the untender Emma Woodhouse and "the strong need to dominate, the offhand cruelty, the protective playfulness, the malice of Jane Austen, the candid Jane Austen of the letters—in which miscarriage is a joke . . . and death equally amusing . . . and marriage also" (*Jane Austen*, 193).

8. As Southam writes, "the case of Jane Austen is more than that of a single author. Her novels revealed to the early nineteenth-century reading public that fiction was capable of unsuspected power, that it was to be taken seriously as a form of literature, and that criticism of the novel could itself be a serious intellectual activity." B. C. Southam, introduction to *Jane Austen: The Critical Heritage*, vol. 1, *1811–1870*, ed. B. C. Southam (London: Routledge, 1987), 1.

9. Hayes, "*Emma*," 13.

10. D. A. Miller, *Jane Austen, or The Secret of Style* (Princeton, NJ: Princeton University Press, 2003), 75.

11. Austen's absurdly compressed endings enact what Barbara Benedict calls the sentimental novel's "framing of feeling," the writer's reconciliation of "the cultural distrust of sentiment and the audience's desire for it" through various means of conventionalization and detachment. Barbara Benedict, *Framing Feeling: Sentiment and Style in English Prose Fiction, 1745–1800* (New York: AMS, 1994), 6. Likewise, in April Alliston's *Virtue's Faults: Correspondences in Eighteenth-Century British and French Women's Fiction* (Stanford: Stanford University Press, 1996), Alliston observes that Austen allows us to mock the clichés of sentimental romance and participate in them at the same time. See also Deidre Shauna Lynch, *The Economy of Character: Novels, Market Culture, and the Business of Inner Meaning* (Chicago: University of Chicago Press, 1998).

12. Claudia Johnson, *Jane Austen: Women, Politics, and the Novel* (Chicago: University of Chicago Press, 1988), 51.

13. Austen exploits the absurdities of this predicament sometimes comically (as when she gleefully mangles Samuel Johnson's dictum of *Rambler* 97, which then goes totally unheeded in *Northanger Abbey*) and sometimes seriously (as when Jane Bennet's uniform cheerfulness of temper is balefully construed by Mr. Darcy as "insensibility").

14. John Bender, *Ends of Enlightenment* (Stanford: Stanford University Press, 2012), 141. In Bender's argument free indirect discourse emerges as the "textual ideology" of the state's "impersonal network of laws, rules, parties, and bureaucratic procedures that intersperse authority throughout everyday life" and whose key feature is "transparency" (142–43). See my discussion in Chapter 3.

15. Miller applies Ann Banfield's concept of "pure narration" to Austen's free indirect discourse (65, 88). See Ann Banfield, *Unspeakable Sentences: Narration and Representation in the Language of Fiction* (Boston: Routledge, 1982).

16. Deidre Shauna Lynch, *Loving Literature: A Cultural History* (Chicago: University of Chicago Press, 2015), 6–7. Lynch's book asks "what an emotional commitment to literature *is*" (14). See also Lynch's introduction to *Janeites: Austen's Disciples and Devotees* (Princeton, NJ: Princeton University Press, 2000).

17. Claudia Johnson, "The 'Twilight of Probability': Uncertainty and Hope in *Sense and Sensibility*," *Philological Quarterly* 62, no. 2 (1983): 171–86, 171. See responses, like Anthony Trollope's, to the novel's infamous ending, in which what "need only be said" is not very much at all, in *Critical Heritage*.

18. Johnson, *Jane Austen*, 49. See also Johnson's "A 'Sweet Face as White as Death': Jane Austen and the Politics of Female Sensibility," *Novel* 22, no. 2 (1989): 159–74, for a reading that considers "the dementia and decay of the wronged woman" as the major topoi of sentimental fiction. Johnson redefines sensibility as "the affective arena of an ideology oppressive to women," through which "the injunctions and priorities which organize women's lives and structure their sense of possibility are written into their own bodies, and thus internalized, concealed, and executed from within" (173).

19. Lynch identifies Elinor and Anne Eliot with the unique qualities of Austen's narrator: an "invisibility, omniscience, and capacity to enter into others' feelings and coordinate and harmonize others' perspectives." Elinor, she writes, serves as a narrative "clearinghouse," uniting subplots through her consciousness (*The Economy of Character*, 233).

20. See especially E. M. Dadlez, *Mirrors to One Another: Emotion and Value in Jane Austen and David Hume* (Chichester: Wiley-Blackwell, 2009); Peter Knox-Shaw, *Jane Austen and the Enlightenment* (Cambridge: Cambridge University Press, 2004); Hina Nazar, *Enlightened Sentiments: Judgment and Autonomy in the Age of Sensibility* (New York: Fordham University Press, 2012); and Gilbert Ryle, "Jane Austen and the Moralists," in *Critical Essays on Jane Austen*, ed. B. C. Southam (London: Routledge, 1968): 106–22.

21. Jane Austen, *Sense and Sensibility*, ed. Edward Copeland (Cambridge: Cambridge University Press, 2005), 300–301.

22. Adela Pinch, *Strange Fits of Passion: Epistemologies of Emotion, Hume to Austen* (Stanford: Stanford University Press, 1997), 19. Considering the long reach of Hume's *Treatise* across romantic literature, including in *Persuasion*, Pinch's study, like Mullan's account of eighteenth-century sensibility, emphasizes the tensions between feeling as a social medium and as a mode of antisociality. Pinch observes how Austenian consciousness "parr[ies] the shocks of social experience," such that it is both "conditioned by the presence of others, *and* . . . constituted *as* resistance to outside influence" (154). Clara Tuite observes that Austenian narration is a "social model of interiority," both "collaborative and conspiratorial"—"a form of sympathy which simultaneously coerces, controls and corrects." Clara Tuite, *Romantic Austen: Sexual Politics and the Literary Canon* (Cambridge: Cambridge University Press, 2002), 67, 75, 69.

23. David M. Black, "Sympathy Reconfigured: Some Reflections on Sympathy,

Empathy and the Discovery of Values." *International Journal of Psychoanalysis* 85 (June 2004): 579–96, 585.

24. *Sense and Sensibility*, dir. Ang Lee (Columbia Pictures, 1995). Prudence is, of course, everywhere in Austen's fiction. For example, when Elizabeth asks her Aunt Gardiner, "What is the difference in matrimonial affairs between the mercenary and the prudent motive? Where does discretion end, and avarice begin?" it is not a rhetorical question. For an illuminating take on the Charlotte Lucas problem see Ruth Perry, "Sleeping with Mr. Collins," *Persuasions* 22 (2000): 119–35.

25. Emma Thompson, *Jane Austen's Sense and Sensibility: The Screenplay and Diaries* (London: Bloomsbury, 1995), 167.

26. See Lauren Kopajtic, "Sovereign Sentiments: Conceptions of Self-Control in David Hume, Adam Smith, and Jane Austen" (PhD diss., Harvard University, 2017). For Kopajtic's take on Hume see "Cultivating Strength of Mind: Hume on the Government of the Passions and Artificial Virtue," *Hume Studies* 41, no. 2 (2015): 201–29. I want to thank Lauren for her immense help with this chapter.

27. Nazar writes that Elinor's doctrine "entails *acting* as though the feelings and opinions of others matter even if they do not or should not" (*Enlightened Sentiments*, 130).

28. Mary Poovey, *The Proper Lady and the Woman Writer: Ideology as Style in the Works of Mary Wollstonecraft, Mary Shelley, and Jane Austen* (Chicago: University of Chicago Press, 1984), 185; Mudrick, *Jane Austen*, 85.

29. Jane Austen, *Northanger Abbey*, ed. Barbara M. Benedict and Deirdre Le Faye (Cambridge: Cambridge University Press, 2005), 256.

30. Elaine Scarry, *The Body in Pain: The Making and Unmaking of the World* (New York: Oxford University Press, 1985), 4.

31. Jane Austen, *Pride and Prejudice*, ed. Pat Rogers (Cambridge: Cambridge University Press, 2005), 408.

32. Jenny Davidson, *Hypocrisy and the Politics of Politeness: Manners and Morals from Locke to Austen* (Cambridge: Cambridge University Press, 2004), 154. See also Johnson, *Jane Austen*, 63: Elinor "has neither smothered her dreams nor even, with all her heroic efforts at screening and concealment, really masked her attachment."

33. Eve Kosofsky Sedgwick, "Jane Austen and the Masturbating Girl," *Critical Inquiry* 17, no. 4 (1991): 818–37, 834.

34. Anne-Lise François, *Open Secrets: The Literature of Uncounted Experience* (Stanford: Stanford University Press, 2008), 82. François engages Stanley Cavell's "Knowing and Acknowledging," in Cavell's *Must We Mean What We Say?* (Cambridge: Cambridge University Press, 1969).

35. For a helpful explication and expansion of this part of the *Treatise* see David Owen, "Hume and the Mechanics of the Mind: Impressions, Ideas, and Association," in *The Cambridge Companion to Hume*, ed. David Fate Norton and Jacqueline Taylor (Cambridge: Cambridge University Press, 2009), 70–104.

36. See especially Pinch, *Strange Fits of Passion*; Catherine Gallagher, *Nobody's Story: The Vanishing Acts of Women Writers in the Marketplace, 1670–1920* (Berkeley:

University of California Press, 1994); and Ian Duncan, *Scott's Shadow: The Novel in Romantic Edinburgh* (Princeton, NJ: Princeton University Press, 2007).

37. Antonio Damasio, *The Feeling of What Happens: Body and Emotion in the Making of Consciousness* (New York: Harcourt, 1999), 145.

38. "Cousins in the fourth degree are connected by causation . . . but not so closely as brothers, much less as child and parent. In general we may observe, that all the relations of blood depend upon cause and effect, and are esteem'd near or remote, according to the number of connecting causes interpos'd betwixt the persons" (I.1.4.3: 13). Fanny Dashwood corroborates Hume's point when urging her husband not to provide for his half-sisters and their mother. Of the three-thousand-pound sum he considers making over to them, per his promise to their dying father, she needles, "What possible claim could the Miss Dashwoods, who were related to [her husband] only by half blood, which she considered as no relationship at all, have on his generosity to so large an amount? It was very well known that no affection was ever supposed to exist between the children of any man by different marriages" (9–10).

39. See Sarah Tindal Kareem's comparative reading of the *Treatise* with *Robinson Crusoe*. Kareem's theory of wonder as a kind of "hesitation" reframes philosophical skepticism as a practice of cognitive "estrangement that momentarily stalls habitual thought processes" or, in other words, "what happens on the way back to reality from estrangement." Sarah Tindal Kareem, *Eighteenth-Century Fiction and the Reinvention of Wonder* (Oxford: Oxford University Press, 2014), 84–85.

40. Pinch reads Hume's exilic gentleman as someone "fleeing" the "claustrophobic" nature of sympathy. The story thus offers, she writes, "a counternarrative to the *Treatise*'s championing of a pervasive, sympathetic sociability, and, perhaps, a hint of *ressentiment* against the social arrangements that his own mechanics of sympathy underscore, in which our feelings of concern always flow toward those greater than us but not toward those lesser" (*Strange Fits of Passion*, 28).

41. Similarly, when Marianne and her mother are mulling over the status of Elinor's relationship with Edward and why the latter has not visited them at Barton Cottage, Marianne remarks " 'How strange this is! What can be the meaning of it!' " without thinking to ask Elinor. Asked by her mother whether Elinor is expecting Edward, Marianne replies, "I have never mentioned it to her, but of course she must" (46).

42. Patricia Meyer Spacks, *Gossip* (New York: Knopf, 1985), 57.

43. Nancy Yousef, *Romantic Intimacy* (Stanford: Stanford University Press, 2013), 122.

44. Miller, *Jane Austen, or The Secret of Style*, 58.

45. Rae Greiner, *Sympathetic Realism in Nineteenth-Century British Fiction* (Baltimore: Johns Hopkins University Press, 2012), 19. Greiner writes of the overcoming of natural insensibility in *TMS*: "Our job in sympathy is to turn nothing into something, often into something *else*—for though our feelings might match perfectly, we can never know for sure. Smith presents this mismatch as an opportunity rather than a problem. When other people's situations rouse our interest, when we contemplate

how conditions of experience shape the attitudes that can be expressed within them, fellow-feeling forges imaginative but no less powerfully affective bonds" (21).

46. Thomas Nagel, "What Is It Like to Be a Bat?" *Philosophical Review* 83, no. 4 (1974): 435–50.

47. See David Marshall's reading of this passage as part of Smith's refutation "that sympathy is selfish rather than altruistic because it springs from self-love." David Marshall, "Adam Smith and the Theatricality of Moral Sentiments," *Critical Inquiry* 10, no. 4 (1984): 592–613, 600.

48. For example, while the spectator feels deep "commiseration," the idiot "laughs and sings perhaps, and is altogether insensible of his own misery. The anguish which humanity feels, therefore, at the sight of such an object, cannot be the reflection of any sentiment of the sufferer" (*TMS* 1.1.1.11: 15).

49. See especially David Marshall, *The Figure of Theater: Shaftesbury, Defoe, Adam Smith, and George Eliot* (New York: Columbia University Press, 1986).

50. Jonathan Lamb, "Imagination, Conjecture, and Disorder," *Eighteenth-Century Studies* 45, no. 1 (2011): 53–69, 57.

51. Greiner, *Sympathetic Realism*, 16.

52. Gordon Teskey, *Allegory and Violence* (Ithaca, NY: Cornell University Press, 1996), 2.

53. George Eliot, *Daniel Deronda*, ed. Terence Cave (London: Penguin, 1995), 469.

54. W. H. Auden, "The Composer," in *Collected Poems*, ed. Edward Mendelson (New York: Vintage, 1991), 181.

55. Of Hume's essentially cognitive theory of sympathy, Nancy Yousef writes, "that human beings perceive one another's pain or joy is a quasi-anthropological epistemic fact in Hume's account . . . but sympathy in itself engenders no wish to do well by the other. The severance of sympathetic insight from ethical engagement is the crucial, distinctive feature of Hume's sentimentalism" (*Romantic Intimacy*, 76). Even in his conception of public sympathy as the ingrained love of law and justice, Yousef finds an "epistemically secure but ethically unstable" answer to the separation between interpersonal perception and ethical obligation—an impasse subsequently taken up in searching accounts of ethics by Wordsworth and Kant (80).

56. Blakey Vermeule, *Why Do We Care About Literary Characters?* (Baltimore: Johns Hopkins University Press, 2010), 49.

57. See Victoria Kahn, *Wayward Contracts: The Crisis of Political Obligation in England, 1640–1674* (Princeton, NJ: Princeton University Press, 2004); and Catherine Gallagher, "The Rise of Fictionality," in *The Novel*, vol. 1, *History, Geography, and Culture*, ed. Franco Moretti (Princeton, NJ: Princeton University Press, 2006).

58. For Hume, emotions and morals are incommensurable phenomena insofar as the former are experiences of the self ("desire and aversion, affection and hatred") whereas the latter are precisely generalized assessments of someone else's circumstances, actions, and manners ("blame or approbation") (*EPM* 9.1: 74). Hume effectively circumscribes Hobbes's landscape of passion and action—in which one moves toward what is helpful (therefore, good and desirable) and away from what is hurtful

(therefore, bad and hateful)—as a theory confined to the individual and therefore totally lacking in moral application: "When a man denominates another his *enemy*, his *rival*, his *antagonist*, his *adversary*, he is understood to speak the language of self-love, and to express sentiments, peculiar to himself, and arising from his particular circumstances and situation. But when he bestows on any man the epithets of *vicious* or *odious* or *depraved*, he then speaks another language, and expresses sentiments, in which, he expects, all his audience are to concur with him" (*EPM* 9.1: 75).

59. Hume nonetheless takes a dig at *Leviathan*: "the descriptions, which certain philosophers delight so much to form of mankind . . . are as wide of nature as any accounts of monsters, which we meet with in fables and romances" (*T* III.2.2.5: 313).

60. Wayne C. Booth, *The Rhetoric of Fiction* (Chicago: University of Chicago Press, 1983), 257, 265.

61. Joanna Picciotto, "Secular Devotions," lecture given at New York University, 1 Feb. 2017. See Picciotto's persuasive reading of the figure of the "pathologically taciturn eyewitness" of Addison's and Steele's *Spectator*, which resonates in the emergence of Austen's impersonal narrative style, in Joanna Picciotto, *Labors of Innocence in Early Modern England* (Cambridge, MA: Harvard University Press, 2010), 512.

62. Booth, *The Rhetoric of Fiction*, 304.

63. "The Janeites," in Rudyard Kipling, *Debits and Credits*, ed. Sandra Kemp (1926; Harmondsworth: Penguin, 1987), 119–40, 137.

64. John Dryden, "A Discourse Concerning the Original and Progress of Satire" (1693).

65. D. W. Harding, "Regulated Hatred: An Aspect of the Work of Jane Austen," *Scrutiny* 8 (March 1940): 346–62, 350. Reprinted in *Regulated Hatred and Other Essays on Jane Austen*, ed. Monica Lawlor (London, Athlone, 1998), 5–25; and in *Jane Austen: The Critical Heritage*, ed. Brian Southam, 2 vols. (London: Routledge, 1987), 2:245–71.

66. See my "Resituating 'Regulated Hatred': D. W. Harding's Jane Austen," *ELH* 77, no. 4 (2010): 995–1014.

67. Second Draft, "JA Apple Blossom" folder, box 30, D. W. Harding papers, Emmanuel College, Cambridge.

68. Linda Hutcheon, *Irony's Edge: The Theory and Politics of Irony* (London: Routledge, 1994), 14–15.

69. Jenny Davidson, "A Modest Question About *Mansfield Park*," *Eighteenth-Century Fiction* 16, no. 2 (2004): 245–64, 252.

70. Philosophers and Austenians have made strong connections between Aristotle (especially of the *Nicomachean Ethics*) and Austen. See David Gallop: "If we can imagine the timeless philosopher choosing among fiction-writers of later ages to illustrate his central ethical doctrines, he could hardly find anyone to match her." David Gallop, "Jane Austen and the Aristotelian Ethic," *Philosophy and Literature* 23, no. 1 (1999): 96–109, 98. See also Anne Crippen Ruderman, in *The Pleasures of Virtue: Political Thought in the Novels of Jane Austen* (Lanham, MD: Rowman and

Littlefield, 1995), where Ruderman quotes Alisdaire MacIntyre's line that "when Jane Austen speaks of 'happiness' she does so as an Aristotelian" (6).

71. "Irony," in *The New Princeton Encyclopedia of Poetry and Poetics*, ed. Alex Preminger and T. V. F. Brogan (Princeton, NJ: Princeton University Press, 1993), 633–35, 634.

72. The ironist (or, in translation, the "mock-modest" or "self-deprecating" person) is more focused on regulating his own powers than on manipulating other people: "Mock-modest people, who understate things, seem more attractive in character; for they are thought to speak not for gain but to avoid parade; and here too it is qualities which bring reputation that they disclaim, as Socrates used to do." Aristotle, *Nicomachean Ethics*, trans. W. D. Ross, in *The Complete Works of Aristotle*, ed. Jonathan Barnes, vol. 2 (Princeton, NJ: Princeton University Press, 1985), 4.7: 1779.

73. Annette Baier, *Death and Character: Further Reflections on Hume* (Cambridge, MA: Harvard University Press, 2008), 4.

74. Park Honan, *Jane Austen: Her Life* (New York: St. Martin's, 1987), 401.

75. Jane Austen, "When Winchester Races," New York Public Library, Berg Collection, uncatalogued MS.

Conclusion: Death Wish for the Novel

1. David Marshall, who notes the Harlowe stamp in Gwendolen's name, reads *Deronda* as a philosophical and literary work that "has its origin in the eighteenth century" and "offers not only retrospective but also prospective views in the history of the novel." David Marshall, *The Figure of Theater: Shaftesbury, Defoe, Adam Smith, and George Eliot* (New York: Columbia University Press, 1986), 195, 193, 205, 206. Of Gwendolen's final epistolary address to Deronda, Adela Pinch writes, "It is strange to feel oneself, at the end of Eliot's intense explorations of thinking about another person in the third person, in the presence of a mode of address reminiscent of the posthumous letters of Clarissa Harlowe." Adela Pinch, *Thinking About Other People in Nineteenth-Century British Writing* (Cambridge: Cambridge University Press, 2010), 155. See also Margaret Doody's "George Eliot and the Eighteenth-Century Novel," *Nineteenth-Century Fiction* 35, no. 3 (1980): 260–91.

2. George Eliot, *Daniel Deronda*, ed. Terence Cave (London: Penguin, 1995), 12, 154.

3. Joseph Roach, *It* (Ann Arbor: University of Michigan Press, 2007), 1, 4, 12, passim.

4. Grandcourt's insensibility is written on his face: "It was perhaps not possible for a breathing man wide awake to look less animated"; "One might be tempted to horsewhip him for the sake of getting some show of passion into his face and speech" (404). Reinforcing the diagnosis of the English as insensible, Eliot depicts "the well-bred Englishman" as a "flaccid" specimen, "whose nullity of face and perfect tailoring might pass everywhere without ridicule" (102, 103). Such "phlegmatic nature" or "the vacuum in gentlemen and lad[ies]" contrasts with the "fervour" or "warm blood" associated with the Jewish characters of the novel (205). We could say that emotion functions as a marker or giveaway, what Eve Kosofsky Sedgwick and

Adam Frank (writing on shame, contempt, and disgust) describe as "a switch point for the individuation of imaging systems, of consciousness, of bodies, of theories, of selves; an individuation that decides not necessarily an identity but a figuration, distinction, or mark of punctuation." Eve Kosofsky Sedgwick and Adam Frank, "Shame in the Cybernetic Fold: Reading Silvan Tomkins," *Critical Inquiry* 21, no. 2 (1995): 496–522, 521.

5. See readings in Sandra Gilbert and Susan Gubar, *The Madwoman in the Attic* (New Haven, CT: Yale University Press, 1979); Jacqueline Rose, *Sexuality and the Field of Vision* (London: Verso, 1986); Peter Brooks, *Body Work: Objects of Desire in Modern Narrative* (Cambridge, MA: Harvard University Press, 1993). Alexander Welsh sums up: "If there is one Victorian plot that openly supports the argument of Sandra Gilbert and Susan Gubar about secret female aggression in the novels of women writers, it is the story of Gwendolen Harleth." Alexander Welsh, *George Eliot and Blackmail* (Cambridge, MA: Harvard University Press, 1985), 271. Incidentally, Eliot's notebooks record passages from Sir James Paget's "Nervous Mimicry." Jane Irwin notes that Paget's essay carefully distinguishes between hysteria and neuromimesis, from which Eliot appears to have modeled Gwendolen's malady; see *George Eliot's "Daniel Deronda" Notebooks*, ed. Jane Irwin (Cambridge: Cambridge University Press, 1996), 351.

6. In the scene of their engagement Gwendolen reverses her decision to refuse Grandcourt and overcomes her feelings of "deep . . . disgust and indignation" (299). Eliot's meditation on the physical phenomenon of desire is evidenced in the manuscript, in which she crosses out "attachment" and replaces it with "attraction." British Library, Western Manuscripts collection, Ten Works of "George Eliot," 1859–1879: Being the holograph copy furnished to the printer by the author, Marian Evans, afterwards Mrs. J. W. Cross. 24 vols. Additional Manuscripts (Add. MS) 34020–43: 1857–79, 34039–42 (300).

7. Anonymous, *The Prude: A Novel by a Young Lady*, pts. 1–3 (London: J. Roberts, 1724–25), 3.5 (emphasis mine).

8. Eliza Haywood, *Love in Excess; or, The Fatal Enquiry*, ed. David Oakleaf, 2nd ed. (Peterborough, Ontario: Broadview, 2000), 86, 38.

9. David M. Black, "Sympathy Reconfigured: Some Reflections on Sympathy, Empathy and the Discovery of Values." *International Journal of Psychoanalysis* 85 (June 2004): 579–96, 585.

10. See Welsh, *George Eliot and Blackmail*, 264: "With the best of motives, he will have watched, talked, and pried his way into this secret, much as if he were inventing psychoanalysis in the Vienna of the eighteen-nineties."

11. Jerome Thale, *The Novels of George Eliot* (New York: Columbia University Press, 1959), 694, 136.

12. Sigmund Freud, "Recommendations to Physicians Practising Psycho-Analysis," in *The Standard Edition of the Complete Psychological Works of Sigmund Freud*, ed. James Strachey, 24 vols. (London: Hogarth, 1958), 12:110 (Freud is quoting himself).

13. Ibid., 114.

14. See also Melanie Klein's model of identification in which imagining the other's situation, interests, and feelings is the only pathway to self-reparation (not self-sacrifice). See Klein and Joan Riviere, *Love, Hate and Reparation* (New York: Norton, 1964), 66.

15. See Eliot's book-length poem *The Spanish Gypsy* (1868) for a possible counter-narrative of "a woman's life," although still locked in a plot of patriarchal violence. Deborah Epstein Nord reads *Deronda* as a revision of *The Spanish Gypsy* in her *Gypsies and the British Imagination, 1807–1930* (New York: Columbia University Press, 2006). Nord argues that "the success of Daniel Deronda's narrative sheds light on the failures of Fedalma's," a "turn[ing] from Gypsy to Jew" that also retracts from its heroine of "gender heterodoxy" (100, 99). On the "self-lacerating strangeness" and "generic weirdness" of *The Spanish Gypsy* see David Kurnick, "Unspeakable George Eliot," *Victorian Literature and Culture* 38, no. 2 (2010): 489–509, 505, 504.

16. For contemporary reactions see *George Eliot: The Critical Heritage*, ed. David Carroll (London: Routledge, 1971), hereafter referenced as *CH*. On hostility to the Jewish plot, Carroll writes that "critics began to wonder if the mysticism of race and nation had sufficient human interest to be the subject of fiction" (*CH* 33). One contemporary reviewer expresses a "conviction that the author has fallen below her usual height" and asks whether that "is owing to any failure of power in herself, or to the utter want of sympathy which exists between her and her readers" (*CH* 376). Another reviewer laments *Deronda*'s "failure . . . to produce the intended effect" (*CH* 404). Leslie Stephen, in a commemorative essay on Eliot, simply omits *Deronda* from the author's list of works, in Gordon Haight, *George Eliot: A Biography* (New York: Oxford University Press 1968), xii. Jerome Thale calls Eliot's hero "a flat failure," adding that "even if the character of Daniel were satisfactory, nothing could make us take Mordecai or the novel's version of Zionism." Thale, *The Novels of George Eliot*, 123. See also Claudia Johnson, "F. R. Leavis: The 'Great Tradition' of the English Novel and the Jewish Part," *Nineteenth-Century Literature* 56, no. 2 (2001): 199–227; and Amanda Anderson, *The Powers of Distance: Cosmopolitanism and the Cultivation of Detachment* (Princeton, NJ: Princeton University Press, 2001).

17. Adela Pinch, *Thinking About Other People*, 145.

18. S. Pearl Brilmyer writes that in *Impressions of Theophrastus Such*, "character is not something one can change at will or easily develop through practices of self-making, or *Bildung*." See S. Pearl Brilmyer, "Sensing Character in George Eliot's *Impressions of Theophrastus Such*," *PMLA* 129, no. 1 (2014): 35–51, 38.

19. David Kurnick, *Empty Houses: Theatrical Failure and the Novel* (Princeton, NJ: Princeton University Press, 2011), 102.

20. In light of Gwendolen's bad acting, Mme Laure's homicide, Mirah's retirement from performance, and the "breaking of the Princess's will to theatrical self-transformation," Kurnick analyzes *Deronda* as "an allegory of the theater being disciplined into contrition by the novel" (97–99). In attending to the theatrical basis of fictionality, Kurnick redirects novelistic drive away from character-based identification, in which "we can choose Daniel or we can choose Leonora," to a "performative desire"

that stages a collective, egalitarian world where, quoting from Eliot, "everything . . . [is] related to everything else" (99). See also David Marshall's claim that *Deronda* "belongs to the theater and has everything to do with the theater" or the "conver[sion of] sentiments into drama" (*The Figure of Theater*, 196, 232).

21. Lisa A. Freeman, *Character's Theater: Genre and Identity on the Eighteenth-Century English Stage* (Philadelphia: University of Pennsylvania Press, 2002), 14.

22. Mikhail Bakhtin, *The Dialogic Imagination*, trans. Caryl Emerson and Michael Holquist (Austin: University of Texas Press, 1981), 5.

23. The Alcharisi makes several such statements: "I parted with you willingly"; "I had joy enough without you then. Now you are come back to me, and I cannot make you a joy"; "I will not pretend to love where I have no love" (623, 663).

24. She had "had the eccentricity of not caring to part . . . and be to him as if she were not" (626, 715).

25. Marshall reads the novel as a study of "the limits of sympathy" and compellingly connects that demonstration to theater, which "represents the ways that we know and do not know ourselves and each other. Theater faces us with the risks of knowing and now knowing. It reveals the risks involved in either being, or being seen by, even the wisest beholder" (240). Marshall usefully draws us to Rousseau's antitheatrical *Lettre à M. d'Alembert sur les spectacles* (1758) (*The Figure of Theater*, 215).

26. Silvan Tomkins aptly observes that "any barrier the parent may place before the passionate wish of the child to identify with and to act like the parents, whether it be because of concern for the child's safety, indifference, hostility, or self-hatred by the parents, is a major source of shame." Silvan S. Tomkins, *Affect, Imagery, Consciousness: The Complete Edition*, 2 vols. (New York: Springer, 2008), 2:402.

27. Denis Diderot, *Paradoxe sur le comédien* (Paris: A. Sautelet, 1830), 7; *The Paradox of Acting*, trans. Walter Herries Pollock (London: Chatto and Windus, 1883), 16. The *Paradox* is a text itself indebted to Richardsonian fiction. As Joseph Roach writes, Diderot "seemed to pattern his world on that of a novel and to imagine himself as a Richardsonian hero" or "the Good-Natured Man," whose overwrought sensibilities hit every note of the emotional scale, "ascending from the rudimentary responsiveness of the nervous system to the highest plane of human sympathy and moral imagination." Joseph Roach, *The Player's Passion: Studies in the Science of Acting* (Newark: University of Delaware Press, 1985), 118–19. See also Michael Fried's long footnote in which he writes that "the *Paradoxe* amounts to a characteristically vigorous and unpredictable development of the notion, implicit from the first in the Diderotian concept of the dramatic *tableau*, of a radical separation between the point of view of the actor and that of the beholder." Michael Fried, *Absorption and Theatricality: Painting and Beholder in the Age of Diderot* (Berkeley: University of California Press, 1980), 220–21n142.

28. Engaging Roach's reading, Abigail Zitin connects Diderot's aesthetic theory to Hogarth's—in particular, to his suggested exercise in *The Analysis of Beauty* of mentally "scooping out objects in order to solicit closer and more careful observation" of their forms. Abigail Zitin, "Thinking like an Artist: Hogarth, Diderot, and

the Aesthetics of Technique," *Eighteenth-Century Studies* 46, no. 4 (2013): 555–70, 557. In this way the mind of the artist comes not only to conjure but also to inhabit the interior of an object and, in so doing, to grasp its full situation: "the imagination will naturally enter into the vacant space within this shell, and mark the opposite corresponding parts so strongly, as to retain the idea of the whole, and make us masters of the meaning of every view of the object, as we walk round it, and view it from without" (Hogarth, *The Analysis of Beauty*, ed. Ronald Paulson [1753; New Haven, CT: Yale University Press, 1997], 21).

29. Daniel Defoe, *Roxana* (1724; Oxford: Oxford University Press, 2008), 147–48.

30. Elizabeth Susan Wahl, *Invisible Relations: Representations of Female Intimacy in the Age of Enlightenment* (Stanford: Stanford University Press, 1999), 13.

31. Toni Bowers, *The Politics of Motherhood: British Writing and Culture, 1680–1760* (Cambridge: Cambridge University Press, 1996), 16.

32. For a reading of Ibsen's Hedda Gabler as a figure of the death drive see Julia Jarcho, "Cold Theory, Cruel Theater: Staging the Death Drive with Lee Edelman and Hedda Gabler," *Critical Inquiry* 44, no. 1 (2017): 1–16, 11. Hedda, another "cold and immovable" criminally minded heroine with "steel-grey" eyes ("cold, clear and calm"), is sister to Gwendolen Harleth, in Henrik Ibsen, *Hedda Gabler and Other Plays*, trans. Una Ellis-Fermor (New York: Penguin, 1950), 349, 272.

33. Dorothy Hale, "Aesthetics and the New Ethics: Theorizing the Novel in the Twenty-First Century," *PMLA* 124, no. 3 (2008): 896–905, 900.

34. Judith Butler, *Giving an Account of Oneself* (New York: Fordham University Press, 2005), 22.

35. Adriana Cavarero, *Relating Narratives: Storytelling and Selfhood* (London: Routledge, 2000), 92. Eliot's 1878 polemical essay against anti-Semitism, "The Modern Hep! Hep! Hep!" extends such an ethic to the sphere of international relations by outlining a model of human rights that calls on the need "to discern likeness amidst diversity" and to recognize the equal rights of other peoples to pursue a separate existence, honor a separate history, and cultivate a separate tradition and "national consciousness," in *Impressions of Theophrastus Such: Essays and Leaves from a Notebook* (Philadelphia: Lippincott, 1901): 168–93, 172.

36. Frances Ferguson, "Rape and the Rise of the Novel," *Representations* 20 (Autumn 1987): 88–112, 109.

37. John Bender, *Ends of Enlightenment* (Stanford: Stanford University Press, 2012), 134.

38. Joseph Roach, "Mother Camp: Walpole, Clive, and the Pleasures of Distress," paper presented at the Annual Meeting of the American Society for Eighteenth-Century Studies, Pittsburgh, PA, March 2016.

Index

PAGE NUMBERS IN ITALICS REFER TO ILLUSTRATIONS.

CPSIA information can be obtained
at www.ICGtesting.com
Printed in the USA
JSHW011731050920
7684JS00002B/7

9 781503 615014